THE GRAMMAR OF
THE ANCIENT
WORLD

THE GRAMMAR OF
THE ANCIENT
WORLD

The ultimate visual guide to the greatest civilizations of ancient times

Editor PROFESSOR DOMINIC RATHBONE

FALL RIVER PRESS

Fall River Press
122 Fifth Avenue
New York, NY 10011

ISBN-13: 978-1-4351-0543-0

Printed and bound in China

10 9 8 7 6 5 4 3 2 1

This book was conceived,
designed, and produced by

Ivy Press
210 High Street, Lewes
East Sussex BN7 2NS
United Kingdom

Creative Director: PETER BRIDGEWATER
Publisher: JASON HOOK
Editorial Director: CAROLINE EARLE
Commissioning Editor: SOPHIE COLLINS
Senior Editor: LORRAINE TURNER
Copy Editor: SIMON SMITH
Art Director: MICHAEL WHITEHEAD
Design: JC LANAWAY
Publishing Coordinator: ANNA STEVENS
Glossary and Index: MIKE DARTON
Picture Manager: KATIE GREENWOOD
Digital Artwork: JOHN MITCHELL

Contents

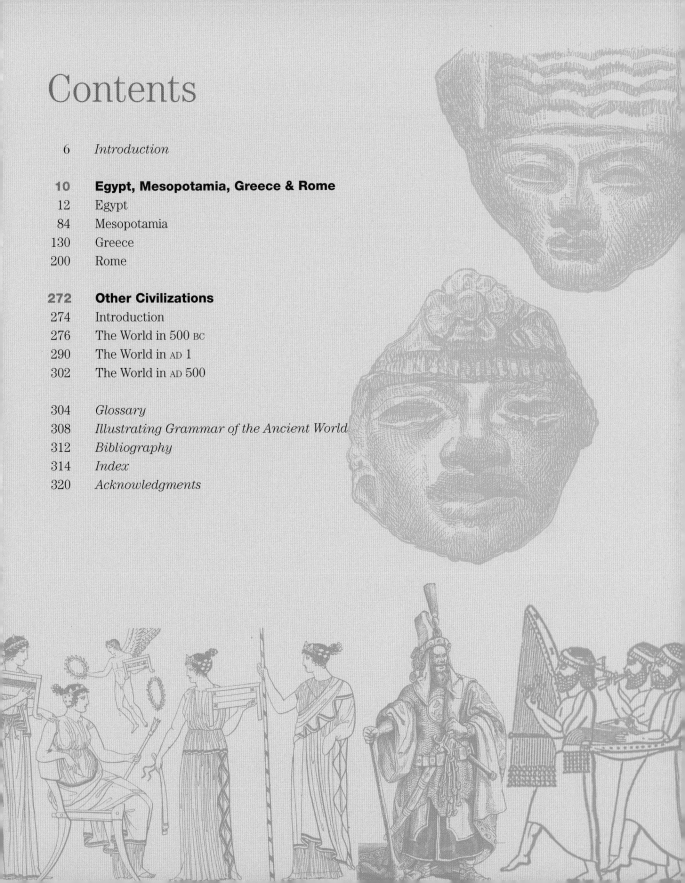

INTRODUCTION

In the 19th century, research into ancient civilizations and publication of the results became a serious business, primarily in Europe and North America. Some scholars studied, translated, and commented on ancient texts in libraries—histories, literatures, and documents. Others mounted expeditions to seek out, record, and, if possible, remove the monuments and material relics of the world's past. Museums filled with ancient artifacts, exotic and mundane, carefully classified and labeled. Libraries filled with books on the art, politics, poetry, religion, technology, and every aspect of long-faded cultures. Public interest was aroused and engaged by press reports and exhibitions of major discoveries, evocative but minutely detailed paintings and prints, such as those of David Roberts and Lawrence Alma-Tadema, while books such as Edward Bulwer-Lytton's *The Last Days of Pompeii* and Oswald Spengler's *The Decline of the West* drew on the past to warn the present of potential doom. With the growth of universities, the concept of the professional academic was created and developed, although the gifted gentleman and lady amateur still made their mark.

On one level this extraordinary cultural revolution, which flourished in this form through to the mid-20th century, can be seen as a product and mirror of the attempted contemporary Western dominance—military, political, and economic—of the rest of the world. Civilizations were "appropriated," linked, and ranked in a genealogical hierarchy, complete with embarrassing "uncles," which both explained and justified the triumph of the West. Of course this is more evident to us with hindsight than it was a conscious program at the time, and it is not the whole story. Archaeologists, historians, and literary scholars have always been an odd bunch, and disagreeing with others' views was (and is) endemic and necessary for making progress in the subject and for developing a career. However primitive we might now find the archaeological techniques used or the historical assumptions made and questions asked, the scholarship, both professional and amateur, of this period had a genuine passion for retrieval and preservation of the remains and memories of ancient civilizations, for advancing knowledge and understanding of their languages, societies, religion, and political systems—in short, their total histories. It also laid down important

ethical guidelines about academic documentation, which still serve—despite the postmodernist championing of relativity in historical outlook and judgment—to calibrate the scale of fiction to fact by which historians still grade each other's reconstructions and fortify their own works by sandbagging weak points with a "probably" or "possibly."

This volume draws on the whole historical and archaeological tradition, old and new. Its coverage extends beyond the traditional Western focus on ancient Greece and Rome by adding chapters on Egypt and Mesopotamia, far older civilizations of developed agriculture, large urban centers, and writing and documentation. A fifth chapter locates these cultures in a broad overview of ancient

world civilizations, from China through Oceania, South America, and Africa to Persia. Once, "ancient" history meant the history of the Greeks and Romans, with walk-on parts for their Persian, African, Germanic, and other neighbors and subjects. Now we want to study the similarities and differences between the contemporary systems of Rome

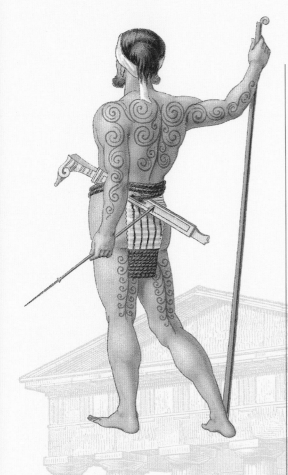

and Han China, or the varying forms and fates of ancient urbanism across several continents. "Ancient" retains its original ending, which is the western fall of the Roman Empire and transition to the embryonic nation-states of medieval Europe, but it now extends back far more widely and broadly, as far as we can go in any place and time where we have the survival of documents that still mark the gray boundary between history and prehistory. Instead of trying to rank past cultures, this volume tries to present them for their own sake.

In homage to the pioneering days of discovery and scholarship, most images are taken from the drawings used as illustrations in 19th- and 20th-century works, because of the facility with which a good illustrator could show details that it was difficult to make clear in a photographic plate (*see also* Illustrating Civilizations of the Ancient World, *pages 308–11*). The modern scholarly narrative identifies what is both enlightening and accurate about these images, explaining how we may now interpret them differently. While illustrating the past as retold today, these drawings remind us of how we have collectively come to visualize it. This, too, is part of our heritage from the ancient world.

EGYPT, MESOPOTAMIA, GREECE & ROME

EGYPT

Egypt, flanked by vast expanses of desert to east and west, is a narrow band of extremely fertile land dependent on the annual flooding of the Nile and the deposit of silt it leaves behind. The earliest hunter-gatherers took advantage of its riches and the remains of agricultural settlements dating back as far as c. 5500 BC have been found. Over the next 2,500 years the people of Egypt learned to exploit the area's natural resources, and established widespread trading contacts.

The civilization we call "ancient Egyptian"—its pharaonic history—flourished from the point at which one state emerged under a single ruler, in around 3100 BC, until 332 BC, when Egypt's invasion by Alexander the Great heralded the beginning of the Greco-Roman period. The pharaonic era was first divided into thirty-one dynasties by Manetho, a priest of the Ptolemaic period in the 3rd century BC and one of Egypt's first historians. Building on his work, Egyptologists subsequently grouped these dynasties, dividing them into Kingdoms (periods of stability, strength, and wealth in Egypt) and Intermediate Periods, which were politically fragmented and unsettled.

The legacy of ancient Egypt is one of unrivaled richness and has enthralled visitors, whether invaders or tourists, for centuries. Many works were published in the 19th century with fine illustrations worthy of the art they recreated. And there is much still to be discovered, as the traditional archaeological bias toward tombs and temples broadens into studies of the secular life and settlements in this most complex of ancient worlds.

TIME LINE
c. 5300 BC–30 BC

c. 5300 BC

Beginning of the Predynastic Period. The emergence of social stratification, craftsmanship, and a recognizable Egyptian culture.

The Narmer Palette

c. 3200 BC

Beginning of the Protodynastic Period (Dynasty 0) and the emergence of writing in Egypt and recognizable pharaonic ruler iconography as exemplified by the Narmer Palette.

c. 3000 BC

Formation of a unified state of Egypt, establishment of capital at Memphis, emergence of monumental architecture in mud brick ,and the beginning of the Early Dynastic Period.

c. 2160 BC

Collapse of the Old Kingdom and the beginning of the politically fragmented First Intermediate Period for which very little evidence survives.

c. 2125–2055 BC

Civil war between the local Theban and Herakleopolitan dynasties based at Thebes (modern Luxor) and Herakleopolis Magna (close to the Fayyum).

Tutankhamun receiving the governor of Nubia

c. 1980–1780 BC

Egyptian construction of mud-brick fortresses in Nubia in order to exploit the area for its gold and manpower, and to control the trade routes south.

c. 1650 BC

Collapse of the Middle Kingdom, supremacy of foreign (perhaps Palestinian) Hyksos kings (15th Dynasty), and the beginning of the politically fragmented Second Intermediate Period.

c. 1465 BC

Hatshepsut sends a trading expedition to Punt, beautifully documented on the walls of her temple at Deir el-Bahri. The most prized commodity imported from this land was aromatic resin for incense.

Imported gold and resin from Punt

c. 1352–1336 BC

Akhenaten builds a new capital at Akhetaten (Tell el-Amarna) and makes significant changes to the art and religion, prioritizing the cult of the sun god Aten.

c. 1327 BC

Tutankhamun is buried in the Valley of the Kings with elaborate funerary goods. He dies around the age of seventeen, after restoring the religion to its traditional polytheistic form after the so-called Amarna heresy.

c. 1069 BC

Collapse of the New Kingdom at the end of the Ramesside Period (the 19th and 20th Dynasties) and the beginning of the Third Intermediate Period, another politically fragmented period of pharaonic history.

c. 747 BC

Conquest of Egypt by Nubian/Kushite rulers (25th Dynasty) from Napata, close to the Nile's Fourth Cataract in modern Sudan. The victory is celebrated on the Stela of Piy.

664 BC

Reestablishment of Egyptian control of Egypt in the form of the Saite 26th Dynasty and the beginning of Late Period. The 26th Dynasty is regarded as a renaissance in pharaonic culture.

c. 610 BC

Foundation of Naucratis, a Greek trading post in Egypt, to which forty years later the pharaoh Amasis (Ahmose II) grants a monopoly over all goods coming by sea from the Mediterranean countries.

601 BC

Nebuchadnezzar leads the Babylonians into battle against Egypt. The location of the battle is unknown, but there are heavy casualties on both sides and the Babylonians withdraw.

400 BC

Egyptian revolts, backed by Atteus, against Persia in the 480s and 450s BC are unsuccessful, but in *c.* 400 BC independence is regained under the 28th to 30th Dynasties.

343 BC

The Persians take control of Egypt once again under Artaxerxes III, heralding the Second Persian Period (or 31st Dynasty). The renewed Persian rule is allegedly harsh.

332 BC

Invasion of Egypt by Alexander the Great (Alexander III of Macedon). His arch enemy was the Persian ruler Darius III (who was controlling Egypt and the Levant), whom he had defeated at the Battle of Issus in 333 BC.

c. 2686 BC

Beginning of the Old Kingdom. The construction of vast stone pyramids for the burials of the rulers, and the flourishing of trade with Nubia and Syria-Palestine.

c. 2667–2648 BC

The construction of the earliest surviving monumental stone structure, Djoser's Step Pyramid at Saqqara, designed by Imhotep, who was later deified.

c. 2589–2566 BC

Construction of the Great Pyramid at Giza for Khufu of the 4th Dynasty. This is the only one of the Seven Wonders of the Ancient World still standing.

c. 2055 BC

Reunification of Egypt under the Theban king Mentuhotep II and the beginning of the Middle Kingdom, a cultural highpoint in Egypt's pharaonic history.

Step pyramid at Saqqara

c. 1985 BC

Foundation of a new capital city at Itj-Tawy and the construction once more of pyramids for the rulers, but now they were built of mud brick cased in limestone.

c. 1560–1550 BC

Expulsion of the Hyksos from their capital at Avaris (Tell el-Daba) by the Theban kings, ensuring an end to foreign rule in Lower Egypt.

c. 1555 BC

Introduction of the horse to Egypt, which together with the chariot became the status symbol of the emerging military elite in the 18th Dynasty.

c. 1550 BC

Reunification of Egypt under one Theban ruler (Ahmose) and the beginning of the New Kingdom, a stable and prosperous period of Egypt's history.

c. 1470–1425 BC

Thutmose III establishes indirect Egyptian control in Syria-Palestine by means of at least sixteen military campaigns.

c. 1274 BC

Ramesses II fights the Battle of Qadesh against the Hittites. The outcome was probably not the great victory he had depicted on the walls of his temples.

c. 1258 BC

Ramesses II signs a peace treaty with the Hittites. This is the only parity treaty between two powers to have survived from the ancient Near East.

c. 1208–1176 BC

Attacks on Egypt by the Sea Peoples, a loose confederation of sea-going Indo-European migrants who were wreaking havoc in the ancient Near East. The Egyptians were able to defeat this threat.

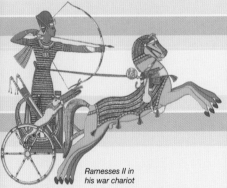

Ramesses II in his war chariot

671 BC and c. 667 BC

Assyrian invasions of Egypt by Esarhaddon (who takes Memphis and forces Egypt to pay tribute). Then Assurbanipal sacks Thebes but is forced to leave Egypt to deal with a rebellion in Babylon in southern Mesopotamia.

Warfare at sea

c. 550 BC

Introduction of demotic script in addition to hieratic, which until now had been the cursive form of hieroglyphs used from the beginning of dynastic history for administrative, literary, and other texts.

525 BC

Persian invasion under Cambyses (heralded by their defeat of the Egyptians at the Battle of Pelusium) and the beginning of the First Persian Period (27th Dynasty). Egypt becomes a province of the Persian Empire.

331 BC

Foundation of Alexandria. The city is planned by Greek architect Deinocrates on a typical Hellenistic rectangular pattern. The island of Pharos was connected to the coast by a dyke, creating a double harbor.

305 BC

Beginning of the Ptolemaic Dynasty ruling Egypt. Alexander had died in Babylon in 323 BC and Ptolemy, son of Lagos, had claimed Egypt when Alexander's generals divided up the Empire.

30 BC

Roman invasion of Egypt under Octavian (who was known as Emperor Augustus from 27 BC) and the death of Cleopatra VII. Egypt becomes a province of the Roman Empire, ruled through a prefect in Alexandria.

GEOGRAPHY

Ancient Egypt

Egypt is located in northeast Africa. It has remarkable natural borders: a difficult stretch of Mediterranean coast to the north; the unnavigable First Cataract to the south (at Aswan); and vast expanses of desert to the east (meeting the Red Sea) and west (to Libya). The geography of this land is unlike any other; most of the country is desert, the Eastern Desert and the Western or Libyan Desert, which becomes the Sahara. The Nile River is the lifeline running through the heart of the country, flanked on either side by a strip of fertile land, opening up to form the marshy Delta north of Cairo.

Plowing with cattle

Delta

The Delta is often described as Lower Egypt. The Canopic, Sebennytic, and Pelusiac branches of the Nile had all dried up by the Islamic Period, leaving only the Damietta and Rosetta branches flowing to this day. This fertile area was known for its marshland, cattle pasture, and vineyards.

Nile Valley

The Nile Valley varies in breadth; in some areas of Egypt the desert cliffs drop almost straight into the Nile, in others there is a considerable expanse of fertile land alongside the river. When the Nile flooded, the valley became a floodplain, and new layers of fertile silt were deposited annually.

Harvesting grapes

EGYPT *c.* 3100 BC–AD 394

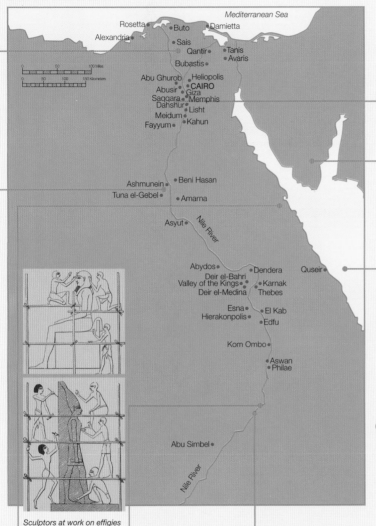

Mediterranean Sea

Rosetta
Alexandria
Buto
Damietta
Sais
Qantir
Tanis
Avaris
Bubastis
Abu Ghurob
Heliopolis
Abusir
CAIRO
Saqqara
Giza
Memphis
Dahshur
Lisht
Meidum
Fayyum
Kahun

Ashmunein
Beni Hasan
Tuna el-Gebel
Amarna

Asyut
Nile River

Abydos
Dendera
Quseir
Deir el-Bahri
Valley of the Kings
Karnak
Deir el-Medina
Thebes
Esna
El Kab
Hierakonpolis
Edfu

Kom Ombo

Aswan
Philae

Abu Simbel

Nile River

Sculptors at work on effigies

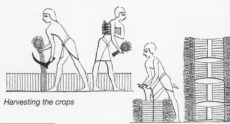

Harvesting the crops

❮ Fayyum

The Fayyum is a large fertile depression in the Western Desert about 37 miles (60 km) southwest of Cairo. Water flows in from the Nile Valley through the Bahr Yussef and drains into Lake Moeris (or Qarun). This area of cultivable land was enlarged and particularly well exploited during the 12th Dynasty and the Ptolemaic and Roman Periods.

❮ Sinai

The Sinai Peninsula to the north of the Red Sea is situated between Egypt and Palestine. The ancient Egyptians exploited this area primarily for its copper and turquoise resources at sites, such as Serabit el-Khadim, Wadi Maghara, and Timna. It also provided the land route for the Egyptians into the Levant.

Egyptian turquoise jewelry

❮ Red Sea

The Red Sea is a salt-water inlet of the Indian Ocean between Africa and Asia. In the north are the Gulf of Suez (leading to the Suez Canal) and the Gulf of Aqaba. The ancient Egyptians built ships at ports, such as Quseir and Mersa Gawasis, in order to sail to the enigmatic land they called Punt.

❮ Wadi Hammamat

The Eastern Desert is crisscrossed with wadis, or dried-up riverbeds. The Wadi Hammamat is the shortest route from the Nile Valley to the Red Sea. The ancient Egyptians used it as a trade route, and quarried a variety of stones and mined gold there.

❮ First Cataract

The First Cataract at Aswan is the most northerly of six cataracts between Egypt's pharaonic southern border and Khartoum in Sudan. It is an area of rapids caused by abrupt geological changes in granite outcrops on the river bed. The river becomes unnavigable in this stretch.

❮ Nile

The inundation began with rain in Central Sudan, which raised the level of the White Nile. A few weeks later, the summer monsoon rain over the Ethiopian Highlands caused a rapid swelling of the Blue Nile and the Atbara Tributary. Until the construction of the Aswan dams, this water flooded Egypt between June and September.

Annual flooding of the Nile

GOVERNMENT

The Pharaoh

After Egypt was unified (*c.* 3000 BC) and became politically stable, the government was led by the ruler, or pharaoh, a title that comes from the ancient Egyptian for "great house" or "palace" (*per aa*). The pharaoh tended to be male because the mythology dictated (the ruler of Egypt was identified closely with the male deity Horus), but at times women did rule Egypt, either as a last resort or as a regent to a minor male successor. The ruler was ultimately responsible for the administration, judicial system, and religious life of the nation. However, during unstable and politically fragmented periods (the "intermediate periods" of pharaonic history) there was no centralized government, no one king ruled over the entire country, and government took place instead at a more local level.

The sphinx
The pharaoh was often represented as a mighty bull but also as a sphinx, a powerful image of the king with the body of a lion. Some queens were represented as sphinxes, but, unlike the often malevolent Greek sphinx, the Egyptian sphinx tended to be male and a protective presence.

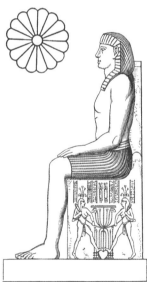

See also
Government,
pages 20–3

Ramesses II
Ramesses II (*c.* 1279–1213 BC) ruled for sixty-seven years. He was trained for kingship during the reign of his father, Seti I (died *c.* 1279 BC). Foreign policy and the economy were high on his political agenda. He fought the Hittites at the Battle of Qadesh (*c.* 1274 BC), the most documented battle in pharaonic history. He also instigated a massive building program throughout Egypt.

The pharaoh's throne
A successful pharaoh ruled over a united Egypt. The king's throne often had a motif encapsulating the royal obligation to ensure the continued union of the two lands (*sema tawy*): hieroglyphic lungs and trachea bound with papyrus and lily, the heraldic plants of the north and south, pulled tight by Hapy, god of the annual inundation of the Nile (*akhet*).

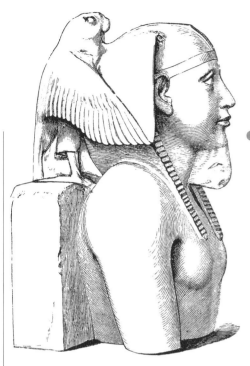

The pharaoh's crown

The tall white crown (*hedjet*) was of Upper Egypt; the red crown (*deshret*) was of Lower Egypt. Even a king of a fully united Egypt might be shown wearing these crowns separately, although they might both be worn as the Double Crown (*pschent*). The Blue Crown (*khepresh*) tends to be associated with warfare. The role of the cobra (*uraeus*) was to protect the king.

Names of the pharaoh

The pharaoh had five names other than his birth name. He was King of Upper and Lower Egypt, and son of the sun god Ra. He was also identified closely with the falcon god Horus through the titles "Horus" and "Golden Horus."

The pharaoh's role

The primary function of the pharaoh was to keep chaos (*isfet*) at bay and maintain order (*maat*) in Egypt and on a cosmic level. One way to achieve this was to minimize potential threats of nature or enemies through royal iconography, in which the king hunted wild animals and executed foreign captives (as here on the Narmer Palette).

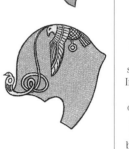

Keeper of order

As supreme judge and high priest of every cult in the land, the pharaoh ensured order throughout Egyptian society and the cosmos. In truth he had deputies to undertake these duties, but temple walls always represented the king performing rituals before the gods, such as the offering of the goddess Maat to a deity in this picture.

Symbols of authority

The crook and flail were symbols of royal authority, and the pharaoh was often pictured holding them crossed over his chest. The hieroglyph for the crook means "to rule." The flail was perhaps originally a shepherd's whip or a fly whisk, but it has also been identified as a goat herder's *ladanisterion*, used to collect the gum resin ladanum.

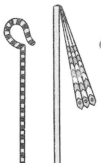

The vulture and the cobra

One of the king's five titles was "He of the Two Ladies." These were the vulture goddess Nekhbet of El-Kab (ancient Nekheb) in the south and the cobra goddess Wadjet of Buto in the Nile Delta. Once again the dual nature of kingship is emphasized, and the king comes under the tutelage (protection) of two ancient deities of the Two Lands.

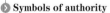

GOVERNMENT

The Royal Family

During the earliest periods of Egypt's pharaonic history, royal family members held all the high administrative and religious offices. However, government reforms following the politically fragmented First Intermediate Period (*c.* 2181–2040 BC) resulted in less royal nepotism and greater opportunities for others. Although women rarely ruled Egypt, royal wives, mothers, and daughters sometimes had considerable political and cultic influence, controlling vast estates with associated industries, such as textile and perfume production. Since kingship was considered divine, royal family members, particularly the queen mother, also had close associations with the divine. To ensure a smooth transition from one king to the next the crown prince might act as coregent with his regnant father. This practice was instituted following the first recorded assassination of an Egyptian king, Amenemhat I (*c.* 1955 BC).

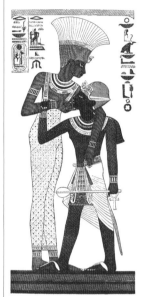

Divine mother of the king
Since it was believed that the pharaoh had divine parentage, he was depicted on the walls of temples throughout Egypt and Nubia being suckled by a number of different goddesses. One of these was Anukis, a goddess of the southern border region of Egypt (and particularly the cataracts), who sometimes appears with the epithet Mother of the King.

The queens' duties
Queens and princesses performed temple rituals in which they shook ceremonial rattles known as sistra. These were particularly associated with the cult of the goddess of fertility Hathor (with whom Queen Nefertari was identified in her temple at Abu Simbel). The hooped sistrum seen above would have had cross wires or rods with disks threaded on them. The head of the goddess features in its design.

The pharaoh's wives
The king would have a chief royal wife and a harem of additional wives, which might include daughters of foreign rulers. Ramesses II, for example, married two Hittite princesses. His chief wife Nefertari (*c.* 1290 BC–*c.* 1255 BC) (below, second left), was honored with a temple at Abu Simbel, and buried in a stunningly decorated tomb in the Valley of the Queens at Luxor.

The pharaoh's palaces
Successful government of Egypt required the pharaoh and his entourage to be peripatetic. For most of Egypt's history, the administrative capital was at Memphis, although Ramesses II built a great new palace capital called Piramesse (modern Qantir) in the eastern Delta. During the New Kingdom the religious capital was at Thebes (modern Luxor), and some of the kings used small palaces attached to the temples built close to their tombs in the Valley of the Kings.

The pharaoh's entourage
Here the pharaoh wears the Double Crown (*pschent*) of Upper and Lower Egypt. He is surrounded by members of his entourage, no doubt some of whom were members of his close family. The highest administrative official in the land was the vizier (*tjaty*) who deputized for the king in most areas of government. From the 18th Dynasty (*c.* 1550 BC) there were two concurrent viziers, one in the north and one in the south.

See also
Government,
pages 18–9
Government,
pages 22–3

The princes' duties
With a harem of wives, a king might end up with a large number of sons. These princes were represented with a distinctive side lock of hair. They were trained in military, priestly, and administrative occupations. Pouring libations before the gods in the temples was one of the rituals deemed crucial for ensuring the continued beneficence of the divine world.

Status symbols
The horse and chariot were introduced into Egypt from western Asia during the Second Intermediate Period (*c.* 1650–1550 BC). From the early New Kingdom (*c.* 1550 BC) the king, royal family, and elite preferred this high-status form of transport, or were carried on the shoulders of servants, accompanied by a fan bearer. Sunshades and fans symbolized fertility and the shadow, which had considerable significance for the ancient Egyptians.

GOVERNMENT

Scribes and Officials

During periods of stability the Egyptian government was highly centralized and incredibly efficient, with the pharaoh central to all aspects of government. The civil service was underpinned by detailed record keeping by a literate minority. As in early Mesopotamia, writing seems to have been used as a means of political control, and scribes were present at all levels of government. An enormous range of titles has survived of those working within the administrative system—unfortunately they are generally not accompanied by job descriptions. Egypt was composed of forty-two nomes, or provinces. Each of these was governed by a nomarch, who held privileges that enabled him to wield control in his local district if the central authority weakened. Women were rare exceptions in the administrative infrastructure, and all the evidence for schooling indicates the education of only boys.

Divine writing
The goddess of writing was Seshat, represented as a woman with a rosette or seven-pointed star on her head. Here she is accompanied by the ibis-headed god Thoth, the patron deity of scribes. Together with the seated god Amun, they write the name of the king on the leaves of the sacred *ished,* or persea tree, recording the king's regnal years and jubilees.

Ka-Aper
A standard means of representing an Egyptian official was striding, left foot forward, holding a long staff in his left hand and often a short scepter of office in his right. This is an acacia wood statue of Ka-Aper, a priest and military scribe who seems to have been involved with the army's campaigns in Palestine, *c.* 2500 BC. The inlaid eyes are particularly lifelike.

The power of the written word
Literacy was such a powerful indicator of status that even high officials chose to be represented sitting cross-legged on the ground as scribes, when in actuality they would have had staff to perform such functions. These men are depicted with rolls of fat that indicate their wealth and sedentary lifestyle. No women are represented in this way.

The scribe's tools

Scribes wrote with a fine rush (*Juncus maritimus*) brush—the reed (*Phragmites aegyptiaca*) pen was introduced to Egypt later by the Greeks. Sometimes scribes are depicted with a brush tucked behind an ear. They used a palette with two cakes of ink—one red, one black–which they would moisten with water. The red pigment was made of red ocher and the black one of carbon.

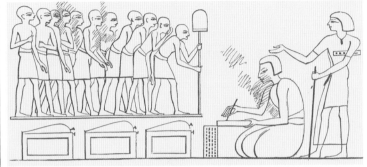

Recording everyday life

Scribes recorded all the minutiae of daily life, such as the registration of able-bodied citizens for corvée duty (forced labor). They did this on papyrus, plastered wooden boards, leather sheets, and ostraca (flakes of limestone and bits of broken pottery). Papyrus was certainly the most valuable writing material, and papyrus rolls were stored in chests like those in front of the seated scribe above.

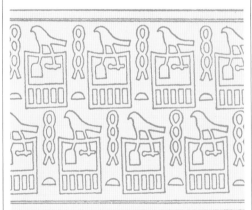

Seals

Early Egyptian officials used cylinder seals, perhaps as a result of Mesopotamian influence in Egypt at this time. The incised seal was rolled over soft mud used to seal a door or receptacle. As here, it is often the impression that has survived rather than the seal itself. The name of the king (Aha) appears inside a *serekh*—which was a frame for the king's name that predated the use of the cartouche—under the falcon god Horus.

See also
Government,
pages 18–21
Work,
pages 46–7

The Viceroy of Kush

Much of Egypt's wealth derived from gold resources in the Eastern Desert. The most productive of these were south of Aswan in the Nubian Desert, so during the periods when Egypt was politically powerful, the rulers made sure they controlled these areas of Nubia. During the reign of Tutankhamun (*c.* 1336–1327 BC), seated here, one of the most prestigious appointments was that of "Viceroy of Kush" (in this case Huy), the Egyptian governor of Nubia.

SOCIETY

Everyday Life

Agriculture was the principal occupation of most of Egyptian society. A high percentage of the population was employed on the estates of the priests, the king, and members of the royal family or elite, therefore the agricultural cycle would have defined their lives. The calendar comprised three seasons, each of four lunar months with three ten-day weeks (an additional five days were added onto the year, but the leap year was introduced into Egypt later by the Greeks). The first season was *akhet*, the flood season. The annual inundation by the Nile was of the utmost importance to the fertility of Egypt because it deposited a new layer of rich silt each year. Then came *peret*, when the crops emerged, and finally *shemu*, harvest time.

The annual flood

Until the completion of the Aswan High Dam in 1971, the Nile flooded every year between June and September, mainly due to heavy summer rains in the Ethiopian highlands. If flood levels were too high or too low, the effect could be devastating for the people of Egypt. Settlements were built on high ground to avoid the floodwaters, and villages might resemble islands during the inundation season (*akhet*).

Divine personifications

The ancient Egyptians created divine personifications of everything that was crucial in their lives, such as the annual flooding of the Nile. The god of the flood was Hapy, represented here with plants on his head, a pendulous breast, and, usually, a somewhat larger stomach than in this picture. The beginning of the flood in Egypt was heralded as "the arrival of Hapy."

Expressions of devotion

The hieroglyph of a lapwing was used to write the ancient Egyptian word for "king's subjects" (*rekhyt*). The raised arms indicate a stance of devotion and adoration; the star also tells us the population are in the act of worshipping. The birds sits on the hieroglyphic sign for "all." So the message is clear: "All subject peoples adore [the pharaoh]."

See also
Society,
pages 26–9
Work,
pages 44–5

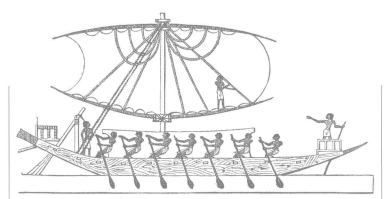

River of life

Daily life revolved around the Nile River and the thick black silt it deposited each year. It was the channel of communication within Egypt and most transportation was riverine. Boats traveling north used oars to negotiate the current, while heading south they used sails to benefit from the prevailing northerly wind.

Preferred meats

Beef and goose were the meats preferred by the wealthy. Other domesticated fowl were swans, ducks, doves, pigeons, cranes, and, from the Roman Period, chickens, although it appears that the warrior-king Thutmose III had brought a chicken home from his military campaigning in Syria, *c.* 1450 BC). Tomb scenes show geese and cranes being force-fed with milled grain and bread pellets.

Beasts of burden

Egypt today conjures up images of camels striding across the desert, but camels did not really feature in the lives of the ancient Egyptians until the Roman Period (from 30 BC). The Nile meant that there was no real need for a large beast of burden, and the donkey was fine for shorter journeys. Depictions of people riding donkeys are rare, but they clearly did. The ancient Egyptian word for donkey was the wonderfully onomatopoeic *aa*.

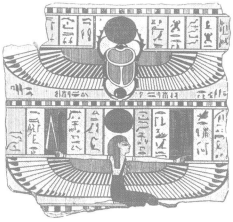

The sun god

There were times when the annual floods were too high or too low, bringing with them devastation and famine, but generally the inundation and strong sun meant abundant harvests. To ensure the continued presence of the sun in their lives the Egyptians worshipped it as a number of deities, one being Khepri, the scarab-beetle god. The beetle's habit of rolling a dung ball was compared with the movement of the sun across the sky.

Cattle count

As is the case in many African tribes today, the wealth of rich men was assessed in heads of cattle, and the cattle count was a favorite subject of tomb scenes. Two main types of cattle were represented, longhorn and shorthorn. Some were confined to stables for fattening and slaughter; others were used for plowing, threshing, and milking.

SOCIETY

Temples and Economic Life

There was almost no coinage in ancient Egypt until the arrival of Alexander the Great in 332 BC. Exchange was by barter, and taxes were paid in kind. Precise areas of land under cultivation were measured and cattle, geese, and other livestock were counted in order to calculate the taxes due. The wealth of Egypt was redistributed through the palace and temples, initially to the considerable number of people employed by them. Royal gift giving was a means of rewarding loyalty and redistributing produce. The temples were also places of storage as well as distribution via a system referred to as the "reversion of offerings." In fact, by the time of the New Kingdom, the temples were the largest employers and were very much the hub of the local economy and society, in a similar manner to medieval European monasteries.

Temple astronomy and festivals

The temple astronomers observed the stars to determine when festivals should take place. Ramesses III's temple at Medinet Habu, for example, celebrated sixty festivals a year. They were an opportunity for the local people to interact more closely with the gods and to benefit from the redistribution of produce. The configurations shown here are the family of northern constellations painted on the ceiling of Seti I's burial chamber in the Valley of the Kings dated *c.* 1280 BC.

Temple staff

The highest ranks in the priesthood, such as those pictured here, were full-time and often hereditary posts. They would perform the rituals before the cult statues of the gods on behalf of the king. However, most who worked in the temples served on a rota system, working one month out of every four. This was worthwhile because temple workers received a share of the temple revenue.

The role of temples

Temples were at the heart of community life. Housing, offices, workshops, and stables abutted their walls. In addition to worship, other aspects of life, such as education, went on within the temple precincts. According to Papyrus Harris of Ramesses III's reign (*c.* 1184–*c.* 1153 BC), Karnak temple employed 81,322 workers over 924 sq miles (2,393 sq km) of arable land, with 433 orchards, 421,362 head of livestock, 65 villages, 83 ships, and 46 workshops.

See also
Society,
pages 24–5
Society,
pages 28–9
Architecture,
pages 66–7

Burning incense

Temples were wealthy establishments. They benefited from Egypt's extensive trade networks. Certain ranks of priest wore leopard skins that were imported from Nubia and countries to the south. Several aromatic substances were burned as incense in temple rituals. The priest here holds an incense burner in his right hand. Resins for this purpose were imported from the eastern Mediterranean, possibly Arabia, and from areas to the south in Africa.

Royal beneficiaries

The pharaoh bestowed gifts on his loyal administrators. Of most significance was the gold *shebyu* collar, which represented an elevation in the status of the subject when presented by the king. The 18th-Dynasty king Akhenaten (*c.* 1352–1336 BC) favoured this means of rewarding his subjects' distinguished service. He is pictured here with his wife Nefertiti and three of their daughters at a "Window of Appearances."

Redistribution of wealth

At the royal gift-giving ceremonies the high officials would receive not only gold collars but also a host of other commodities. A sizeable share of these would then be redistributed among the members of the household, staff, and dependants of the elite man. Scribes were ever present to record the various stages of the economic process.

Spiritual cleansing

The most common priestly title was *wab* (pure or purified). Each temple had a sacred lake in which the priests could cleanse themselves. They also tended to shave their heads. Inscriptions at the Ptolemaic and Roman Period temple at Esna inform us that those entering the temple were expected to have cut their nails, removed all body hair, and washed their hands in natron.

SOCIETY

Family Life

Marriage was fundamental to Egyptian society, with the family as the basic social unit. Unlike the king, men tended to have one wife at a time, although divorce and early death (particularly of women in childbirth) might result in more than one spouse in a person's lifetime. A woman's social status and position in the household were dependent on her ability to conceive; the function of a wife was to produce children, and divorce might be demanded if a woman was unable to do so. It was expected that children would look after their parents in old age and, most importantly, provide them with a proper burial and then remember them after death with offerings and invocations. Sons took over their fathers' professions. In fact, the reputation of the family hinged upon producing the next generation.

Gender representations
In images people were represented in accordance with the conventions of Egyptian art, and depictions were highly stylized and idealized. Men were usually portrayed with reddish brown skin and women with paler, yellow skin. When a couple were seated next to each other, they were always represented with the man in the dominant position in front of the woman.

See also
Society,
pages 24–7
Architecture,
pages 70–1

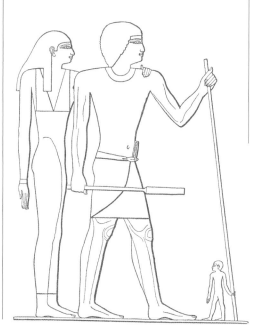

Marriage and setting up home
Marriage had social importance, but it appears to have had no religious significance. As far as we know it was not accompanied by any form of religious ritual. The emphasis was on the initiation of a new household. Two of the common terms used to express the concept of marriage from the New Kingdom onward were "to enter a house" and "to set up a home."

Life after death
A recurring scene on the walls of nonroyal tombs is the depiction of fishing and fowling. The tomb owner is always accompanied by his family, and although he engages in activities he no doubt performed during his lifetime, and wishes to enjoy in the afterlife, the scene is also steeped in the symbolism of fertility, and thus rebirth, after death.

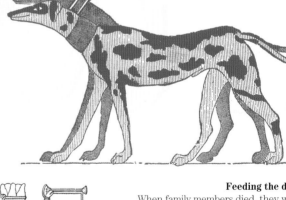

The role of dogs
Dogs were beloved pets and often accompanied their owners on hunting expeditions. They were also used as guard and police animals. One word for a dog was the onomatopoeic *iuiu*. Nearly eighty dog names have been recorded, including Blacky/Ebony, Good Herdsman, Brave One, Reliable, Lord, Northwind—and Useless!

Domesticated animals
The ancient painters were decidedly more true to life in their portrayals of the animal world than they were in their depictions of the human body. Family life might include pets, which were often named and sometimes buried in style. Cats (descended from the African wild cat *Felis silvestris libyca*) held a special place in Egyptian life. They were mostly lithely built tabbies and were called by the onomatopoeic term *miu*. On hunting trips they were used to flush out birds from the marshes.

Feeding the dead
When family members died, they were often buried together in one tomb. A wealthy family would own estates, which might continue to provide offerings for their funerary cult. The ancient Egyptians believed that they would require sustenance in the afterlife, so processions of offering bearers were depicted on the tomb walls, carrying a range of produce, including bread, cakes, beer, fruit, and fowl.

WARFARE

Weapons and Armor

During the Dynastic Period (*c.* 3000–*c.* 1550 BC) there was remarkably little change in Egyptian weaponry, with weapons remaining similar to those used elsewhere in Africa and in the Near East. Since the late Predynastic Period (prior to the formation of a unified state), the Egyptians had fought with maces, axes, spears, bows and arrows, and throw sticks. They continued to do so up until the New Kingdom, at which time Egypt experienced innovations in military technology thanks to Western Asiatic (Palestinian, Syrian, Mitanni, and Hittite) influences in Egypt. During the 18th Dynasty, Egypt had far greater contact with Palestine and Syria than ever before. The horse, chariot, and body armor were introduced into Egypt, and the bow, shield, dagger, and short sword were developed.

See also
Warfare,
pages 32–5

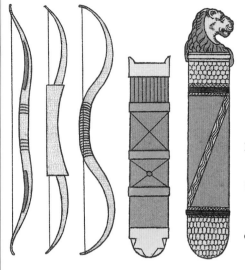

Development of the bow
During the Dynastic Period archers used a "self" (or simple) bow of wood strung with twisted gut. Later they used a recurved bow (see the three bows on left) of two convex sections, offering greater force and range. The composite bow was introduced in the New Kingdom. Strips of horn and sinew were glued to a wooden self bow, resulting in the more elastic recurved and triangular composite bows, giving much greater range than before. Two quivers are also shown here.

Arrows and arrowheads
Arrows were usually made of hard-stemmed reeds. These were fletched with three feathers and tipped initially with flint, bone, ebony or ivory points. By the Middle Kingdom (*c.* 2055–1650 BC) archers used copper and bronze arrowheads, which might be barbed, wide or narrow.

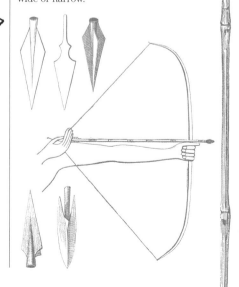

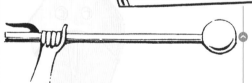

The mace
As a wooden handle inserted into a stone head, the mace was the simplest of the weapons used by the ancient Egyptians. It was most popular during the Predynastic and Protodynastic Periods (up until *c.* 3100 BC) during which time the mace head developed from being disk- to pear-shaped. The mace became a symbol of domination, and the pharaoh was depicted wielding it long after it had fallen out of general use.

The throw stick
The throw stick (a curved wooden blade) was used as a weapon during the Predynastic Period, but by the Dynastic Period its primary use was for hunting birds. Tutankhamun was buried with a large number of these, some very elaborate, inlaid with ivory and ebony and gilded.

Close-quarter combat

Daggers were ideal for close-quarter combat and despatching the fallen enemy. Blades were always short and double-edged, and designed for stabbing rather than slashing.

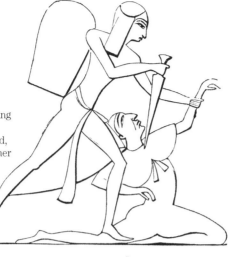

Shields

From the late Predynastic Period to the Middle Kingdom, the Egyptians used 3–5 ft (1–1.5 m) long shields made of cowhide stretched over a wooden frame with a handle at the back. Their top edge was curved or pointed. In the New Kingdom a shield with a tapered lower half was introduced.

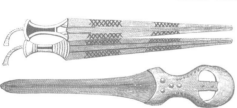

Daggers and knives

Early on the Egyptians made very fine flint knives and daggers, and continued to do so even with the advent of copper and bronze. The innovations in military technology during the early New Kingdom brought with them a new form of dagger, with the narrow blade and tang cast in one. Handles were made of wood, bone, or ivory.

Armor

Egyptian soldiers did not wear armor until the early New Kingdom, when for the first time linen or leather jerkins, with small bronze or hard-leather, overlapping scales riveted to them were used. Bronze-scale armor was used most frequently by the Persians, and it is possible that most of the scale armor found in Egypt had originally belonged to foreigners.

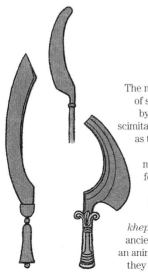

Khepesh

The most specialized form of sword or dagger used by the Egyptians was a scimitar-like weapon known as the *khepesh*. It had a curved bronze blade modeled on an Asiatic form, which appeared in Egypt during the Second Intermediate Period. The name *khepesh* derives from the ancient Egyptian word for an animal's foreleg, because they have a similar shape.

Battle-axes

The axe was one of the most commonly used weapons. In the Old Kingdom its copper head was semicircular. By the Middle Kingdom it had developed the longer bronze or copper blade with concave sides and a curved edge. Another type was the "scalloped" or "tanged" axe head, which was attached to the wooden haft with three tangs.

WARFARE

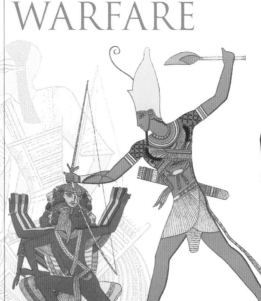

Soldiers and Captives

There seems to have been no need for a permanent standing army in Egypt until the early 18th Dynasty (1550–1292 BC), when burgeoning Egyptian imperialism led to the establishment of a large professional army. Before then, apart from a small royal bodyguard, young men were conscripted on an ad hoc basis for military campaigns. From the beginning of pharaonic history, Nubian mercenaries served in the Egyptian army, particularly the Medjay, a nomadic group originally from the eastern deserts of Nubia. By the New Kingdom, many nationalities fought for Egypt, including Syrians, Libyans, and Hittites. Then, during the 26th Dynasty (664–525 BC), Ionians, Carians, and Phoenicians began to feature in the Egyptian Army. The image of the bound captive appears frequently in Egyptian art as a symbol of Egypt's (and the pharaoh's) supremacy. Prisoners of war were usually forced to join the Egyptian Army or given as slaves to distinguished soldiers.

See also
Warfare,
pages 30–1
Warfare,
pages 34–5
Work,
pages 46–7

Depictions of foreigners
As far as the ancient Egyptians were concerned, those who lived outside their borders were potential enemies or threats to Egypt's sense of order, so it was of magical significance to represent them with their arms tied behind their backs or in a subordinate position beneath the pharaoh. The foreigners commonly represented in this way were a generic Nubian (from southern Egypt) and Asiatic (Palestinian/Syrian).

War captives
Prisoners of war were usually brought back to Egypt with their hands manacled before or behind them. Egyptian artists portrayed people from western Asia or the Levant with a distinctive facial shape, hairstyle, skin color, and clothing. High-status prisoners might be executed and their bodies displayed as a warning to others.

Confounding the enemy
Some pharaohs did indeed lead their troops into battle, but whether a king was a true military leader or not was not an issue in the art of the day. It was a standard image for all kings to be represented smiting the enemy. Here he grabs the hair of the foreigners in one hand and raises a mace-*khepesh* (a stone mace head combined with a curved metal blade) ready to strike.

⟩ War chariots

In the fifth year of Ramesses II's reign, a great battle took place between the Egyptians and the Hittites, the Battle of Qadesh on the Orontes River in Syria. As was customary, the Egyptian chariots were manned by a driver and a warrior, while the Hittites appear in threes—a driver, a spearman, and a shield bearer holding a distinctive shield.

Military elite ⟩

A new warrior class emerged in Egypt in the New Kingdom, modeled on the Asiatic military elite. Their status symbol was the chariot pulled by two horses, and they were known in Egypt as the *maryannu* (young heroes). The greatest of the military pharaohs was Thutmose III (*c.* 1479–1425 BC). He led sixteen campaigns into Syria-Palestine, creating an Empire and extending Egypt's influence in the Near East.

⟩ Mercenaries

The mercenaries who fought on behalf of the Egyptians at the Battle of Qadesh all had distinctive appearances and weaponry. These were Libyans, Syrians, and the Sherden (leading this group), the last-named probably originating from northern Syria, although they are often associated with Sardinia. Their helmets were particularly unusual; they were of metal or leather surmounted by horns and with a central disk.

WARFARE

Battles and Spoils of War

The Egyptians were adept at defending their borders. It is not known for sure whether the Hyksos of the western Asiatic invaded Egypt in *c.* 1650 BC, but they certainly emerged as the dominant force in the Delta region for a period of one hundred years. The better-documented invasions by Nubians, Persians, and Assyrians did not take place until Egypt's Late Period, a good 2,300 years after the formation of the Egyptian state. Alexander the Great went on to conquer Egypt in 332 BC and the Romans wrangled control from the Greeks in 30 BC. During prosperous periods the Egyptians were highly successful at controlling trade networks and natural resources beyond their borders. During the Middle Kingdom, they built large mud-brick fortresses in Nubia, and a policy of expansionism and imperialism was certainly exercised in Syria-Palestine during the New Kingdom. Well-documented battles at Megiddo (*c.* 1482 BC) and Qadesh (*c.* 1274 BC) provide considerable evidence for Egyptian military tactics and techniques.

Second Battle of Qadesh
Ramesses II, shown here fighting in the Battle of Qadesh, portrayed the battle as a great Egyptian victory over the Hittites when it appears to have been at best a stalemate (the Hittite records survive to set the record straight). Ramesses had marched his 20,000-strong army up through Palestine and Lebanon, but he was caught off guard by the Hittite chariotry, and he was saved from a crushing defeat only by the arrival of Egyptian reinforcements heading inland from the Phoenician coast.

See also
Warfare,
pages 30–3

First Battle of Qadesh
Ramesses II is famous for his Battle of Qadesh (*c.* 1274 BC), but his father Seti I had been decidedly more successful at his very own earlier Battle of Qadesh (*c.* 1294 BC), which resulted in an agreement between the Hittite king Muwatallis and Seti over the division of Syria-Palestine between the two superpowers.

Siege of Dapur

Ramesses II laid siege to the city of Dapur in Syria (above). The Egyptians dug a ditch around the city they were attacking. They constructed an enclosure wall of locally felled trees, and made use of scaling ladders. The best-documented siege was the one by Thutmose III of Megiddo (in modern Israel).

Divine campaigns

The four divisions of Ramesses II's main army were named after four of the most important deities: Amun, Ra, Ptah, and Seth. The warrior kings of the New Kingdom campaigned in the name of Amun (pictured below on the left) and his temples at Luxor benefited greatly from the imperial wealth flooding into Egypt.

Maritime warfare

The earliest, properly documented sea battle was fought between the victorious Egyptians (on the left) and the "Sea Peoples" during the reign of Ramesses III. These "Sea Peoples" or "Northerners," as the Egyptians called them, were a loose confederation of seafaring Indo-European migrants that were wreaking havoc in the eastern Mediterranean.

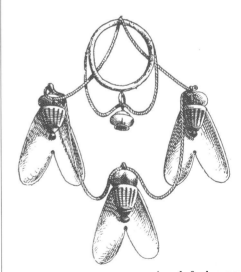

Awards for bravery

The "Flies of Valor" were gold pendants in the form of flies awarded to soldiers for bravery. Presumably the symbol of the fly was chosen for its persistence and determination. The pendants pictured here were found on the body of a queen named Ahhotep (*c.* 1550 BC). It is not known whether she actually did wage war, but she may well have been involved in the Theban campaign to expel the Hyksos from the Delta at the end of the Second Intermediate Period.

RELIGION

Mythology

Ancient Egyptian religion was polytheistic and the ancient Egyptians created order within their complex pantheon of gods and goddesses by grouping deities into family units. To a certain extent, the divine realm reflected that of mortals. Myths describe the antics of the deities, their displays of emotion, and the often difficult, as well as positive, relationships between them. These myths were probably generated by the educated temple priesthoods at cult centers throughout Egypt, and they were constructed in order to provide explanations for the fundamentals of human existence. They contain carefully constructed metaphors and provide a window into the ancient Egyptian mind. Several explanations as to how the universe came into being survive, each associated with different important cult centers, but sharing common ground.

Khnum

Khnum was the ram-headed creator god of the southern region of Egypt, with cult centers at Esna and Elephantine. He was associated with the cataract at Aswan and the annual flooding of the Nile. He was said to have modeled all aspects of the universe out of clay on a potter's wheel.

Holy triad

By the New Kingdom, Amun, the local god of ancient Thebes (modern Luxor), had emerged as the preeminent deity in the state pantheon. He was worshipped at Karnak Temple in Luxor as a member of a triad with his consort, the mother goddess Mut, and their child deity, Khonsu.

The Heliopolitan myth

In the myth of Heliopolis (ancient Inunu, now in a Cairo suburb), the self-engendered creator god Atum gave form to Shu (the god of air) and Tefnut (the goddess of moisture), who in turn gave birth to Geb (the earth god) and Nut (the sky goddess). Shu forced them apart by lifting Nut up above the earth.

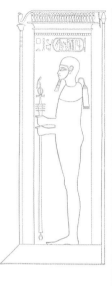

Ptah speaks

Ptah was the self-engendered creator god of Memphis, who brought the universe into being by conceiving all aspects of it in his heart and then by speaking his thoughts out loud. Everything came into being when Ptah declared its name.

See also
Religion,
pages 38–41

Representations of night

Nut could also be represented as a cow, still supported by her father Shu with his arms outstretched. The ancient Egyptians explained nighttime darkness by suggesting that Nut swallowed the sun in the evening, after which it traveled through her body (often in a boat), and she gave birth to it at dawn.

Rebirth

Nut could also be depicted stretched out across the ceilings of royal burial chambers and inside the lids of coffins and sarcophagi. She is shown swallowing and giving birth to the sun, but she was also considered the divine personification of the burial chamber and sarcophagus, and the inference is that, like the sun, the dead person beneath her would be reborn from her.

Hathor

Hathor could be represented as a woman or a cow or as a woman with cow's ears. She was the goddess of fertility, music, dance, mining regions, foreign lands, and the land of the dead. Each year her cult statue was taken from the inner sanctum of her temple at Dendera onto the roof, where she bathed in the energizing rays of the sun at dawn, shown here as Nut gives birth to the sun.

Horus and Seth

The king of Egypt was identified with the falcon god Horus; both could be depicted wearing the Double Crown of Upper and Lower Egypt. In Egyptian myth, following the death of the god Osiris, there were a series of confrontations between his son Horus and his brother Seth. Reliefs in the temple of Horus at Edfu show him, assisted by his mother the goddess Isis, harpooning Seth, who takes the form of a hippopotamus.

Divine kingship

The office of kingship was considered divine in ancient Egypt. The king was able to make use of Ptah's characteristics, *heka* (divine energy), *sia* (divine knowledge), and *hu* (divine utterance), and interacted closely with the gods. Here the 18th-Dynasty king Amenhotep II (reign *c.* 1420 BC) is being purified by the falcon-headed god Horus and the ibis-headed god Thoth.

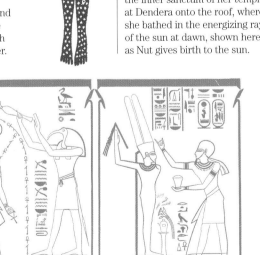

RELIGION

Funerary Religion

The ancient Egyptians believed that when they died, if all went according to plan, they would reemerge into an afterlife of plenty. Funerary spells—the so-called *Coffin Texts* and *Book of the Dead*—describe this well-watered place with its abundant grain and fruit trees as a place where the dead could lead the life they had enjoyed on earth, only better. It was deemed essential that the body and name of the dead person be preserved, and that he or she was buried in accordance with the correct rituals, together with food supplies and other basic necessities. It was only the upper echelons of Egyptian society who could afford elaborate mummification and a decorated tomb. Most Egyptians would have been buried in shallow graves in direct contact with the sand (perfect for the desiccation of the body) and with life's bare essentials.

Anubis
The jackal-headed deity was Anubis, the god of cemeteries and embalming. The body was embalmed with natron, a naturally occurring salt, and wrapped in linen bandages. The mummification process took seventy days, the period of time that Sirius was out of sight prior to its heliacal rising, which heralded the annual Nile flood, and thus the start of the New Year.

The Four Sons of Horus
For much of pharaonic history, the lungs, liver, stomach, and intestines were removed from the body, embalmed separately, and placed in what Egyptologists call canopic jars. They were protected by four guardian deities (shown above), collectively known as the Four Sons of Horus, from left to right, Qebesenuef, Duamutef, Hapy, and Imsety.

Opening of the Mouth
The Opening of the Mouth ceremony was the final rite performed on the mummified body before it was placed in the tomb. Various implements, including a model adze and a snake-headed wand, were held up to the nose and mouth of the deceased to restore the senses and reanimate him or her for the afterlife.

See also
Religion, *pages 36–7*
Religion, *pages 40–1*
Architecture, *pages 68–9*

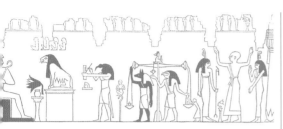

The divine tribunal

The ancient Egyptians believed that after death they would be judged on their lifetime in order to determine whether they could pass on into the afterlife. The divine tribunal was presided over by the god of the dead, rebirth, and fertility, Osiris. The heart of the deceased was symbolically weighed against the feather of *maat*, the symbol of truth, justice, and order.

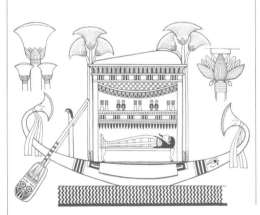

Ka and ba

The ancient Egyptians believed that when they died their *ka*, or vital force, remained intimately linked with their physical body, while their *ba*, or unique personality, was mobile. The latter was represented as a bird with a human head and sometimes arms and is shown here enjoying the water and shade offered by a manifestation of the goddess Nut as a sycamore tree.

Ammit

Ammit literally means Devourer. She was a terrifying presence at the divine judgment, poised ready to devour the heart of the deceased if it was weighed down by misdeeds. She was a composite creature—part crocodile, part leopard or lion, part hippopotamus. The ancient Egyptians believed that the heart was the seat of all thought and emotion: no heart meant no afterlife.

Abydos

Abydos was the legendary burial place of the god of the dead, Osiris, and it became a particularly important place of pilgrimage during the New Kingdom (*c*. 1550–*c*. 1069 BC). Tomb scenes show the mummified body of the deceased being taken by boat on a symbolic post-mortem pilgrimage to Abydos.

Coffins

Coffins were either rectangular or anthropoid. Deities, amuletic symbols, and hieroglyphic inscriptions were emblazoned on the more costly coffins. In the Ramesside Period (*c*. 1295–*c*. 1069 BC) it is known that a coffin cost about 20 *deben*, the price of a donkey, a small cow, or a bed.

RELIGION

Private Religion

Interaction between the ancient Egyptians and their gods was an important aspect of daily life, but this rarely took place in the great temples of Egypt. Unlike mosques and churches, the temples of ancient Egypt were not places of communal worship. The local community might experience their local deities when the sacred statues and shrines were brought out of the temples on festival days—on such occasions they could consult a statue of a god directly and the priests would manipulate it to respond. Ordinary people were also able (later in pharaonic history) to engage in rituals in the outer parts of temples. Certain deities were more closely associated with the household and daily life, particularly those vulnerable stages of the human life cycle, such as pregnancy, childbirth and early childhood. Spells, amulets, and magical rituals were very important at these times.

See also
Religion,
pages 36–9
Architecture,
pages 68–9

Greeting the sun
The ancient Egyptians were great observers of the natural world, and they incorporated much of what they saw into their belief system. Baboons were seen to chatter and rise up on their hind legs at dawn, so the ancient Egyptians associated this posture with worship of the sun, and with gods and goddesses in general.

Festivals
At festivals, the priests carried the sacred shrine out of the sanctuary, often to visit another temple. This portable shrine tended to be in the form of a boat (referred to as a bark or barque). It housed the cult statue of the god, which was always concealed from view. These divine outings were often occasions for oracular consultation.

Bastet the cat goddess
Herodotus discussed Egypt at length in Book II of his *Histories*. He described the festival of the protective cat goddess Bastet at Bubastis (Tell Basta) in the eastern Delta. Apparently thousands of people attended her annual festival, and more wine was consumed during that festival than in all the rest of the year put together.

Serket

The protective goddess Serket was represented as a scorpion, semi-scorpion, or as a woman with a scorpion on her head. To placate her was to help guard against the worrying possibility of scorpion stings. Small, votive scorpions were deposited at shrines from the earliest times, and myths and spells were devised to help the ancient Egyptians overcome what was clearly one of their most common fears.

Bes

Bes featured in the daily lives of the ancient Egyptians as a household god, offering protection at vulnerable times, such as sleep or childbirth. He appears on fragments of wall paintings from houses and in the decoration on headrests, beds, and chairs.

Cippus of Horus

A Cippus of Horus is a magical stela covered in hieroglyphic spells to help safeguard against scorpions and snakes. Water was poured over the Cippus, imbuing it with the magical power of the spells and accompanying imagery. This water could be collected and either applied to the body or drunk.

Heket the midwife

The frog-headed goddess Heket was the goddess most closely associated with midwifery. In the "Tales of Wonder" on the Middle Kingdom Westcar Papyrus, she is one of three divine midwives disguised as dancing girls that appear to deliver triplets. They speed up the delivery, cut the umbilical cords, and wash the babies.

The scarab

The scarab was an amulet that was also used as a seal, with the design for the impression incised on the base. This beetle (*Scarabaeus sacer*) was the means of representing the solar deity Khepri, who was also associated with creation and rebirth.

The Eye of Horus

In Egyptian mythology Horus had his left eye damaged by the god Seth, but since it was healed by the goddess Hathor it was associated with healing and well being by the ancients. Their word for the Eye of Horus was *wedjat*, meaning 'whole', and it was often worn as an amulet.

WORK

Farming

Most of the population of ancient Egypt spent their lives working the land. The thick silt deposited by the Nile inundation each year was rich and fertile, and the land was irrigated by using canals to direct the floodwaters into basins. The water was retained for forty to sixty days before it was released back into the river. The stages of the agricultural cycle are well represented in scenes on the walls of elite tombs. The land was tilled and seed sown. Then the crops were harvested, threshed, winnowed, sieved, and stored. The ancient Egyptians expressed their dependence on the land in tomb scenes, and in so doing they hoped to ensure that the crops would continue to flourish in this life and the next. The main crops were emmer wheat, barley, and flax.

Plowing and sowing
A shallow wooden plowing ard was usually pulled by cattle harnessed by a yoke attached to their horns (as here) and later by the more efficient shoulder yoke. Farmers practiced broadcast sowing by scattering seed corn (probably in spikelets) from bags held or hung around the shoulder.

The shaduf
The shaduf was introduced to Egypt during the 18th Dynasty and is still used there today. It is a pole and lever device to lift a bucket of water from the river or a canal to higher land. It is more suitable for watering gardens than fields.

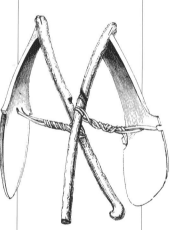

Tilling the soil
Very little tillage was necessary on well-irrigated land, but ancient Egyptian farmers did use wooden hoes to till the land to create a loose, friable soil. This would have improved cereal yield by providing an adequate seed cover for germination, aerating the soil, and encouraging strong root development. Cast-bronze hoes are also known from the New Kingdom.

Help in the afterlife

To avoid having to work the land in the afterlife, wealthy Egyptians were buried with *shabtis* (figurines) made of faience, stone, wood, pottery, bronze, wax, or glass. These often held a hoe and a pick and were inscribed with a spell ensuring that they would do any hard work for the deceased in the next life.

The crops

Emmer wheat and barley would have been harvested between early February and late May. Sickle blades were originally of chipped stone, handheld or set in a wooden handle or the lower jawbone of an animal. Later sickle blades were also made of copper and then bronze. Here the cereal is being cut low down; the straw could be used as fuel, fodder, roofing, and temper in mud brick, plaster, and pottery.

Granaries

Grain was probably stored in spikelet form rather than as clean grain, to protect it against insects, fungi, and other pests. Granaries were often domed, probably to allow air to circulate and ensure a cool interior. The grain was fed in through doors near the top (accessed via a ladder or staircase) and removed through doors near the bottom. Cereals were probably dehusked at a domestic or household level, using a pestle and mortar.

Harvesting the grain

The pictures above show only the cereal ears being harvested. They were then spread over a threshing floor and trampled by hoofed animals (usually cattle) to separate the emmer spikelets and hulled barley grains from the cereal straw. Farmers then used winnowing fans or paddles to separate the threshed cereal from the remaining straw and other light debris. Scribes (bottom left) were always on hand to record the quantities.

See also
Work,
pages 44–7

WORK

Hunting and Animal Husbandry

The ancient Egyptians devoted considerable time and energy to procuring their food supplies, and they engaged in hunting, fishing, and fowling from the earliest times. To these activities they added animal husbandry in some regions from *c.* 4900 BC. The deserts and marshy areas of the Delta and Fayyum were perfect hunting environments, while even more important for the diet of the ancient Egyptians (particularly those who couldn't afford the luxury of meat) were the fish that could be caught in the Nile, Delta, and off the Mediterranean and Red Sea coasts. Nets, traps, and hooks were all used. The marshy areas were also perfect for cattle pasture. The ancient Egyptians also kept and bred sheep, goats, pigs, geese, ducks, pigeons, and, from the Roman Period, chickens.

Fishing

The ancient Egyptian fishermen used hand nets (triangular frames of sticks with deep nets attached), but they also used seine nets, as pictured here, from at least 2600 BC. These large nets were weighted at the bottom to make them hang vertically and had floats along their upper line. They were usually worked from the river or canal bank, but large rafts or boats might also be used.

Netting birds

The scenes of tomb owners hunting birds with throw sticks in the marshes clearly depict leisure activities. Snaring fowl as a food resource, however, was done using large clap nets, as above, by a papyrus thicket. Papyrus grew abundantly in the Fayyum and Delta areas. This was used not only to make papyrus paper, but also to make boats, sandals, basketry, matting, and ropes.

Hunting with bows

Predynastic rock art in the Western and Eastern deserts show men hunting with bows and arrows, and this continued throughout the Pharaonic Period. It would not have been necessary to use arrowheads for smaller prey; it would have been sufficient to sharpen the end of the reed arrow to a point. These arrows were usually carried by the huntsman in leather or linen quivers slung across their backs.

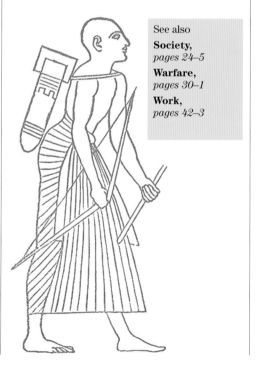

See also
Society,
pages 24–5
Warfare,
pages 30–1
Work,
pages 42–3

Cattle

These long- and shorthorn cows are clearly being fattened for slaughter. The longhorn cattle were domesticated in Predynastic times and were perhaps descended from aurochs. The shorthorn variety was gradually introduced from the Old Kingdom onward, eventually becoming more common. During the 18th Dynasty, the humped zebu was introduced from Syria as a draught animal. Cattle were imported, particularly from Nubia.

Wild prey

Desert animals hunted by the ancient Egyptians included antelopes (addax, oryx, and roan), hartebeests, gazelles (Soemmering's, slenderhorn, and dorcas), dama deer and ibex. They also snared smaller prey, such as hedgehogs, hares, and rabbits. Dogs often accompanied the hunters; by the Dynastic Period, hunting dogs tended to be of a greyhound or saluki type.

Branding

Cattle and oxen let out to pasture were often branded with the mark of their owner, usually on their forehead or haunches. A number of bronze cattle brands have survived from ancient Egypt—for example, in the form of a pair of ox horns, a lion's head (perhaps the goddess Sekhmet), and geese (the sacred animal representing the god Amun).

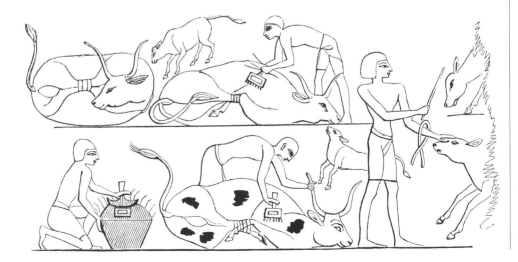

WORK

Professions

There is a wonderful piece of Middle Kingdom literature designed to indoctrinate young men with the joys of becoming a scribe, which is known today as "The Satire of the Trades." A host of possible occupations are described in disparaging terms, while the merits of a scribe's position in life are heavily emphasized. Boys usually followed in the footsteps of their fathers, perhaps to become potters, stonemasons, craftsmen, soldiers, barbers, musicians, gardeners, cobblers, or washermen, to name but a few. The chief role of women in Egyptian society was to run households and produce children, but they might also have professions, such as musician, dancer, mourner, perfume maker, or textile manufacturer.

Male musicians
Male musicians (especially harpists, as here) often seem to have been blind. This may have been so that they could serve as temple musicians and play before the cult statue without laying their "impure" eyes upon the god. Male drummers, for example, might also beat a rhythm for marching soldiers, oarsmen, or agricultural workers.

See also
Government,
pages 22–3
Warfare,
pages 32–3
Work,
pages 42–3

Female musicians
Bands of skilled female musicians and dancers could be hired to perform at parties, and are shown playing a variety of instruments. Women also worked as temple musicians, singers, and dancers. These women are often shown participating in processions on religious festival days. The deities were believed to "feed" on music, dance, and incense.

The army

Each division of the army was commanded by a general (the great Overseer of the Division), who tended to be a son of the king. The basic military unit consisted of a platoon of fifty infantrymen, each under the command of a Chief of Fifty. There were usually five platoons in a company and about twenty companies in a division. There were separate companies of elite troops and chariot warriors.

Mourning

Women were frequently employed at funerals as professional mourners. They wept and wailed, threw dust on their heads, and bared their breasts. Until the New Kingdom the two chief ritual mourners at funerals seem to have been priestesses impersonating the goddesses Isis and Nephthys (who, according to the mythology, had mourned the death of the god Osiris). In New Kingdom tomb scenes, the chief mourners are sometimes identified as wives and daughters of the deceased.

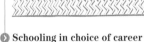

Schooling in choice of career

Schooling texts have survived that were transcribed by schoolboys who, at the same time as mastering the written word, were told of the hardships of some occupations, especially the soldier, in the hope they would work hard and become scribes or civil servants. In one description of army life the soldier is said to be laid down and beaten like a piece of papyrus (overlapping strips of papyrus stem were beaten to make paper).

Army life

A soldier's life was not easy. Military training camps were tough places with rigorous drill practice and regular physical punishment. The military campaigns themselves were grueling and grisly. But for those who shone in battle and made it home, there were rewards to be had: personal advancement, the spoils of war (including prisoners of war), gold, and gifts of land and livestock on retirement.

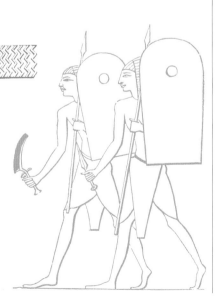

TECHNOLOGY

Stoneworking

The ancient Egyptians were extraordinarily adept at quarrying, transporting, and working stone. Egypt was rich in stone on both sides of the Nile Valley. It was first used for building architectural features of Early Dynastic royal and aristocratic tombs at Abydos and Saqqara (after *c.* 3000 BC); then in the ingenious 3rd-Dynasty Step Pyramid at Saqqara (*c.* 2650 BC), not to mention Khufu's Great Pyramid at Giza (*c.* 2560 BC). The most commonly used building stones were limestone (quarried mainly in the hills bordering the Nile Valley from Cairo to a little beyond Esna); sandstone (especially beyond Esna to Aswan); and pink and gray granite (mainly in the Aswan region). The Egyptians also sculpted stone statuary, sarcophagi, obelisks, and vessels out of a range of stones, including quartzite, graywacke, siltstone, alabaster, diorite, basalt, breccia, porphyry, serpentine, and dolorite.

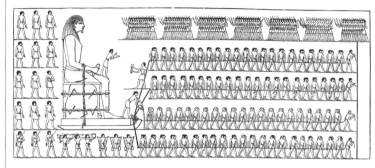

Manpower

On land, the great weights were shifted by sheer manpower alone, dragging massive stone blocks on rollers and sleds with papyrus- or linen-cord rope. In the Middle Kingdom tomb of Djehutyhotep (*c.* 1850 BC), there is a scene of 172 men dragging a colossal alabaster statue weighing around 69 tons (70 tonnes) along a 9-mile (15-km) route.

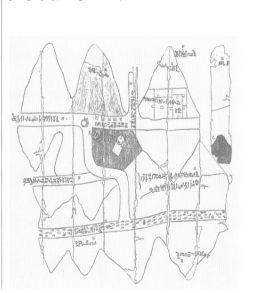

The Turin Papyrus

This, the so-called Turin Papyrus map, is the only topographic map to survive from ancient Egypt. In fact, it is one of the earliest maps in the world with real geographical content. It shows a 9-mile (15-km) stretch of the Wadi Hammamat in the center of the Eastern Desert (between the Nile Valley and the Red Sea), in which the ancients quarried *bekhen*-stone (a metagraywacke sandstone and siltstone) and mined gold.

Entering the Great Pyramid

The original entrance to Khufu's pyramid at Giza is located on its north face in the sixteenth course of masonry. It is surmounted by four relieving blocks designed to support and distribute the extraordinary weight of masonry above. This entrance was originally sealed and covered in limestone casing.

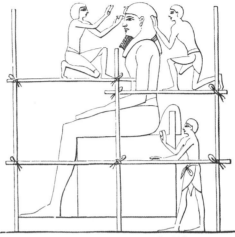

See also
Technology,
pages 50–3

Inside the Great Pyramid

The burial chamber inside the Great Pyramid is built entirely of pink granite. Its flat ceiling is made of nine enormous blocks with a combined weight of more than 400 tons (408 tonnes). The ancient architects are thought to have constructed five relieving chambers over this ceiling to help it resist the incredible pressure bearing down on it.

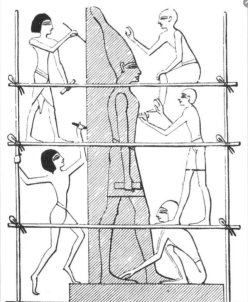

Cooperative effort

Statues were mostly produced by teams of sculptors working together in temple and royal workshops. Most surviving statues are of stone, but they were also made in wood and metal. For carving colossal stone statues, it was necessary to construct wooden scaffolding around the piece. This kind of scaffolding was also used by craftsmen decorating the walls of tombs and temples.

Statue decoration

It might seem hard to believe, but many of the statues were not originally the subtle hues we appreciate today, but were once painted in vibrant colors, which have faded over time. The eyes of statues were often inlaid with white and black stones, such as calcite and obsidian, and the inclusion of rock crystal created an even more lifelike effect. Sometimes a copper rim around the eye imitated the malachite worn as eye makeup.

Sculptors' tools

Sculptors could carve soft stones, such as limestone and sandstone, with copper and bronze chisels, but the really hard stones could not have been cut with metal tools. For these, dolorite, granite, and flint tools were used together with a quartz abrasive. The final smoothing to create a polished surface was carried out with sandstone rubbers or sand.

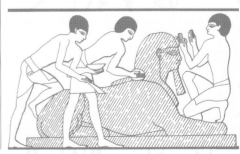

Pyrotechnology

The Egyptians were working with metal, clay, and faience at least as early as 4000 BC. They had also begun to make jewelry by the early Predynastic Period. Faience is a nonclay ceramic made of quartz or silica (mainly sand) with an added alkali and lime. The technology of faience-making is similar to that of glassmaking, but the ancient Egyptians did not master that skill until the New Kingdom. The introduction of glassmaking skills may well have been the result of the 18th-Dynasty pharaoh Thutmose III's military campaigns in Mitanni, north of Mesopotamia. It is possible glassmakers were brought back to Egypt as captives. The most common names for glass, *ehlipakku* and *mekku*, were taken from Hurrian and Akkadian, the ancient languages of Anatolia and Mesopotamia.

The potter's art
Potters mostly used alluvial Nile-silt clay available throughout the Nile Valley. They also used marl clay, which was stonelike before treatment and came from the desert edge and under cultivation near the desert. The New Kingdom potters used turntables; they would not have been truly able to throw pots until the development of the kick wheel.

Faience
Faience makers added natron (a naturally occurring salt) or the ash of certain halophytic (salt-loving) plants, and perhaps lime to sand or crushed quartz pebbles. They mixed these with water to form a malleable paste, which could be hand-modeled or molded, and then fired at 1470–1830°F (800–1000°C) to form pieces, such as this dish.

Glass
Like faience, glass was made of silica, alkali (plant ash or natron), and lime (probably present as an impurity in the sand). It tended to be colored, such as this core-formed polychrome vessel, using colorants, such as copper, cobalt, and manganese. Glass objects were also made in molds or cold cut from glass blocks.

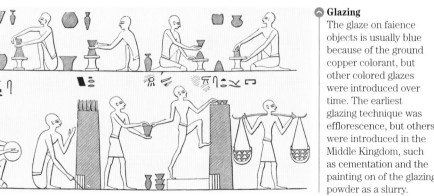

Glazing
The glaze on faience objects is usually blue because of the ground copper colorant, but other colored glazes were introduced over time. The earliest glazing technique was efflorescence, but others were introduced in the Middle Kingdom, such as cementation and the painting on of the glazing powder as a slurry.

Personal adornment
Jewelry dating from all periods of early Egyptian history has survived because the ancient Egyptians chose to be buried with it. Personal adornment was clearly highly regarded and was important in terms of identification and status, even in the afterlife. Jewelry was worn by men, women, and children.

Metalwork
The ancient Egyptians were master metalworkers, developing their skills early on. By 3300 BC they were melting, casting, and smelting metals from ores. The first metals they processed were gold and copper, which was especially hard because of its natural arsenic content. They also worked with electrum, silver, iron, tin, bronze, lead, and platinum. This is a bronze vessel.

See also
Technology,
pages 48–9
Technology,
pages 52–3

Decorative jewelry
Jewellers inlaid semiprecious stones (particularly carnelian, turquoise, and lapis lazuli), glass, and faience into gold, silver, and electrum. The technique of *cloisonné* was used from at least as early as the early Old Kingdom. Metal cells, or *cloisons*, were filled with colored inlays cemented into position.

Bellows
Middle Kingdom Egyptian metalworkers used skin bellows to intensify the heat of their hearths. By the 18th Dynasty, they were using more effective dish bellows (pottery, wood, or stone dishes fitted with skin or leather coverings, connected by reeds or pipes to clay nozzles into the hearth).
In the 19th Dynasty, metalworkers developed sophisticated mud-brick shaft furnaces.

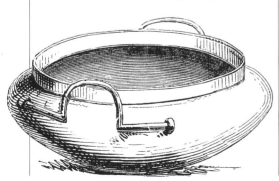

TECHNOLOGY

Carpentry, Leather, and Textiles

Carpenters, joiners, shipwrights, and wood carvers worked with native and imported timber. Trees growing in Egypt included the date palm, dom palm, sycamore fig, tamarisk, and acacia. These woods were used mainly for furniture, coffins and statuary. Palm trees and acacia could be used for roof joists, columns, and boatbuilding, but for large-scale construction and the best-quality coffins the Egyptians relied on cedar, imported from the Lebanon. They also imported pine, juniper, and cypress from the Levant and ebony from tropical Africa. Other groups of craftsmen included tanners, spinners, and weavers, who made leather and linen for the production of clothing and a variety of other finished goods.

Boatbuilding

Boats of reeds, rushes, papyrus, and wood were used for fishing, for crossing the river, and for transport up- and downstream. Acacia was often used for shipbuilding, but the largest surviving vessels are of cedar. The most famous example of an Egyptian boat is that buried in pieces alongside the pyramid of Khufu at Giza, which had its large planks of wood sewn together with ropes.

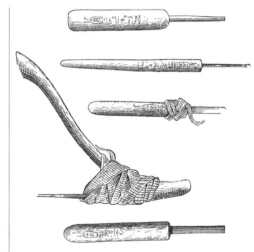

Chests

A variety of wooden chests and boxes were produced by carpenters to store anything from household and temple goods to archives of papyrus rolls. Boxes on carrying poles were used to transport loads over long distances. The chests shown here have shrine-shaped lids. They were usually fastened shut by a cord around the handles, sealed with clay.

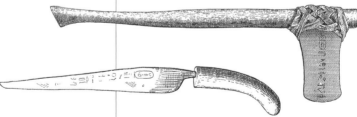

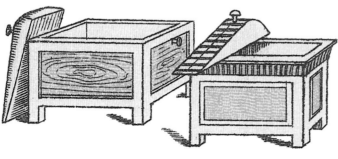

Carpenters' tools

Carpenters worked with a variety of metal tools including axes, adzes, saws, chisels. and awls. Before the use of bronze, the natural content of arsenic in the copper resulted in hard tool heads and blades. Bronze was initially imported from Syria, but in the New Kingdom Egyptian metalworkers began to alloy copper with tin to produce their own. All tool blades were strengthened by annealing.

Making chariots

Chariot makers constructed light, wooden
semicircular chariots. They were open at the back,
and had an axle with a pair of four- or six-spoked
wheels. The wheels usually had a diameter of around
3 ft (1 m), assembled from small pieces of wood and
bound together with leather tires. A long pole
attached to the center of the axle would be
yoked to two horses.

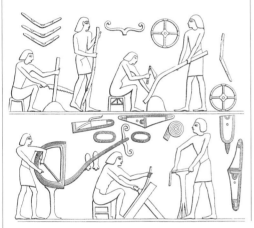

Making coffins

Tamarisk, fig, and
cedar were used by the
coffin makers. Here the
carpenter on the left has
created a vise by lashing
his plank to a post stuck
in the ground. He uses
a large saw with both
hands. The handle would
be wood and the blade
either copper or bronze.
The teeth of the saw
were directed toward
the carpenter, so he
would have to draw the
saw backward to cut
the wood.

See also
Technology,
pages 48–51

Weaving flax

Flax was the principal
fabric source in ancient
Egypt. Until the end of
the Middle Kingdom,
linen production was
carried out exclusively
by women (who
even held the title
"Overseer of the House
of Weavers") using
horizontal ground-looms.
By the New Kingdom,
both men and women
wove cloth, using
vertical upright looms
introduced into Egypt
from the Near East
during the Second
Intermediate Period.

Tanning

Tanners produced leather
from the skins of sheep,
goats, and cattle by
treating the hides with
juice from the fruit of the
acacia tree. Leather
workers used metal hide-
scrapers, leather-cutting
knives, awls, and needles.
Leather was used for
sandals, furniture (for
example, to cover stools),
tools (to lash blades to
hafts), chariot equipment
(including harnesses and
whips), clothing, writing
materials, quivers,
and tents.

TRADE

Egypt and the Near East

Egypt had trading contact with Western Asia and the Levant from the Predynastic Period. Predynastic Egyptian graves have yielded lapis lazuli from Badakhshan in Afghanistan, obsidian from Anatolia (as well as nearby Ethiopia), silver from western Asia, stone cylinder seals from Mesopotamia, and storage vessels from Syria-Palestine and Mesopotamia. Of particular importance was the importation of cedar wood from Lebanon. This exchange of commodities brought with it exchanges of ideas, and this cross-cultural contact can be seen to be expressed on luxury objects of the late Predynastic and Protodynastic Periods. It has been argued that the cultural transfers, particularly from Mesopotamia and Elam, were the catalyst for state formation as well as writing and monumental mud-brick architecture in Egypt from *c.* 3100 BC. Trade with the Near East flourished through the stable periods of dynastic history.

See also
Trade,
pages 56–9

Pictures of foreigners
The ancient Egyptians interacted with their neighbors to the northeast and frequently portrayed them in their art. In addition to the characteristic facial features, beard, hairstyle, and skin color, "Asiatics" tended to wear more brightly colored clothing than the Egyptians, who preferred white linen garments.

Imported goods
This un-Egyptian style of elaborate metal vessel is depicted arriving into Egypt from western Asia during the New Kingdom. Unfortunately the ancient Egyptians used the same word (*inw*) to describe all commodities arriving into Egypt, whether they were traded goods, tribute, or plunder, so it is difficult to determine the precise nature of these foreign wares.

The Narmer Palette
The Narmer Palette is an Egyptian ceremonial schist palette used for pigment grinding, dating to the reign of one of Egypt's earliest kings, Narmer (*c.* 3100 BC), shown on this side of the palette wearing the Red Crown of Lower Egypt. The area in which pigment was ground is encircled by the necks of two mythical animals found on contemporary Sumerian and Elamite cylinder seals.

Horses

From the New Kingdom onward, horses similar to the modern Arabian horse were imported to Egypt from Syria. Yoke measurements of surviving chariots reveal that these horses had an average height of 53 inches (135 cm). Horses were also favored war booty and prestige gifts between rulers in North Africa and the Near East.

Goods in and out

Scribes recorded the extraordinary range of luxury goods arriving into Egypt from far-flung places. Unfortunately the Egyptians were not keen to record what was leaving Egypt in exchange (assuming that goods were), so scenes such as this in the tomb of the 18th-Dynasty vizier Rekhmire (c. 1479–1400 BC), presumably give us a biased view of what was actually going on.

Transporting metal

The ancient Egyptians imported both finished vessels and different metals in unworked form. The man at the front of this procession carries copper in the form of an ox-hide ingot, a common way of transporting metals at the time. The Egyptians had their own copper in the Eastern Desert and Sinai, but it was also imported from Cyprus and the Near East.

Exotic animals

The ancient Egyptians prized exotic animals imported from far-off lands. Here a Syrian elephant (much smaller than the African elephant) and a yellowish brown isabelline bear bring up the rear. Bears were never native to Egypt, and this particular animal is likely to have been tame, so it would have been a special attraction to the Egyptians.

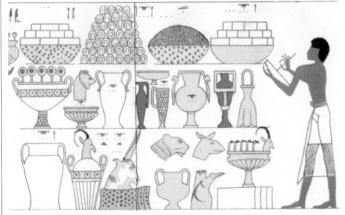

TRADE

Egypt and Nubia

Nubia is a term used to describe the Nile Valley south of Aswan and the First Cataract, the southern border of Egypt, as far as the Fourth Cataract in Sudan (although sometimes as far south as Khartoum). Egypt interacted with Nubia throughout pharaonic history, and during its more stable and politically powerful periods exercised control over Nubia, particularly over Lower Nubia, the region between the First and Second Cataracts. The Egyptians' primary concern was the exploitation of the Nubian gold mines, but the Nubians were also middlemen for trade with sub-Saharan Africa, and control of these trade routes was highly attractive to the Egyptians. In the Middle Kingdom the Egyptians began to build huge mud-brick forts in Nubia, and by the New Kingdom the Egyptian rulers were commissioning the building of stone and rock-cut temples there, the most impressive being Ramesses II's great temple at Abu Simbel.

See also
Work,
pages 44–5
Trade,
pages 54–5
Trade,
pages 58–9

Nubians in art
Nubians were depicted in a different manner to Egyptians, with distinctive physical features and clothing. Here their hairstyles and feathered headdresses are characteristic. In the 18th Dynasty giraffes were brought from Nubia as trading goods or tribute. It is possible that they became pets on the estates of royalty and the elite.

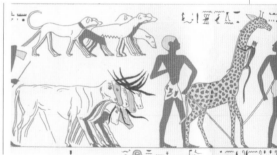

Cataracts of the Nile
The First Cataract of the Nile at Aswan marked the border between Egypt and Nubia. This is the first of six cataracts; the sixth is about 45 miles (75 km) north of Khartoum in Sudan. These are rocky areas of rapids caused by abrupt geological changes. The First Cataract comprises granite boulders, which make the river unnavigable in that area.

Gifts from the south
The best-known scene of Nubian tribute or trading goods arriving into Egypt is in the tomb of the 18th-Dynasty vizier Rekhmire. Giraffes, green monkeys, cattle, and saluki dogs were all brought from Nubia. Monkeys became the exotic pets of the wealthy and salukis were prized hunting dogs.

Exotic goods

Other luxury goods imported from Nubia were giraffe tails (carried in the right hand of the man leading this procession), which were used as fly whisks, ebony, ivory, animal skins (particularly leopard skins, which were worn by certain ranks of priest), and yet more exotic animals, including baboons, leopards, and cheetahs.

Ramesses in Nubia

Ramesses II chose to make his presence felt in Nubia. He built a number of temples there, including this one at Wadi el-Sebua, dedicated to the Egyptian gods Amun-Ra and Ra-Horakhty, and the deified pharaoh Ramesses. This temple would have been lost beneath the waters of Lake Nasser if it had not been moved, block by block, in 1964 to a more elevated site 2½ miles (4 km to the west.

Ostriches

Ostrich feathers and eggs were both imported from Nubia. The eggshells were used for manufacturing luxury items, such as containers and beads. The feathers were used in fans for high-status individuals—Tutankhamun was buried with several fans of this kind, one of which still had the feathers preserved when Howard Carter discovered the tomb in 1922.

Meroitic Nubia

An important period of Nubian history was the Meroitic Period, from the end of the 4th century BC to the mid-4th century AD. During this time, the Nubian rulers were buried in pyramids at Meroe between the Fifth and Sixth Cataracts. Here Amani-tore (early 1st century AD), a *kandake* (female ruler or royal woman), is portrayed in a powerful pose on the temple at Naqa.

TRADE

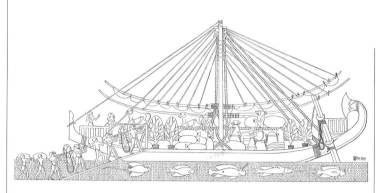

Egypt and Punt

The Egyptians visited a place they called Punt for at least 1,500 years, from the 5th Dynasty (*c.* 2500 BC) until the 20th Dynasty, although Punt continues to get mentioned in texts up until the Ptolemaic Period (after 305 BC). The precise location of Punt is unknown; some suggest it was in Eritrea or Somalia, or possibly it was on the Arabian Peninsula. Wherever it was, the purpose of the visits was trade. As always, we have a clearer idea of what the Egyptians imported than of what they exported, and Punt was the source of exotic and precious goods, particularly aromatic resins (*antyw*), generally understood to be myrrh, although some scholars identify it as frankincense. Other products imported from Punt included gold, silver, electrum, lapis lazuli, ebony, ivory, antimony, and malachite for eye paint, herbs, throw sticks, slaves, ostrich eggs and feathers, animal skins, cattle, dogs, and wild animals.

Sailing to Punt

All the evidence indicates that the Egyptians navigated the Red Sea to reach Punt. The best recorded of these trips took place during the eighth or ninth regnal year of the 18th-Dynasty pharaoh Hatshepsut (*c.* 1465 BC). Wonderfully detailed scenes of the ships, commodities, and the land of Punt itself survive on the walls of Hatshepsut's temple at Deir el-Bahri, on the west bank of the Nile at Luxor.

See also
Trade,
pages 54–7

Transporting goods

All commodities were transported the length of the Egyptian Nile Valley by boat. The cataracts at Aswan and farther south made navigation more difficult, so donkey caravans tended to work the trade routes into Nubia. Although Punt may have been in east Africa, there is no evidence that the Egyptians journeyed there via Nubia.

Hatshepsut's expedition

The leader of Hatshepsut's expedition to Punt was the Royal Chancellor Neshi (*c.* 1465 BC). According to the inscriptions, he was to extract tribute from the Puntites, who must pledge their allegiance to the distant Egyptian ruler, but, in reality, it was probably a trading mission involving a fair exchange of commodities. The expedition was accompanied by a considerable number of soldiers (pictured here), presumably for show or protection—or possibly to ensure the Puntites gave generously.

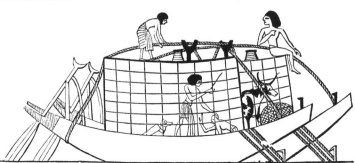

Gold and resins

Gold was usually imported from Punt in the form of rings. The *antyw,* or aromatic resins, arrived in lumps in baskets or modeled into elaborate forms, such as these obelisks. Perhaps the red granulations were believed to resemble the flecked color of pink Aswan granite favored for the carving of obelisks, particularly during the 18th Dynasty.

Luxury items

In addition to the resin, the *antyw* trees themselves were also imported from Punt. They were tapped by making an incision in the tree bark and the gum resin then oozed out and hardened. Ostrich feathers and eggs, and exotic animals, such as the cheetah shown here, were also brought from Punt.

Flora and fauna

The Egyptian craftsmen responsible for the scenes of Punt on the walls of Hatshepsut's temple at Deir el-Bahri paid extraordinary attention to detail. The fish beneath the ships in the sea are accurate depictions of the maritime life of the Red Sea, and the flora and fauna of the country itself are depicted with great care. These are some of the Puntite plants from those scenes.

Hathor

The Egyptian goddess Hathor was worshipped as the patron deity of foreign lands, and particularly their goods, whether they be acquired by trade or mining. It was in this capacity that she was regarded as the Lady of Punt. She was also the "Lady of Fragrance," appropriate for her association with a land that yielded aromatic resins.

Antyw

Antyw was highly prized because it was used to produce incense for temple rituals and the funerary cults of the upper echelons of Egyptian society. It was burned in many styles of incense burner, one of which is depicted here. It was also employed in expensive perfumes and fumigations, in mummification, and in medicine.

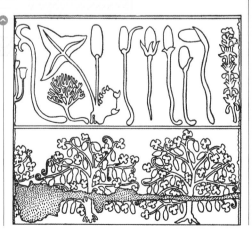

LEISURE

Music

Music was an essential element of Egyptian culture and religion. Numerous depictions of musicians survive, as do a number of the musical instruments themselves, but unfortunately there is no preserved musical notation so, although we know the words to the songs they sang, we have no idea of the tunes they played. Music was important in the temples, and musicians featured prominently at festivals because music pacified and gladdened the hearts of gods and mortals alike. Musicians are depicted in the households of the wealthy and often performing at banquets. Music clearly had erotic connotations and often the musicians were scantily clad, nubile young women.

Musicians
By the New Kingdom, the majority of musicians depicted are women. They performed in groups at banquets, often accompanying dancers. In this scene from the Theban tomb of Nebamun, three of the band are clapping, the fourth plays a double flute. It is rare to see representations of full-frontal faces in Egyptian art. A song is written in hieroglyphs above their heads.

See also
Work,
pages 46–7
Leisure,
pages 62–5

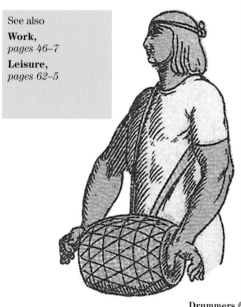

The goddess of music
The goddess Hathor features in multiple contexts. She was, among other things, the goddess of music and happiness, a provider of joy and pleasure, in which music featured heavily. She was also Lady of Drunkenness and Song. Female musicians were an important element in her worship as well as in the temples of other deities.

Drummers
Various percussive instruments were played by the ancient Egyptians. Certainly by the Old Kingdom they were playing rectangular and round-framed hand drums beaten with their hands and not sticks. The earliest form of drum was the barrel-shaped one depicted here. They also produced rhythms with clappers of bone and ivory, and ceremonial rattles or sistra.

Flutes

The oldest instrument played in Egypt was the single flute. By the time of the Old Kingdom, single and double flutes or pipes were played. They were made of reed or wood, and were blown from the side like a modern flute or from the end like a recorder. This end-blown flute is similar to the *ney* that is still being played throughout the Middle East.

Harps

The large floor harp had become popular in Egypt by the Old Kingdom. By the New Kingdom, a number of new types of musical instruments were being played by Egyptian musicians. These included a small shoulder-held harp, which seems to have come from the Near East. Often harps were elaborately painted, inlaid, or carved.

Lyres

Yet another musical instrument with its origins in the Near East was the lyre. It appears in Mesopotamia from the 3rd millennium BC and had made its way into Egypt by the New Kingdom. These instruments could be ornamental, often with carvings in the form of animals.

Lutes

The lute was another of the musical instruments introduced to Egypt from the Near East during the New Kingdom. Egyptian lutes had a long, slender neck and an elongated, oval resonating body made of wood. They apparently made a sound like a mandolin crossed with a banjo.

Female lutenists

Depictions of women playing the lute could have heavy erotic connotations. Such female musicians are often naked except for a heavy wig and some jewelry, or they are wearing decidedly transparent fine linen garments. Nubile female lutenists are found incorporated into the design of toilet articles, such as cosmetics spoons.

Tuning and playing techniques

The lyre continues to be played in East Africa today, probably reflecting the ancient diffusion of the instrument via Egypt. The tuning and playing techniques of modern lyres in East Africa are certainly thought to be similar to those of ancient Egypt and Greece, where this instrument was particularly popular.

Festivities and Banquets

The ancient Egyptians appreciated the exotic and the erotic, and their festivities were steeped in sensuality. They laid particular emphasis on the senses of smell and taste. Their ideal would have been to perfume the banqueting room with imported fragrances, such as myrrh and frankincense. The evidence for private partying survives mainly in the form of banqueting scenes on the walls of nonroyal tombs. Perhaps these are depictions of funerary banquets or an ideal life that the Egyptians hoped to enjoy after death. This evidence is restricted to the wealthy, but no doubt sociable gatherings with alcohol, music, and dance took place at all levels of society with varying degrees of luxury and extravagance.

Narcotic flowers

The ancient Egyptians may well have added small quantities of narcotic substances to their drinks, especially to wine. One plant depicted in the banquet scenes, and in close association with alcohol, is the blue lotus, or more correctly the lily (the *Nymphaea caerulea* shown here with papyrus plants), which is now thought to release narcotic properties when the blossom is dropped into wine.

Festive flowers

Flowers are ever present in the party scenes. Servants decked the guests with garlands. Sometimes a single bud or a blossoming flower attached to the front of a floral headdress dangles over a guest's forehead. Often a flower was presented to each guest to hold during the entertainment, usually comprising music and dance.

Nefertem

The god of perfumes was Nefertem. He was also the divine personification of the blue lotus, which is actually a type of water lily. He was associated with the rising sun, especially the first sunrise at the time of creation, and was usually represented as a man with a lotus/lily blossom emerging from the top of his head.

Sweet smells

Servants anointed the wigs of partygoers with a sweet-scented ointment. Depictions showing cones on top of wigs are interpreted as being made of fragranced fat, which slowly melted as the party heated up, but perhaps they are overemphasized in the art to stress the wealth, sensuality, and delightful smell of the individuals in question.

Dance of death

These are a particular type of dancer called *muu*-dancers, who are distinguished by their kilts and reed headdresses. They did not perform at parties but at funerals, and their ritual dances were deemed crucial to the successful outcome of the funerary rituals. They played the role of divine ferrymen, ensuring the safe transportation of the deceased into the afterlife.

Binge drinking

Although the surviving ethical texts extol the virtues of abstemiousness, the ancient Egyptians clearly did overindulge at parties. Unfortunately this servant did not get the bowl to her mistress in time! Inscriptions accompanying these scenes tell us that guests might desire to drink to drunkenness. Beer and wine were both enjoyed at these festive occasions.

See also

Leisure,
pages 60–1

Leisure,
pages 64–5

Food,
pages 74–5

Dance and performance

Dancing featured in the religious and social lives of the ancient Egyptians. In the banquet scenes wealthy guests are shown watching dancers as entertainment. Men tended to dance with men and women with women. Dances varied from slow and postured movement to lyrical, fluid, or gymnastic performances. In fact, much of the dancing was more like acrobatics.

LEISURE

Games, Hobbies, and Toys

In their leisure time the ancient Egyptians enjoyed a range of games, some more active than others. Board games were popular from the beginning of pharaonic history and could be played by all levels of society on a range of boards, from those marked out with a finger in the sand to the costly ebony and ivory game boxes buried with Tutankhamun. Children played with toys that in their simplest form could be animals modeled out of mud (such as those found in the Middle Kingdom settlement of Kahun), or the more complex mechanical ivory dancing toy pygmies from the contemporary tomb of a girl called Hapy at Lisht. More physical games were also enjoyed, including acrobatics, wrestling, and juggling. The elite could relax on their estates in their well-tended yards. As today, wealthy men seemed to relish hunting and fishing as sport, which for others would have been hard work and subsistence activities.

Senet

The game most commonly represented in tomb scenes is the thirty-square game called *senet*. Two players usually started with seven playing pieces of different forms. Movement of the pieces was determined by throwing knucklebones or casting sticks. The aim was to be the first to remove all one's pieces from the board.

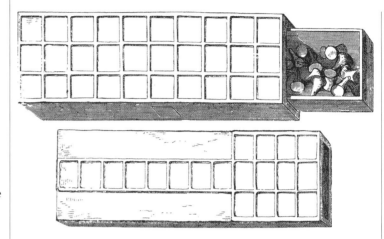

Game boards
Game boards could be boxes with drawers for storing the playing pieces. *Senet* had thirty squares; a similar game was one that had twenty squares, often erroneously called *Tjau* instead of *Aseb*. It may have come to Egypt from western Asia. Both boards would have had hieroglyphic signs marked on some of the squares.

Games and pieces
Playing pieces varied for different games. Those shown above were used for *Senet* and the Game of Twenty Squares. There was another game called *Mehen* that was played during the Old Kingdom. The circular board was in the form of a coiled snake and players had to get their pieces (tiny lions and small balls) from the tail to the head of the snake.

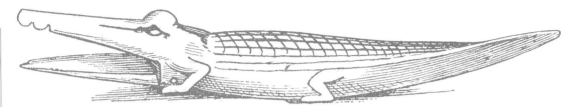

Children's toys

Animal toys were particularly popular. This wooden crocodile is not unique in having a movable lower jaw; similar examples include a mouse and a feline. A wooden female figure survives who appears to grind grain when a string is pulled. Children also played with spinning tops, skittles, and puppets.

See also
Leisure,
pages 60–3

Activity sports

More active games often involved acrobatics, rhythmic throwing and catching, and juggling, as shown in the two pictures below. A variety of balls have survived; the best-quality ones are made of leather straps sewn around a core of straw, reeds, hair, yarn, or chaff. The girls below have a distinctive hairstyle, presumably linked to this particular activity.

Dolls

It is difficult to interpret these female figures with certainty. They tend to have emphasized pubic regions and, to a lesser extent, breasts. The example on the right may be a votive object known as a fertility figurine, but the one on the left is often described as a paddle doll. Rag dolls also survive, sometimes with changes of outfit.

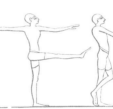

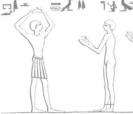

Fishing

Only the wealthy are shown fishing as a leisure activity. This gentleman is seated on a fine, carved chair by a pool, presumably in his yard. Fishing rods are depicted for the first time in tombs of the Middle Kingdom, but it is not until the New Kingdom that the tomb owner (rather than a fisherman) is depicted with a rod.

ARCHITECTURE

Temples

From the New Kingdom onward, Egyptian temples were built in a fairly uniform layout. A processional way (often lined by sphinxes) led to a great gateway (a pylon) and then a series of open and closed courts before the roofed interior with the inner sanctum at its heart. Temples were designed to reflect the universe at the time of creation. Every temple was believed to stand on the primordial mound (the floor level rose toward the sanctuary) and every temple complex had a sacred lake that symbolized the primeval waters of Nun. The undulating mud-brick walls surrounding some sacred precincts have been interpreted as the waters of chaos lapping at the mound of creation. Inside the enclosure wall the temple buildings evoked a marshland, with columns and walls decorated with a variety of plant life, and stars painted on the ceilings imitated the night skies.

Luxor Temple
Luxor Temple has a rare north–south axis, running parallel to the river. Although primarily a temple dedicated to Amun by Amunhotep III (*c.* 1390–*c.* 1352 BC), the First Pylon was added by Ramesses II. This entrance was marked by a pair of obelisks and guarded by colossal statues of the king.

The Temple of Philae
The temple of Philae on an island in the First Cataract is one of Egypt's most picturesque sacred sites. Here the cult of the goddess Isis survived later into Roman times than that of any other Egyptian deity. The entire temple was moved onto the higher neighboring island of Agilika in the 1970s, when Philae was submerged by the formation of Lake Nasser.

Temple facade
The temple was the "horizon of the god." The form of the pylon gateway reflected the horizon hieroglyph, *akhet*. The pylon was usually of stone with a great cedar door, flanked by cedar flagstaffs from which pennants fluttered. The pharaoh was depicted on it smiting foreigners and offering to the gods.

Columns

Stone columns were usually carved in the form of trees or plants, such as these, with papyrus-bud (left) and open-flower capitals. These were the most commonly used types in ancient Egypt. The column shafts and architraves were often covered in scenes and inscriptions, usually in painted relief.

⊙ Temple courts

The first court in any conventional temple was a Peristyle Court, open in the middle and surrounded by a colonnade. A temple might have more than one such court. It would presumably have been more accessible to the public than the darker, more mysterious roofed areas deeper inside the temple.

⊙ Other column styles

Stone columns were also carved in imitation of bundles of papyrus stems tied together. The capitals represented their unopened flower buds. The papyrus stem has a triangular cross section that was carefully copied. Less common column types imitated lotus/lily plants (usually in bundles), or had smooth, cylindrical shafts with palm-frond capitals.

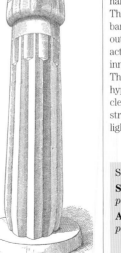

⊙ Hypostyle hall

The final peristyle court led into the first (sometimes only) hypostyle hall, a roofed hall thick with columns. This hall was an effective barrier between the outside world of secular activity and the shadowy inner world of the gods. The lighting in the hypostyle hall was clerestory, creating striking effects with light shafts.

See also
Society,
pages 26–7
Architecture,
pages 68–71

ARCHITECTURE

Tombs

The late Predynastic Period brought with it social stratification and the emergence of an elite that desired ever grander burials. The ruling class of the Early Dynastic Period chose to be buried in tombs with monumental mud-brick superstructures, which are known today as mastabas. These developed into stepped pyramids and the geometrically true, smooth-sided pyramids in the Old Kingdom for royal burials (the high officials continued to be buried in mastabas). The rock-cut tomb in the desert escarpment was favored by nobles throughout the Pharaonic Period, and during the New Kingdom the pharaohs were buried in the most famous of this type, the tombs in the Valley of the Kings at Luxor. Throughout pharaonic history, the luxury of burial in a tomb was restricted to a privileged minority.

Step pyramid
The step pyramid was an impressive focal point of the royal funerary complexes of the 3rd Dynasty. The earliest and best preserved of these structures is that of the 3rd-Dynasty king Djoser (who reigned in the 2640s BC). It is located at North Saqqara and is acclaimed as the world's first monumental building in stone.

Transitional design
The pyramid at Meidum provides evidence for the transitional phase from stepped to smooth-sided pyramid. It began as a stepped pyramid, cased in the best-quality limestone from the Tura quarries, and then the steps were filled in to form a true pyramid under the 4th-Dynasty king Sneferu (*c.* 2613–*c.* 2589 BC).

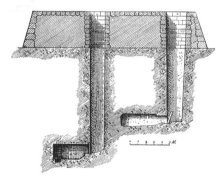

Mastaba tombs
The mastaba tombs take their name from the Arabic word for bench (due to the form of the tomb superstructure). Initially they consisted of brick burial chambers in pits dug in the desert, lined with wooden paneling or granite, with simple superstructures of rectangular mud-brick enclosures filled up with sand and gravel with niched facades.

The Bent Pyramid

Sneferu's Bent Pyramid at Dahshur is another example of early experimentation in pyramid design. Presumably the pyramid turned out to be unstable and so had to be completed at a shallower angle (forty-three degrees rather than the original fifty-four degrees). This pyramid has retained more of its fine Tura limestone casing than any other pyramid.

The Pyramids at Giza

The Great Pyramid was built by King Sneferu's son Khufu (*c*. 2589–*c*. 2566 BC) on the Giza plateau. It is the only one of the Seven Wonders of the Ancient World still standing. The pyramid's height would originally have been 479 ft (146 m), and it is said to be constructed of 2.3 million blocks of limestone. The sphinx is associated with the neighboring Pyramid of Khafre.

Tombs

By the New Kingdom pharaohs were no longer buried in pyramids, but in tombs cut into the desert cliffs in the Valley of the Kings. Nobles were buried in smaller versions of these during the Pharaonic Period. Some Middle Kingdom important local people were buried at Beni Hasan in elaborate rock-cut tombs with fabulous views over the Nile Valley.

See also

Religion,
pages 38–9

Architecture,
pages 66–7

Houses

Egyptian domestic buildings were
constructed mainly of sun-baked, mud brick,
but also of reeds, papyrus, and wood with
some stone features. Reeds and papyrus
were woven to make matting, which could
be used over a frame of native timber, then
the whole was covered with mud.
Agricultural workers lived in small villages
close to the land they farmed. Towns and
cities would have had varied populations and
were often cosmopolitan. Excavation of the
18th-Dynasty city of Akhetaten (Tell el-
Amarna) in Middle Egypt has revealed that
the poor lived in cramped housing abutting
grand estates of the wealthy, rather than in
segregated slums. And another excavation at
Deir el-Medina revealed a village where tomb
workers and their chiefs lived. However, few
settlements have survived because they were
built in the floodplain from vulnerable
materials, in areas that are still inhabited,
making archaeology nearly impossible.

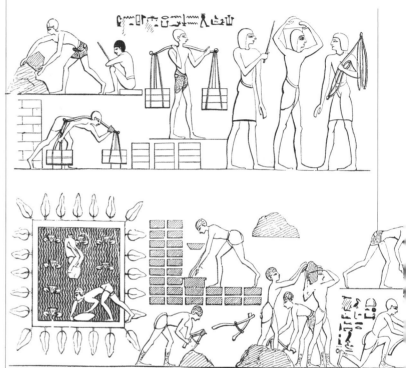

Domestic housing

Houses grew up outside
the walls of the temples.
As here, the tops of the
temple pylon, obelisks,
and flagpoles would have
been visible behind the
enclosure wall. Windows
in houses were small,
high in the walls, and
without glass panes.
Window frames and
grilles tended to be
wooden, although stone
window grilles have
been discovered at
Tell el-Amarna. As
in temples, rooms of
different heights allowed
clerestory lighting.

Making bricks

Rectangular bricks were
made of Nile mud, sand,
plant fibers or small
stones and fragments
of brick. Clay was
sometimes a major
component, which made
a yellowish brick. They
were produced using
a rectangular wooden
mold (open top and
bottom, with a handle
at one corner), and were
mostly sun-dried rather
than fired.

Air-conditioning

Some depictions of houses show triangular structures on the roofs. These are ventilation shafts, a type of trap door with a vent to direct the cooling north breeze down into the house. They have also been identified in house remains at Tell el-Amarna. Before the arrival of air-conditioning, these were a feature of houses throughout the Near East.

Country estates

The country houses of the wealthy were set on estates with all kinds of luxuries, including vineyards as here. Most images of houses on the walls of tombs suggest a detached residence within a compound. There is archaeological evidence for such town houses at Tell el-Amarna, but it must be remembered that one of the functions of tomb scenes was to express an idealized version of reality.

Wealthy homes

Larger houses were often two or three stories high. Even in the palaces, walls were of mud brick, plastered and painted, or decorated with beautiful faience tiles and inlay. Wonderful examples of these forms of interior decoration have been excavated at Tell el-Amarna. Some of the column capitals in the Great Palace there were inlaid with a design in alternating blue and red glass.

See also
Society,
pages 28–9
Architecture,
pages 66–7

FOOD

Food Preparation and Dining

Egypt's food supplies were very much dependent on the annual flooding of the Nile, but on the whole Egypt was a fertile and productive land and famine was rare. Scenes of animal husbandry were commonly depicted in tombs, and they were always accompanied by detailed imagery of butchery. Similarly, scenes of fishing were accompanied by those of the preparation of fish for eating, and fowling scenes appear alongside depictions of plucking and preserving. Pictures of food preparation are far more common than scenes of cooking and eating. In early instructional literature, the maxim "Gluttony is despicable" rings out. But despite this, excessive food consumption is evident among those who could afford it. At elite banquets the favored meats seem to have been beef and goose, but it is likely that such delicacies were rarely sampled by the majority of the population, who must have been reliant on fish for their protein.

Slaughter
The animal was laid on its back with its lower legs trussed. Its throat was turned to one side and cut, severing the carotid artery (as is done in Egypt today). The butcher pumped the animal's foreleg to drain the blood from the body, thus preventing spoilage of the meat. A priest might test the blood and entrails for purity.

Preserving fish
Fish were usually gutted through an incision along the vertebral column. They were then laid flat or hung to dry, with the head and backbone often left intact. Fish were commonly preserved by salting. They could be rubbed with salt and hung out to dry or left for several days between layers of salt in large, sealed vessels. A fisherman's catch was recorded by scribes and a portion of it distributed to officials. He could then trade the remaining fish (either fresh, or dressed and preserved) for other commodities—for example, one fresh mullet for a jar of beer, or a basket of dried mugils for an amulet.

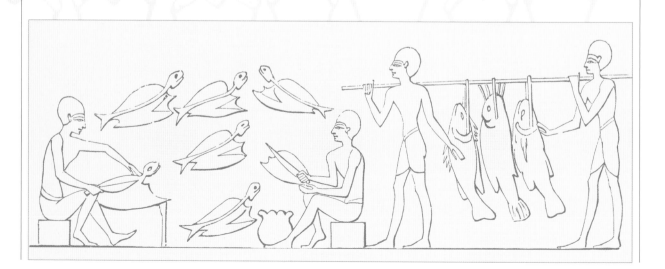

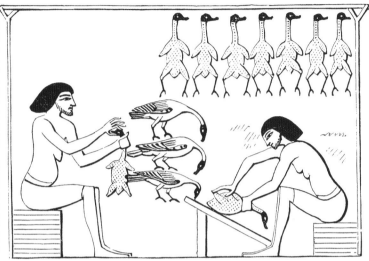

Butchering poultry
Poultry was killed by strangulation, then plucked and eviscerated through a slit in the ventral surface. When poultry is shown hanging, it was probably a temporary measure to enhance the flavor. For the meat to dry in this way, it would have to have been cut into strips. Wet and dry salt curing was also used in meat preservation.

See also
Work,
pages 44–5
Food,
pages 72–3

Food preparation
The archeology of settlements, such as Tell el-Amarna, has yielded evidence for mortar and quern emplacements, hearths, and bread ovens. The last-named were often located on the flat roofs of houses. On a domestic level, women would have been responsible for preparing the food. The men pictured here are preparing and cooking food on a grander scale.

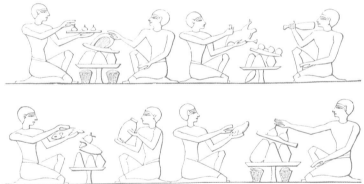

Table manners
The Egyptians tended to live close to the ground. Their furniture, including tables, chairs, and stools, was low, although mats and cushions on the floor were commonly used. They also preferred to eat with their fingers, so napkins and finger bowls at meals must have been essential.

FOOD

The Fruits of the Land

Fruit, vegetables, beans, and herbs grew abundantly in Egypt. Celery, onions, leeks, garlic, lettuce, cucumbers, radishes, brown beans (called *ful* in Egypt today), chickpeas, and lentils were all eaten flavored with parsley, marjoram, coriander, and dill. Popular fruit were pomegranates, figs, grapes, dates, and *nabk* berries. Grapes were turned into wine, and the Egyptians were also partial to what the Roman scientist and historian Pliny (1st century AD) called "artificial wine," made from dates, figs, and pomegranates. The Egyptians made beer from barley and wheat, which they sometimes flavored with pomegranates, figs, mint, honey, or grape juice. The Greek scholar Athenaeus (2nd–3rd century AD) described Egyptian beer as very strong, provoking dancing and singing.

Palm fruit

Date palms (on the left) and *dom* palms are seen here growing side by side. The fronds differ in appearance, and the *dom* palm tree has a distinctive forked trunk. Dates were eaten fresh and dried and were made into jam. The shiny brown *dom* fruit— which, fresh off the tree, are hard and woody— were made into cake.

Figs and baboons

Two types of fig trees grew in ancient Egypt: the true fig (*Ficus carica*) and, more commonly, the wild fig or sycamore fig (*Ficus sycomorus*) with oval leaves. This man is having trouble harvesting the fruit before the baboons get to it. They are likely to be of the type known as Anubis baboons.

Food offerings

In Egyptian art, food appears more frequently on offering tables than on dining tables. Sustenance, particularly meat, fruit, vegetables, bread, beer, and wine, were considered the most important offerings to make to the dead and the gods. In this fragment of wall painting, the tomb owner can just be made out on the right.

See also
Leisure,
pages 62–3
Food,
pages 72–3

Viticulture

Egypt's winemaking regions were the oases in the Western Desert and the Delta, where wine was being produced from as early as the 1st Dynasty (*c.* 3000 BC). As here, vines were often grown on artificially raised areas and were trained over a trellis. Grapes were usually harvested in late summer, seemingly by men.

Second pressing

After treading, the remains of the crushed grapes were placed in a cloth or sack press (maybe made of linen or basketry), which was twisted until no further juice came out. Here one end is twisted while the other is secured. Alternatively, poles were attached to either end of the cloth or sack and were then twisted in opposite directions.

Viniculture

Grapes were trodden under foot in large vats. As here, the treaders might hold onto ropes hanging from a crossbar above the vat. The extracted juice left the vat through spouts, and after several days of primary fermentation in wide-mouthed jars, the containers were sealed or the liquid transferred to other jars for storage.

COSTUME

Clothing

Ancient Egyptian clothing was predominantly of linen, and evidence for the use of linen extends back to 5000 BC. Fabric was not often dyed, but was produced in a range of natural colors, from white through to brown (depending on the maturity of the flax and how it was prepared). Some cloth was deliberately bleached white using the naturally occurring salt, natron (a compound of sodium carbonate and sodium bicarbonate). Fabric texture also varied. There were four qualities: smooth (or ordinary) cloth, thin cloth, fine thin cloth, and royal linen. According to the art, the finest quality was so sheer that it was very nearly transparent. Cotton was unknown in Egypt until the Ptolemaic and Roman Periods, but clothing was also made out of wool (from sheep and goats) for warm clothing, leather (for example, for loincloths) and, to a much lesser extent, coir-type fibers, such as grass, reed, and hemp.

Kilts

Generally, clothing was very simple. Men working in the fields and craftsmen would wear a basic short kilt or loincloth. Officials, such as the man to the right, with his staff and scepter denoting status, would wear a more elaborate pleated kilt knotted at the waist in a particular way.

See also
Costume,
pages 78–9
Daily life,
pages 82–3

Overskirts and tunics

From the Middle Kingdom onward, high-status men would often wear a long, transparent overskirt over their kilts. Pleats were certainly favored, and striped or pleated fine shawls were worn by men and women. Linen shirts or tunics have survived from the Early Dynastic Period (*c.* 2800 BC) onward. Plain or pleated ankle-length tunics became popular during the late 18th Dynasty.

Finest fabrics

The Egyptian artist would often show the skin color beneath the linen garment in order to imply just how fine (and thus expensive) the clothing was. Fashions in elite attire changed over the years, so observation of clothing can be a useful means of dating a tomb scene or statue.

Figure-hugging clothing

In the Old Kingdom the fashion for women was a very tight-fitting dress, known as a sheath dress, with broad shoulder straps. In artistic representations, this type of dress accentuates the female form, leaving nothing to the imagination. Presumably this was an artistic device to emphasize female fertility and sexuality, for in reality a dress this tight would have hindered all movement.

Pleated dresses

Women began the New Kingdom wearing sheath dresses, but these were soon replaced by increasingly elaborate, pleated dresses. Cloth was wound around the lower torso and draped over the shoulders so that the two weft fringes hung down the front. It was knotted or tied with a sash beneath the breasts.

Pharaonic costume

From the Old Kingdom the pharaoh wore a corselet, kilt, and girdle. Pharaonic costume, including that of the royal family, became more elaborate by the Ramesside Period (the 19th and 20th Dynasties). The kilt was more complicated and the pendant apron larger and more decorative. The corselet was eventually replaced by a short-sleeved jerkin.

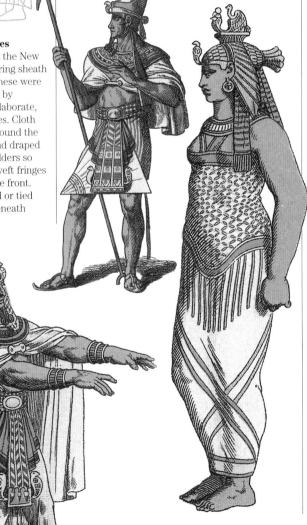

Stagewear

Artists frequently stressed the erotic nature of music and female musicians by depicting them in clothes so sheer that their bodies were clearly visible beneath. This lute player is performing at a banquet wearing a large cloak wrapped and knotted around her body, leaving her right shoulder exposed.

COSTUME

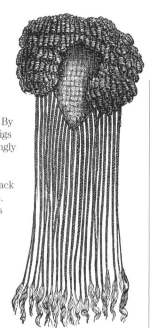

Accessories

Both men and women accessorized their outfits with sandals, wigs, and jewelry. Sandals were, of course, practical and are known to have been worn by quarrymen in the Eastern Desert, but those depicted wearing them in the art tend to be royal and high-status individuals, and sandals (or an accompanying sandal bearer) are an indicator of this status. Wigs may have served a practical function to protect the head against the strong sun and to guard against head lice, but they were clearly also a fashion accessory and closely associated with female sexuality. Jewelry could be made of a range of materials. Certain items had associations of relative status—for example, broad collars indicated high status. Girdles, anklets, bracelets, armlets, rings, necklaces, diadems, earrings, and studs were also all worn by those who could afford them.

Rings

Rings of bronze, silver, gold, faience, and glass, have all survived. Among these are gold rings with turquoise, quartz, and amethyst beads as bezels. These can be in the form of scarabs, perhaps of lapis lazuli or green jasper, which sometimes swivel to reveal an underside with an incised spiral motif or arrangement of hieroglyphs.

See also
Costume,
pages 76–7
Daily life,
pages 82–3

Pendants

A fabulous range of pendants survive from ancient Egypt, which would have been strung on necklaces and collars. Floral motifs feature most heavily, followed by animal designs. Some materials were particularly popular for necklaces at certain points of pharaonic history; for example, amethyst was fashionable during the Middle Kingdom.

Wig style

As with jewelry and clothing, there were fashions in wigs, too. By the New Kingdom, wigs had become increasingly elaborate and might have long braids covering the upper back and often the breasts. Sometimes the braids were gathered in bundles toward the bottom of the wig, forming bangs.

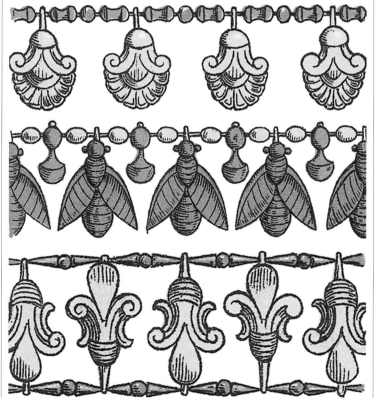

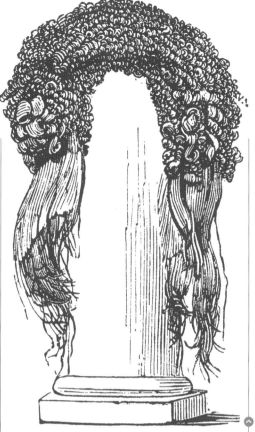

Wig construction
Wigs were usually made of human hair, which was coated with beeswax and resin and attached to a net of braided human hair—although vegetable fibers, such as date palm, were sometimes used for padding. There is no evidence for wool or any other animal hair being used.

Women's wigs
The wigs depicted in the art are for the most part considerably more attractive than those that have actually survived. Women's wigs tended to be heavy and ornamented with hair-rings, diadems, and other jewelry. These elaborate wigs were restricted to the wealthy; those less affluent had to make do with false braids and curls.

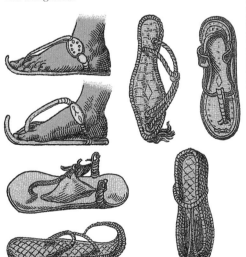

Sandals
The ancient Egyptians wore sandals rather than shoes. They were made of wood, goatskin, or fibers from palm trees or the papyrus plant and were held on the foot by simple straps. Many of the sandals that have been discovered come to a point at the toes.

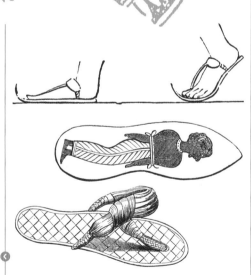

Stamping on the enemy
Sometimes a pharaoh might wear sandals with images of bound captives on the soles, so that with every step he took he was symbolically crushing the foreigners who were considered potential enemies of Egypt. A pair of marquetry-veneered sandals was found in Tutankhamun's tomb decorated with a Nubian and Asiatic prisoner on each of the upper soles.

DAILY LIFE

Furniture

Actual items of furniture have survived from ancient Egypt, as have numerous depictions of different kinds of furniture, especially on the walls of nonroyal tombs. Furniture was made from various woods: acacia, tamarisk, willow, sidder, sycamore fig, and imported Lebanese cedar, North African ash, Turkish oak, and Ethiopian ebony. Elements of furniture were made of ivory, reed, rush, and leather. Furniture probably did not feature too heavily in the lives of most Egyptians, for whom it would have been an unnecessary luxury, and the majority would have slept and sat on low mud-brick platforms, mats, and cushions.

Linen chests

Chests found in tombs have normally been plundered, but boxes of this type probably originally contained bedding and linen. One side panel of the gable-shaped lid opens; it was "locked" by winding cord around the two mushroom-shaped handles set into the center of the lid on either side of the ridge. The cord was then sealed with clay.

Royal furniture

Royal furniture was in a league of its own. It was gilded, inlaid with colored glass or faience, veneered with rare timbers, exquisitely painted, or decorated with royal insignia or, as here, bound captives, lions, Horus falcons, cartouches, solar disks, and the "unification of the two lands" motif, *sema tawy*.

Perpaut's chest

This elaborate chest was found in the 18th Dynasty Theban (Luxor) tomb of Perpaut (*c.* 1400 BC). The geometric pattern painted on the lid was popular in this period. The long sides have painted scenes of Perpaut and his wife accepting offerings from their son and daughters. The end panels have scenes of gazelles feeding from an ornamental tree.

Lion-leg chair

Chairs of this type would have been found in the houses of the wealthy elite. They have short, lion-shaped legs set on small copper drums. The seat is made from a rush weave that passes through holes bored along the inside edge of the seat frame. The joints are wedged rather than glued.

See also

Architecture,
pages 70–1

Daily life,
pages 82–3

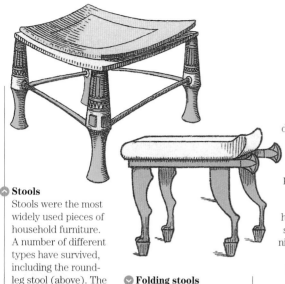

Stools

Stools were the most widely used pieces of household furniture. A number of different types have survived, including the round-leg stool (above). The hand-carved legs were sometimes inlaid with ebony and ivory, and a sheet of leather was stuck onto heavily plastered seat rails to form a seat.

Folding stools

The folding stool was first used in the Middle Kingdom. It was a mobile seat because it was light and easy to handle when folded. New Kingdom versions of this model are more elaborate, with the vertical spindles often finished with goose heads (below, left). Some headrests were also designed to fold and be easily portable (below, right).

Bes and Taweret

Headrests were sometimes decorated with images of the household deities Bes and Taweret. These apotropaic deities were believed to protect the sleepers through the potentially dangerous darkness of night. It was hoped they would keep away scorpions, snakes, intruders, nightmares, and demons. The protective deities are often portrayed looking menacing and brandishing knives.

Headrests

Egyptians used headrests instead of pillows. These were usually made of wood, but examples have survived (from the tomb of Tutankhamun) in materials, such as alabaster and even glass. Some were padded, but they mostly appear not to have been. They are still used today in some countries, such as Kenya.

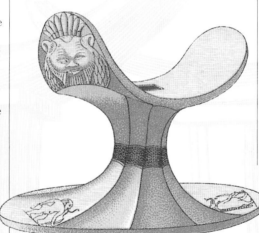

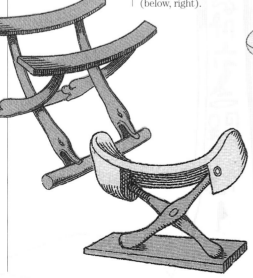

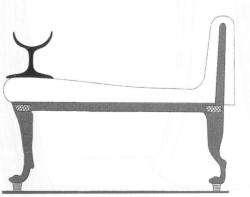

Beds

Beds were often designed with bull- or lion-shaped legs, and by the New Kingdom had a footboard attached to the bed by large right-angled braces that were dowelled to each edge of the footboard and the side rails. Bed frames usually sloped slightly toward the footboard and had cord or leather webbing and some form of mattress.

DAILY LIFE

Household Objects

Personal adornment was important to the ancient Egyptians. Both men and women wore cosmetics, presumably to enhance their appearances, but eye paints would also have served a practical purpose. The malachite-based green eye paint (*udju*) would apparently have had antibacterial and disinfectant qualities (it occurs as an ingredient in prescriptions for eye medicines in the magico-medical papyri), and this and the galena-based eye paint (*mesdemet*) would have trapped dust and sand and would have protected the eyes against flies and the glare of the sun. The malachite-based variety seems to have been the most popular until the mid-Old Kingdom, but by the New Kingdom galena had almost completely replaced it. A range of toilet articles are among the objects of daily use found in an ancient Egyptian household, but because the wealthy ancient Egyptians chose to be buried with them, they are more often found in tombs rather than houses.

See also
Costume,
pages 76–9
Daily life,
pages 80–1

Cosmetic jars ⌃
A range of elaborate cosmetics vessels has survived from ancient Egypt. Small pots with flat bottoms, wide rims, and flat circular lids were commonly used for storing cosmetics during the Middle Kingdom and early New Kingdom. The kohl tube became popular in the New Kingdom. The more decorative ones were in the form of palm columns or were held by monkeys.

Cosmetic spoons
Some of the most beautiful toilet objects of the New Kingdom are the wooden "cosmetic spoons." They are elaborately carved—in this example, in the form of a young woman picking lilies. The bowls of these spoons may have contained cosmetic creams, and some had swiveling lids.

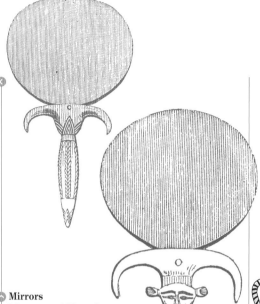

Mirrors
Mirrors would have been affordable by a minority because they were highly polished metal disks, usually of bronze, attached to ornamental handles. The papyrus motif (a symbol of vitality) was frequently used in the design of the handle, as was Hathor, goddess of beauty and fertility. The word for mirror was *ankh*, the same as for life.

Hair combs
Combs were made of ivory and wood. Despite the wearing of wigs, people clearly cared about the appearance of their real hair and could call upon the services of a hairdresser. Prescriptions survive for anti-alopecia, anti-balding, and anti-graying remedies. There are also recipes for washes to make hair grow thicker and stronger.

Storage
All kinds of household objects were stored in chests and boxes. Some boxes had interiors divided into compartments, perhaps to hold a range of different pots. Reeds, bound together with rush or papyrus, were used to make simple boxes from Predynastic times. Here a combination of reeds and wood has been used.

Vases
Since vases and pots often had tapered bottoms, they required support. A hole could be dug into the ground in which to stand the vessel, or it could be put in a stand. Thin strips of lumber were mortised, tenoned, and dowelled together to make these, and the frame was then gessoed and painted.

MESOPOTAMIA

Mesopotamia might justly be called the cradle of civilization. Intensive agriculture, industrial production, urbanism, and national government all started here, and many innovations in technology, mathematics, law, and science sprang from the establishment of sedentary society. The period from 3000 BC to 539 BC encompasses several different civilizations, some controlling relatively small regions, others exercising power over extensive territories and numerous subject peoples.

Mesopotamia was ruled by several nonnative dynasties, but each was assiduous in maintaining and adopting the culture that they found in preference to the one they had left. The early history of Mesopotamia is one of small, settled societies, their unification under a central power, the subsequent collapse of this state under the influence of external pressures, and then the reestablishment of a unified power. From about 1800 BC, Mesopotamia was divided between Babylonia in the south and Assyria in the north, with relations between the two varying from peaceful coexistence to open warfare. From around 780 BC, Assyria reigned supreme, controlling an Empire that stretched from the Arabian Gulf to the Mediterranean and southern Asia Minor. By 612 BC, the Assyrian Empire was no more and Babylonia took control of the Near East. This is the period of Nebuchadnezzar and Belshazzar, which established Babylon forever after as a byword for splendor, power, and, ultimately, decadence. But in 539 BC the Persians conquered Babylon, and Mesopotamia as an independent entity ceased to exist.

TIME LINE
c. 6000 BC–539 BC

Cuneiform inscription embedded in a terra-cotta brick

c. 6000 BC

Beginnings of pottery making and metallurgy, with arable farming and animal husbandry now well established.

c. 5000 BC

Farming communities developing in southern Mesopotamia and evidence of religious shrines.

c. 3000 BC

The first cities appear, and society becomes more complex; evidence of towns in northern Mesopotamia.

c. 2900 BC

Beginning of Early Dynastic Period; city-states in southern Mesopotamia and evidence of warfare; cuneiform script developing; most of the population now lives in cities.

c. 2600 BC

Dynasties of kings enumerated in Sumerian King List.

2600–2334 BC

Early Dynastic III; larger political units emerging; writing system fully developed; southern Mesopotamia united under Lugalzagesi (2340–2316 BC), king of the city-state of Umma.

2193–2153 BC

Collapse of the Akkadian Empire; Sumerian city-states regain their independence; Akkad overrun by invading Guti from the east.

2153–2112 BC

Gutians control parts of Sumer.

2112–2004 BC

Third Dynasty of Ur; Sumer and Akkad reunited under Ur-Nammu; his successor Shulgi (2094–2097 BC) gains control of part of Elam in southern Iran.

2004 BC

Ur sacked by Elamites; Ur III ends.

1781–1750 BC

Hammurabi controls all of southern Mesopotamia; after the death of Shamshi-Adad, his kingdom extends into Assyria as well.

1750–1600 BC

After Hammurabi's death in 1750 BC, Babylonian Empire gradually declines; Assyria descends into anarchy with a series of usurpers.

1600–1200 BC

Kassite Period in Babylonia; the Kassites were settlers who gained control after the brief Hittite invasion that ended with the sacking of Babylon in 1595 BC.

1155 BC

Babylon sacked by the Elamites; end of the Kassite Period.

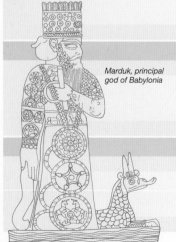

Marduk, principal god of Babylonia

1150–950 BC

Period of decline in Babylonia; Assyria maintains relative prosperity under a succession of strong kings until the death in 1076 BC of Tiglath-Pileser I (1114–1076 BC), after which it too declines.

950–609 BC

Neo-Assyrian Period, when Assyria begins to revive under a succession of strong rulers.

726–627 BC

Height of Assyrian power; Babylonia resists Assyrian domination, assisted by the Elamites, resulting in periodic conflicts.

683 BC

Sennacherib razes Babylon to the ground in response to persistent rebellions.

A city plundered by the Assyrians

646 BC

Assurbanipal defeats Elam, razes Susa to the ground, and restores the statue of Marduk, patron deity of Babylon, to the temple there.

612 BC

After the death of Assurbanipal, the Assyrian Empire quickly collapses under the twin threats of the Medes and the Babylonians; in 612 BC the capital, Nineveh, is captured.

c. 4000 BC

Early Uruk Period; large numbers of settlements in southern Mesopotamia, wheel-made pottery, animals being used for transport and plowing.

c. 3500 BC

Emergence of writing and economic specialization; urbanism and temple complexes developing.

Early rendering of an ox-drawn plow

2334–2193 BC

Akkadian Empire established by Sargon; Akkad (central Mesopotamia) and Sumer (southern Mesopotamia) unified; Mesopotamian sphere of influence extends from the Arabian Gulf to eastern Anatolia.

2004–1780 BC

Old Babylonian Period; Isin becomes dominant city-state in southern Mesopotamia; emergence of Assyria from *c.* 2015 BC.

1813–1781 BC

Northern Mesopotamia united under Shamshi-Adad I (flourished in late 18th century BC); Assyria controls northern and central area from the Euphrates to the Zagros Mountains.

1792 BC

Hammurabi becomes king of Babylon and begins to build his Empire; takes control of Isin in 1787 BC.

Stele with a portrait of Hammurabi

1500–1350 BC

Assyria conquered and ruled by the Mitanni, their neighbors to the west.

1350 BC

Collapse of Mitanni Empire; beginning of Middle Assyrian Period under Assur-uballit I (1363–1328 BC); Kassite rule maintaining peace and prosperity in Babylonia.

1300–1225 BC

Border disputes between Assyria and Babylonia escalate into frequent warfare; Babylonia often allied with the Elamites against Assyria.

880–824 BC

Assyria becomes a dominant power in the Near East under Assurnasirpal II and Shalmaneser III; friendly relations maintained with Babylonia for most of this period.

823–811 BC

Reign of Shamshi-Adad V in Assyria marks a decline in relations with Babylonia, which he attacks and defeats.

780–727 BC

Some decades of decline in Assyria are brought to an end by Tiglath-Pileser III (reigned 744–727 BC), who reorganizes and rebuilds his kingdom.

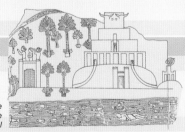

Contemporary picture of a ziggurat from the palace of Assurbanipal

668–627 BC

Reign of Assurbanipal, under whom the Assyrian Empire includes all of Mesopotamia, Elam, Egypt, the Levant, and Anatolia; in 648 BC Assurbanipal deposes his brother from the throne of Babylon and assumes direct control.

609–539 BC

Neo-Babylonian Period; Babylon seizes the Empire of its erstwhile northern ruler; Nebuchadnezzar extensively rebuilds Babylon in great splendor.

587–539 BC

Exile of the Jews in Babylon.

556–539 BC

Reign of King Nabonidus, who spends ten years campaigning in Arabia, leaving his son Belshazzar as regent. In 539 BC Cyrus II of Persia defeated Nabonidus and captured Babylon.

GEOGRAPHY

Mesopotamia

Mesopotamia—literally "the land between the rivers"—was the name given in Classical times to the region bounded roughly by the Tigris and Euphrates rivers in what is now southern Iraq, where the earliest culturally advanced societies known to us flourished for over 5,000 years. The earliest settlements were in the southern part of the region, known as Sumer, where the development of irrigation-fed, large-scale agriculture led to the beginnings of urbanism. The region enjoyed the most fertile land in the Near East, and was the focal point of trade routes from Anatolia to the Arabian Gulf and through Persia to the Indus Valley. The people of Mesopotamia and their rulers made good use of these advantages, with results that were productive in many ways of Western society as we know it today.

Euphrates

The more important of the two main rivers, the Euphrates flowed more slowly and in more channels than its companion and its periodic flooding deposited fertile silt on the plain between the two rivers. This process of deposition also raised the bed of the river above the level of the surrounding land, so that it was a straightforward matter to breach its banks in order to build irrigation canals.

Tigris

Faster flowing and more deeply channeled than the Euphrates, the Tigris was less suited to irrigation in southern Mesopotamia. The main population centers on the river were the great Assyrian cities in the north.

Oxen were used for plowing floodplains

MESOPOTAMIA *c.* 3000–539 BC

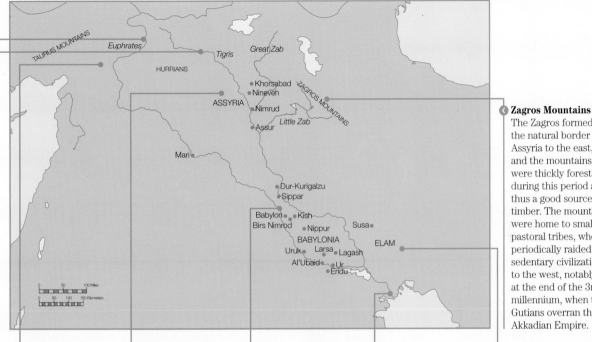

- TAURUS MOUNTAINS
- Euphrates
- Tigris
- Great Zab
- HURRIANS
- Khorsabad
- Nineveh
- ZAGROS MOUNTAINS
- ASSYRIA
- Nimrud
- Little Zab
- Assur
- Mari
- Dur-Kurigalzu
- Sippar
- Babylon
- Kish
- Birs Nimrod
- Nippur
- Susa
- BABYLONIA
- ELAM
- Uruk
- Larsa
- Lagash
- Al'Ubaid
- Ur
- Eridu

50   100 Miles
50   100   150 Kilometers

Zagros Mountains

The Zagros formed the natural border of Assyria to the east, and the mountains were thickly forested during this period and thus a good source of timber. The mountains were home to small pastoral tribes, who periodically raided the sedentary civilization to the west, notably at the end of the 3rd millennium, when the Gutians overran the Akkadian Empire.

Anatolia

At its greatest extent Mesopotamian influence reached as far as Anatolia, and the Taurus Mountains were an important source of minerals, particularly copper, gold, and silver. The Taurus were known from the time of Sargon of Akkad as the Silver Mountains.

Ruins at Dur Kurigalzu, built as a defense against Assyria

Assyria

The heartland of Assyria was centered on the Tigris and its tributaries, the Greater and Lesser Zab. The plains between the northern Tigris and Euphrates provided grazing for sheep and goats but the land was not irrigable, so cultivation was only possible along the rivers and farther north, where rainfall was more reliable.

Carved relief of one of the famous gardens of Babylonia

Babylonia

The alluvial plain where the Tigris and Euphrates came closest together was the focus of Babylonia, comprising the earlier kingdoms of Sumer and Akkad. Since the rainfall was not enough to support agriculture, irrigation channels were developed to spread the river water across the plain. Flood control was most important when crops were to be harvested.

Chaldea

The coastal area of Mesopotamia, known from the middle of the 2nd millennium as Sealand, a marshy area of reed beds and date palms where the two main rivers ran into the Gulf of Arabia. It is likely that the Gulf coastline was as much as 93 miles (150 km) farther inland at the beginning of the 4th millennium than it is now.

Pigs rooting among the reed beds of Chaldea

Elam

The region to the east of Babylonia, separated from Mesopotamia by marshland to the south and the Zagros farther north. Elam enjoyed sufficient rainfall to allow cultivation of crops without irrigation, as well as grassland for pastoralism from earliest times. Elam's relations with Babylonia varied, but it was almost always hostile to Assyria.

GOVERNMENT

Kings

The term king can have various applications during the 2,500-year period considered here. Early Mesopotamian cities had chiefs, clearly identifiable from documents and inscriptions, who had responsibility for the upkeep of infrastructure, such as irrigation canals, and the administration of justice and bureaucracy. Later, when larger areas came under the rule of individuals, such as Sargon (2334–2279 BC) and Hammurabi (*c.* 1792–1750 BC), the king of a city was more like a governor who owed loyalty to the central authority. The king's authority was divinely ordained, and he was the representative of the city's god. In Assyria the king was presented for the blessing of the god Assur at the beginning of his reign and was thereafter judged to be the rightful ruler, whereas in Babylonia the king was required to submit to the validation of the city god in a ceremony held every new year.

Hammurabi

Hammurabi (1792–1750 BC) was the first significant King of Babylon, who began the process that saw the city established, sometimes in fact but always in reputation, as the preeminent city of the Near East for nearly 2,000 years. During the first few years of his reign, he set the administration of his city-state on a proper footing and jockeyed for position among the contending kingdoms in the region. By the end of his reign, he had united all of Babylonia under his rule, had taken control briefly of Assur and Nineveh in the north and had fixed Babylon as the rightful seat of kingship in southern Mesopotamia.

See also
Government,
pages 92–7
Leisure,
pages 112–15

Gudea of Lagash

Gudea was King of Lagash, a city-state in southern Mesopotamia, from 2141–2122 BC and many statues of him survive. Gudea reigned after the Kingdom of Akkad, established by Sargon and his successors, had been destroyed by the invading Gutians, after which the city-states of southern Mesopotamia regained their former autonomy.

Nebuchadnezzar I

The first Babylonian king to bear this name, Nebuchadnezzar, had a reign (604–562 BC) that was distinguished by his decisive defeat of the Elamites, whose sacking of Babylon around 1150 BC had marked the end of the long-lived Kassite Dynasty in Babylonia. Among the trophies that the Elamites had carried off to their capital Susa, were the stelae on which Hammurabi's law code was inscribed and the statue of Marduk, which Nebuchadnezzar was able to retrieve. This boundary stone records the granting of certain privileges to one of the king's campaign generals.

Assurbanipal

King of Assyria (668–627 BC), Assurbanipal shared the rule of Mesopotamia with his brother Shamash-shuma-ukin (reigned 668–648 BC), King of Babylonia, under a treaty established by their father Esarhaddon (reigned 681–669 BC). However, the military might of the Assyrian held the reins of power, and a Babylonian revolt in 652 BC put down by Assurbanipal led to the defeat and death of his brother.

Sennacherib

Sennacherib, the King of Assyria (reigned 704–681 BC), is shown seated on his throne dressed to preside over a festival. The son of Sargon II, Sennacherib had a reign that was marked by campaigns to subdue threats to the southern part of his kingdom from the Babylonians and their Elamite and Chaldean allies, campaigns that culminated in the complete destruction of Babylon in 689 BC and in Sennacherib's assumption of the ancient title of King of Sumer and Akkad.

Sargon II

This image from a bas-relief from the royal palace at Dur Shurrakin shows Sargon II, the King of Assyria from 721 to 705 BC. Sargon's king name was clearly chosen to link him with the great Sargon of Akkad, the first king to unite Mesopotamia under a single rule near the end of the 3rd millennium BC. Sargon's ancestry is uncertain, and he may have been a usurper. He assumed the kingship of Babylonia and Assyria in 709 BC, but was eventually killed in battle on the northern frontier, an unusual fate for a Mesopotamian ruler.

GOVERNMENT

Institutions

The two main institutions in Mesopotamia were the temple and the palace. Although some land was privately owned, the majority of the land belonged to one or other of these institutions, who then leased plots to their tenants. Large numbers of people were employed in the service of the temple, and the temple administrators were in turn responsible for the redistribution of agricultural surpluses. The Mesopotamians would not recognize the distinction we make between religion and secularism, and the service of the city god was not so much a matter of religious faith as simply the central fact that structured their lives. The balance of power between temple and palace fluctuated over time, with the later Assyrian and Babylonian kings asserting themselves over the power of the temple. But since the king had to have the support of the city god, in practice there was always a close relationship between the two institutions.

See also

Government,
pages 90–1

Government,
pages 94–7

The role of the king
The king was closely associated with the city god, and a statue of the king would share the temple space with the image of the god, symbolizing this relationship. He was effectively the god's agent, and his duties included improving the fertility of the land, defending his people from their enemies, promoting justice, and building and maintaining the temple. The inscription on this statue of Gudea proclaims that he built the temple dedicated to Ningirsu, the tutelary deity of Lagash, and on his lap there is a tablet with a building plan inscribed on it.

Serving the city god
Early Mesopotamian society was highly centralized, and because the city-state was understood to be the fiefdom of the city god, the temple exercised a large measure of control over the economic life of the citizens. This upper-class individual is bringing an animal to sacrifice. Making a regular offering to the temple was a sign that you were a member of the community and thus enjoyed the various rights that went along with this. It also generated surpluses that the temple redistributed to its own personnel and to those who ran the state bureaucracy.

Constitutional monarchy

The power of the king over his subjects was mediated by a number of factors. A strong king must have been advantageous to a city-state in terms of controlling resources in competition against other states, but as late as 2300 BC the person chosen as the ruler of Kish took the name Iphur-Kish or "Kish assembled," indicating that he ruled by the will of the people. The central ideology that everyone, including the king, was in the service of the god never wavered throughout Mesopotamian history, and even the Assyrian kings with their immense military strength were careful to restore the ancient Babylonian temples as an assurance that they enjoyed divine approval.

The court

With the emergence of more extensive and unified states from the beginning of the 2nd millennium BC, the role of senior officials became significant. The authority of the king would be passed down a chain of command from the vizier, who had direct access to the king, to the governors of the provinces. Since most bureaucrats were illiterate, the scribes who were attached to the court had considerable power. Eunuchs were favored as senior officials since there was no possibility of them entertaining dynastic ambitions.

Propaganda

Royal inscriptions were an important way of sustaining the ideology of kingship, and it seems that almost any surface that could be used to extol the king's piety, virtue, power, and, by extension, right to govern would receive an inscription. This stela of Shamshi-Adad V (823–811 BC) records the uprisings in Assyria toward the end of the reign of his predecessor, Shalmaneser III (858–824 BC), and the success of the new king in reestablishing order throughout the kingdom.

GOVERNMENT

Bureaucracy

The Mesopotamian passion for keeping records is well attested by the large numbers of tablets that survive. Many of these are, understandably, economic documents, with records of transactions, taxes paid or owed, goods despatched or received. Once people had moved away from subsistence agriculture, it was essential to keep track of surpluses and how they were distributed. There are also lists of everything imaginable. Some, such as the Sumerian King List from the end of the 3rd millennium BC, had a clear purpose in demonstrating the legitimate lineage of the earliest kings to rule southern Mesopotamia as a single entity. However, there are also lists of trees, types of fish, animals, countries, even simply of related words and phrases, with no evidence of analysis or any kind of narrative. The Mesopotamian scribe was a devoted cataloger of the world around him, a collector of information rather than a philosopher.

See also

Government,
pages 90–3

Government,
pages 96–7

Lion weight
A standardized system of weights and measures was recognized early on as essential for purposes of trade and administration. Although different kingdoms used different systems, there is evidence that the Mesopotamian system was the most widespread in the Near East. Tables of equivalents enabled different systems to be combined. Weights from southern Mesopotamia were generally duck-shaped, whereas in the north they were made in the shape of lions, as in this example.

Seals
Various methods were used to establish ownership of goods and to validate decisions and official documents. The earliest known method of recording a transaction was the use of pebbles or tokens placed inside a bag or jar, which was then sealed with a piece of clay impressed with a mark that signified the owner and the kind of things being counted.

Cylinder seals

From the beginning of the 3rd millennium BC cylinder seals began to replace the earlier stamp seals. A stone or bronze cylinder was carved with an inscription and an image representing the authority of the owner of the seal, often showing a person being brought into the presence of a god or a king. This cylinder would leave an impression when rolled over a flat piece of clay, which would then harden and become permanent. Thousands of such seals and seal impressions have been recovered by archaeologists and are an important source of information about many aspects of Mesopotamian life and government.

Clay tablets

Perhaps the most significant advantage for the historian of Mesopotamia is that the written documents were made using clay, which when baked hard is virtually indestructible. Thus we have documents from Sumeria from the beginning of the 3rd millennium BC, whereas documentation from Egypt for the same period is lacking because the writing material, papyrus, has long since disintegrated. Clay tablets were the most common material for documents right up to the birth of Christ, when the cuneiform script had largely been superseded by the cursive script of Aramaic and related languages.

Scribes

The role of the scribe was important in a period when very few people could read or write. Economic transactions were meticulously recorded on behalf of the twin Mesopotamian institutions, the temple and the palace, and scribes could attain positions of some influence. As shown here, details of the spoils of war were recorded, even to the extent of accounting for the numbers of enemy dead by counting the heads.

GOVERNMENT

Writing

The development of writing is probably the single most important contribution by the Mesopotamians to what we might call civilized culture. Writing was not invented for religious or literary purposes, however, but in order to keep accounts. From images representing merchandise and quantities, within a couple of centuries writing had developed toward using symbols instead of pictures, and then toward being able to represent sounds as well as ideas. The cuneiform system is immensely complicated, having some five hundred different basic signs, and scribal training in the *edubba*, or school, took several years. The scribal schools were instrumental in preserving the heritage of Sumerian culture and disseminating it throughout western Asia.

See also
Government,
pages 90–5
Daily life,
pages 124–5

Cuneiform
From around 2500 BC the writing system developed away from pictograms toward a symbolic representation of words using wedge-shaped symbols marked into the clay with the end of a cut reed or stylus. This system was able not simply to represent a single word, but could show phonetic values—that is, the shapes could represent sounds as well as words. Over time the cuneiform symbols were simplified and conventionalized, allowing much greater facility for representing different languages.

Early pictograms
The earliest Mesopotamian writing system used pictograms, similar to the Egyptian system of hieroglyphics, with a shape or picture for each word or idea. This script is known as Uruk IV, from the place in southern Mesopotamia where it was first found, and dates to around 3000 BC. The inscriptions found were chiefly lists of livestock or agricultural equipment.

Akkadian hymn tablet
Translating the cuneiform script was a challenge for 19th-century scholars. The library of Assurbanipal discovered at Nineveh included tablets with texts in both Akkadian and the earlier Sumerian language, both written using the cuneiform script. Having parallel texts meant that if one language was known already, the other could be derived from it by a process of comparison.

Prism of Sennacherib
Inscriptions were frequently made on cylinders and prisms, which were placed in the foundations of temples and palaces. The inscriptions gave details of who erected the building and for what purpose, but they also gave a history of the ruler's deeds and ancestry, presumably as a memorial should the building be destroyed. These prism cylinders have been invaluable in reconstructing Mesopotamian history.

Numbers
The cuneiform system of numbering was similar to that of the Romans, although more cumbersome. Before cuneiform, numbers were represented on tablets by a combination of impressed circles and crescent shapes, though clearly this system could only be used for the simplest transactions.

1		11		100	
2		12		200	
3		20		300	
4		30		400	
5		40		500	
6		50		600	
7		60		700	
8		70		800	
9		80		900	
10		90		1000	

WARFARE

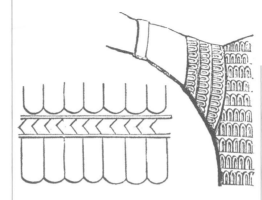

Arms and Armor

As soon as resources began to be appropriated by one group or another there were bound to be conflicts. Texts relating to wars are known from the earliest times, although a war, such as that between the southern cities of Lagash and Umma in the mid-3rd millennium, would probably have been a single engagement lasting a few hours with a hundred casualties at the absolute most, because the military equipment available would not have permitted anything more substantial. However, by the time of the Assyrian kings of the 1st millennium, the period for which we have the greatest amount of visual evidence, warfare was much more technologically advanced.

Body armor
Body armor consisted of a belted tunic with metal plates sewn onto it, which reached down below the waist, although some reliefs show it reaching to the knees. The upper arms were bare and a skirt was worn beneath the tunic down to the knees. Soldiers of all classes are most frequently shown barefoot, but sometimes they have sandals that are little more than a heel piece with straps across the foot.

Shields
The earliest shields were round bucklers made of hides or wickerwork and later wholly of metal. By the time of Sennacherib, the shields had become much larger, about 5 ft (1.5 m) in diameter and of a convex shape. They seem to have been made of wicker with metal rims and banding, presumably because a metal shield of this size would be impossible to maneuver. They were fitted with a strap so that they could be slung over the shoulder when on the march. Later still the Assyrian spearmen had tall, rectangular shields.

Helmets
The helmets seen most often in bas-reliefs are of a simple, conical shape with flaps to cover the ears. Sometimes soldiers, particularly archers and slingers, are depicted wearing close-fitting caps of leather rather than helmets. Spearmen from the time of Sargon II onward had helmets with crescent-shaped crests designed to deflect blows and offer greater protection.

See also
Warfare,
pages 102–3
Costume,
pages 122–3

Spearmen

The spearmen were the backbone of the Assyrian army, using weapons that were about 6 ft (2 m) long. The spear had a counterweight at the end so that the center of gravity was farther back along the shaft, allowing the spearman to keep as great a distance as possible between him and the enemy. Cavalry had longer spears, over 10 ft (3 m) long. Shorter javelins are also depicted on the reliefs, but these are usually part of the armory of the charioteers and are never shown being actually thrown as weapons.

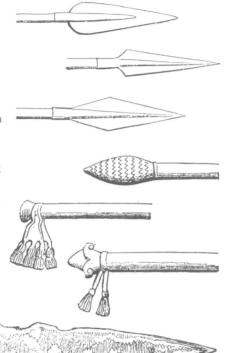

Static shields

As well as the shields carried by the spearmen, the Assyrians had much larger shields made from wicker that curved over at the top to protect archers from weapons fired from above. These were placed on the ground and the archer would fire from behind the shield while his attendant held it upright.

Archers

Assyrian archers at the time of Sargon seem to have been of various classes, some better armored than others. The bow was quite short, little more than 3 ft (1 m) in length, and so shorter than those used by the Egyptians. Archers are often depicted in pairs, and the archers of the higher class have attendants who hold their shield or protect their backs. The arrows were carried in quivers that were ornamented with rosettes and banding, and they were probably made of wood rather than metal because no actual examples have been found.

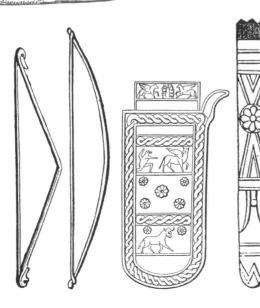

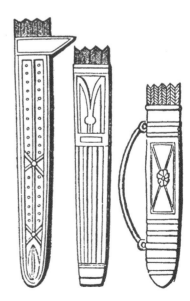

WARFARE

Methods

Although the Median conquerors of Assyria in the late 7th century BC claimed to have been the first to put an Asiatic army on an organized footing, the Assyrian army of the Sargonid kings was certainly organized into divisions of cavalry, spearmen, and archers, with subdivisions within those groups. There is evidence from reliefs of spearmen organized in phalanxes and of cavalry advancing separately from infantry. War was a seasonal event, carried out in spring and early summer when mountain passes became negotiable and before the heat of the summer set in. At the height of their Empire in the 1st millennium, the Assyrians were the most feared and accomplished military nation in the Near East.

See also
Warfare,
pages 98–9
Warfare,
pages 102–3

Phalanx
The use of organized squadrons of infantry was common from the earliest period. The stele erected by King Eannatum of Lagash to celebrate his victory over the rival city-state of Umma around 2450 BC shows a phalanx of spearmen advancing in close array.

Chariots
The war chariot was the preeminent weapon, used by the king and senior officers in battle, and mentioned frequently by the Assyrians themselves as well as by their enemies as the emblem of Assyrian military might. Usually shown being drawn by two horses, although occasionally three, the chariot carries the archer, his attendant—who holds the shield—and the charioteer himself. Although its speed and elevated view of the battlefield would have been useful, in practice the mounted cavalry and foot soldiers would probably have been more effective, and by the time of Sargon the chariot's emblematic purpose seems to have outweighed its military usefulness.

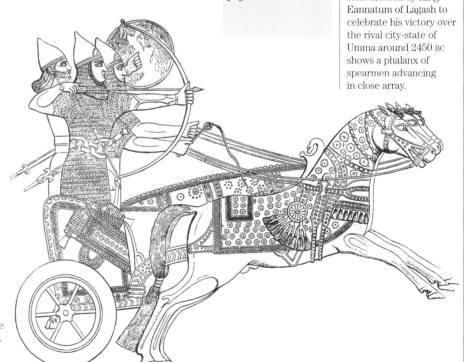

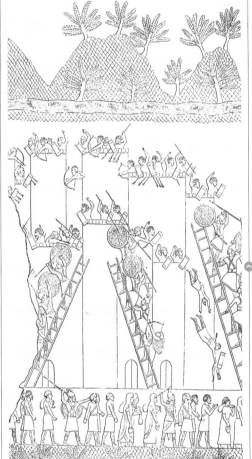

Battering rams
Judging by the wall reliefs, the Assyrians used battering rams effectively. They are shown as having four or six wheels, with a protective canopy over the top and one or more projecting rams. A ramp of earth would allow the ram to be directed at the weaker upper walls of the besieged city.

The siege
The besieged city is a frequent subject of Assyrian wall reliefs. They generally offer a narrative of the entire event, as in the example above, with the invaders scaling the walls using ladders, the bodies of the defenders strewn about the battlefield, and captives being led away.

Undermining city defenses
As well as scaling ladders and battering rams, the Assyrians would attack the base of the city walls at close quarters. Usually the soldiers are shown under the protection of the tall, curved wickerwork shields, although the soldiers in this depiction seem to be heedless of their own safety.

WARFARE

Captives and Plunder

The purpose of war was to secure resources or territory, or to protect trade routes or to quell rebellion, and the aftermath varied depending on the original purpose. The administration of a large Empire required loyal vassals, and this was unlikely to be achieved by large-scale destruction in the wake of a military victory. Hence, regardless of the Assyrian reputation, there is evidence that conquered cities were allowed to keep their privileges if they agreed to pay appropriate tribute. It was the persistent threat from Babylon that finally persuaded Sennacherib to raze the city entirely, although even after that his successor Esarhaddon rebuilt the city and the temple and restored the statues of their gods that Sennacherib had taken back to Nineveh.

Taken into captivity

The defeated citizens were frequently taken back to the Assyrian homeland. Some might be made slaves, but others were settled in new homes, and it is clear from Assyrian documents that this was a policy to pacify potentially rebellious peoples and widen the Assyrian sphere of influence. Men who had useful trades were especially valued and assimilated to the home city. These deportations were one important way in which language exchange took place, with sometimes entire populations being transplanted.

Enemy prisoners

The Assyrians have a reputation for brutality, although it is difficult at this distance in time to ascertain how justifiable this is. Reliefs show prisoners being executed, usually by bludgeoning but sometimes by decapitation, and prisoners are also shown impaled on spikes outside captured cities. Numerous inscriptions of the Sargonid kings recount how the victors put out the eyes or cut off the noses of the vanquished, but it seems that it was the ruler and his close retinue who would be made an example of in this way, and then only in the case of cities that had persistently rebelled against Assyrian authority rather than newly conquered rulers.

See also
Warfare,
pages 98–9
Warfare,
pages 100–1

Animals

Flocks of sheep and other animals appropriated from the vanquished were also accounted for by the scribes. The enemy's horses were particularly prized, but camels, although captured in large numbers after raids on the Arabs by the Sargonid kings, were little used in Mesopotamia and certainly not by the military.

Destruction

When everything worth taking had been taken, the defeated city would be destroyed. The standard inscription formula recounting a victory stated: "The land X I plundered, I devastated the whole of it." When Sennacherib captured Babylon in 689 BC, his soldiers were particularly thorough, burning the city, hurling the rubble into the Euphrates, and finally engineering a flood that "made it like a meadow."

Spoils of war

Valuables and treasure were removed from a defeated city in great quantity. The ubiquitous presence in the reliefs of scribes and images of weighing scales suggest that some measure of the booty was apportioned to the king, but some was certainly allowed to be kept by the soldiers themselves. The most important plunder would be images of the city's gods, the removal of which condemned the defeated population to continued misfortune and marked the triumph of the victor.

RELIGION

Deities

Mesopotamia was polytheistic throughout the period dealt with here, though the relative importance of the gods being worshipped varied over time and there was some hybridization of divine attributes. The earliest gods were related to fertility and nature, not surprisingly given the dependence of the people on the produce of their land. Later the astral deities were more significant. Each city had its own god who lived in the temple, and it was the duty of the people of the city to serve him or her. The calendar of festivals and presentation of offerings to the temple structured and ordered Mesopotamian life, as did the temple's role as landowner and administrator. How much this official religion was internalized or significant to ordinary citizens is impossible to say, but as mentioned earlier the idea of a separation between "religious" life and "secular" life was not one that would have been understood at this time.

Marduk

Marduk's elevation to becoming the national god of Babylonia took place at some time during the last third of the 2nd millennium, as part of a deliberate effort on behalf of the kings of Babylon to endow the city with the dignity and authority previously associated with Nippur, the city of Enlil, who was the national god of Sumer. Marduk's symbol is the dragon and his temple, Esagila, housed a gigantic statue of him, which according to Herodotus was made of gold and seated on a gold throne.

Assur

The most important Assyrian god, Assur, is represented by a ring with the wings and tail of a bird, sometimes with a human figure inside the ring. This emblem is found on reliefs and royal stelae and even on the military standard of Sargon himself. Assur is always associated with the king, and the Assyrian king owed his legitimacy to Assur's approval, being presented before his shrine at the outset of his reign. Assur's status as national god is reflected both in the name of the kingdom and in the fact that no single cultic center is associated with him.

Nabu

Nabu, the god of wisdom, was the son of Marduk and his main cultic center was Borsippa in Babylonia. Nabu was also the patron deity of the scribes, which might explain why his popularity increased in the 1st millennium, almost to the point of rivaling Marduk himself.

See also

Religion,
pages 106–7

Architecture,
pages 118–19

Ishtar

Goddess of fertility, love, and, in other guises, war, Ishtar was particularly associated with the city of Uruk and the planet Venus. She was frequently depicted riding on her sacred animal, the lion, and by the 2nd millennium her worship was so widespread throughout Mesopotamia that her name came to mean simply goddess.

Sin

Sin, or Nanna, the moon god, was the father of Shamash and Ishtar and was represented by a crescent moon. Here he presides over the scene of an official being presented to Ur-Nammu (2112–2095 BC), King of Ur, at the end of the 3rd millennium. His chief cultic center was Ur, and the position of the high priestess of Ur, instituted by Sargon of Akkad, was one of great dignity and power in Babylonia, being the direct gift of the king and frequently held, in the later 3rd millennium, by a royal daughter.

Shamash Chaldea frontis

God of the sun and of justice, Shamash is the third of the astral gods (Sin is god of the moon and Ishtar is goddess of Venus). Shamash's cultic center was Sippar. He is commonly represented with a rod and a ring, or as a disk with rays of fire coming from it, clearly visible in this relief from Sippar from the reign of the Neo-Babylonian king Nabopolassar (625–605 BC). Shamash features on the stela of Hammurabi that contains his law code, legitimating the king's claims as a just ruler.

Adad

The weather god, Adad, was often associated with the group of astral deities. His symbol was forked lightning and his emblematic animal was the bull. Adad was an important god to the Assyrians and to the West Semitic peoples, and the Yahweh of the early Hebrew religion shares some characteristics with him, riding the clouds and speaking in a voice of thunder.

RELIGION

Demons and Protectors

Regardless of their experience of official religion, the Mesopotamians were sufficiently aware of the dangers and threats of daily life to have developed a whole range of protective rituals. Belief in demons as personifications of such events as bad weather and illness was widespread, and the use of incantations and magic rituals was common, as was the recourse to talismanic protective objects, often statues. Another important aspect of Mesopotamian religious belief was the idea that the will of the gods could be established through divination. Countless texts have been found listing the meaning of divination rituals, most commonly extispicy, the examination of the entrails of animals, but also analyzing the patterns made by incense smoke or oil in water or natural events. This was considered a scientific rather than a magical process, in keeping with the literalistic religious outlook of the period, and the examination of celestial bodies for divinatory purposes led to a considerable body of astronomical knowledge.

Demon of the west wind
Numerous statues of this bizarre creature, Pazuzu, have been found. It was hung in houses as a protective talisman, because the wind from the southwest, from Arabia, would have been hot and dry and potentially disastrous to the crops of southern Mesopotamia. An inscription on the back includes a magic formula to break the wings of the west wind, making the demon powerless against the owner of the talisman.

See also
Religion,
pages 104–5
Daily Life,
pages 124–5

Domestic protectors
Clay models of dogs were very common as protective amulets. The clay was first ritually sanctified with incantations and censing, before being shaped into animals and inscribed and then baked hard. The inscriptions say such things as "Capturer of the enemy" or "Don't stop to think, bark!" When completed, the amulets were placed with additional ceremony in whatever parts of the house they were to protect, commonly the doors and windows, although sometimes they were placed in the foundations of the house.

Winged bull
Statues of this creature, called *lamassu*, were commonly placed as guards at the entrance gates of palaces and temples, and a pair can be seen restored to their original positions at the entrance of the Northwest Palace at Nimrud.

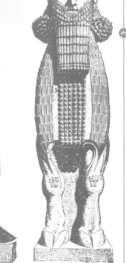

Eagle-headed man

Composite creatures are common in reliefs and cylinder seals both from northern and southern Mesopotamia. Eagle-headed men, winged lions with human heads, scorpion men, goat-fish—the Mesopotamian imagination abounded with such strange and frequently threatening beings, and numerous protective incantations have been found offering exorcism against these assailants from another world.

Sargon before the sacred tree

The significance of the sacred tree can be judged from the fact that the king is depicted venerating it. Here Sargon II of Assyria stands before the sacred tree with his right arm raised in the formulaic gesture of worship. Some kind of ceremony involving the presentation of fruit to the king before the tree is known from reliefs, but its meaning is unclear.

Ea-Han

Not all of the otherworldly monsters were threatening. Ea-Han, the fish-man, was supposed to have emerged from the Persian Gulf when the peoples of southern Mesopotamia were living as savages, and he revealed to them the principles of civilization, including law, literacy, agriculture, and building cities.

The sacred tree

This religious symbol appears on cylinder seals from the earliest periods and remains a common motif well into the 1st millennium. Its significance has not been definitely established, though it seems reasonable to assume that it began as some kind of fertility symbol, much like the maypole. From simple designs that resemble date palms or conifers, the iconography of the sacred tree developed, so that later versions are highly decorated and stylized.

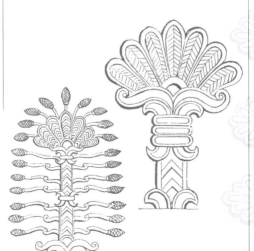

WORK

Farming and Fishing

The fertile alluvial soils of southern Mesopotamia were ideal for growing crops, but the water supply was deficient because, unlike in Egypt, there was no consistent annual flood that would irrigate the land. Instead, flooding was erratic and could be catastrophic. The need to control the supply of water for crops led to the formation of mutually supportive groups of people to build and maintain canals, which led, in turn, to the requirement for some kind of authority to oversee the process. The consequent increase in productivity created surpluses that meant some people did not have to farm the land, but could instead perform other tasks, including that of mediating with the gods to ensure the harvest in exchange for a share of the surplus. Thus agricultural organization was the trigger for the elements of what we regard as civilization, of which Mesopotamia is arguably the cradle.

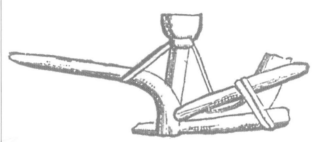

Seed plow
The development of the seed plow marked a great advance in Mesopotamian agriculture. Seed was poured into the hopper (funnel-shaped receptacle) as the plow was pulled along and directed more efficiently into the drill. The staple cereal crop was barley, which was more tolerant of the saline soil of Babylonia than other cereal crops.

See also
Technology,
pages 110–11
Leisure,
pages 112–13

Plowing
It is not known exactly when the plow was invented, although it is highly likely that some kind of primitive plow was in use by the beginning of the 6th millennium BC. Together with irrigation, the ox-drawn plow was the key to the development of large-scale agriculture and, ultimately, urban development in Mesopotamia.

Domestic animals
The main herd animals—sheep, pigs, goats, and cattle—are known to have been domesticated around 6000 BC, and all were kept by the Mesopotamians. A broad distinction can be made between Babylonia, which was chiefly arable, and the more hilly Assyria, which was more pastoral, but the distinction largely disappears from the beginning of the 2nd millennium BC. Ducks and geese are also mentioned in texts, though chickens seem to have arrived from the East relatively late during the 1st millennium.

Working animals

The ox was the main work animal, and donkeys were used as beasts of burden. Horses were mainly used for military purposes to draw chariots; they only started to be used for mounted cavalry from the beginning of the 1st millennium BC.

Milk

Milk was not drunk in Mesopotamia because the climate was not conducive to its storage. It was, however, used to make yogurt, ghee, and cheese. A frieze from the middle of the 3rd millennium BC shows a cow being milked and men making milk products. It also indicates that the Sumerians had observed that placing a calf near the mother stimulated her milk flow.

Fruit trees

The most important tree was undoubtedly the date palm, as a source of food, wood for construction, fibers for rope, and leaves for roofing. Date palms were abundant in southern Mesopotamia and required little cultivation, and there are some 150 words for the various types of palm and their products recorded from the 2nd millennium BC. Other fruit trees were also grown, and there is evidence as here of the Mesopotamian skill in cultivating and training vines.

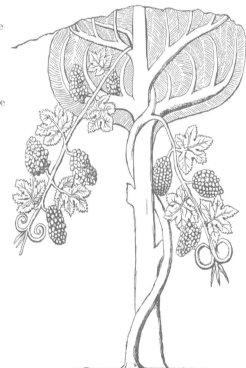

Fishing

Fish was the primary source of protein from the earliest period of Mesopotamian history, and fifty different types of fish are known from Sumerian texts. After the Old Babylonian Period, however, fish and fishing are rarely mentioned, suggesting that fish became less important as a food source outside the extreme south of the region. An inscription from Neo-Babylonian Uruk suggests that the word "fisherman" had the connotation of a lawless person, the implication being perhaps that people reliant on fish for their sustenance did not share the civilized outlook of the Babylonians farther north.

TECHNOLOGY

Transport, Tools, and Craft Goods

A wide range of specialized occupations was facilitated by the agricultural revolution in southern Mesopotamia. The Mesopotamians had mastered pottery by the 6th millennium BC, they were proficient in working metal and stone, were ingenious in their applications for the abundant deposits of clay, and had sufficient grasp of chemistry to make sophisticated use of glass. They had made and recorded astronomical observations and they could predict lunar eclipses by the mid-1st millennium BC, and in mathematics they developed a place-value system, had tables of square roots and cube roots, recognized Pythagoras' theorem as a practical fact (although they had no theoretical proof of it), and knew the value of π (pi) to an accuracy of about 0.6 percent.

Water transport

The Mesopotamians were not renowned as a maritime people, although they did navigate the two great waterways that marked out their territory. They used a type of coracle for conveying small loads, and these are often seen carrying war chariots in battle reliefs. They also used rafts buoyed by inflated animal skins, and the same buoyancy aid was also used by soldiers crossing rivers and, as here, by fishermen.

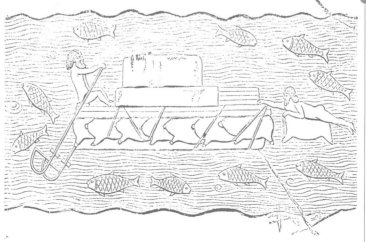

Heavy lifting

The enormous stone colossi that guarded the gates of palaces were transported in a rough-hewn state and completed in situ. The statues were moved on a wooden sled using a system of greased wooden rollers and levers, with large numbers of slaves employed to haul the monuments from the quarry to the building site.

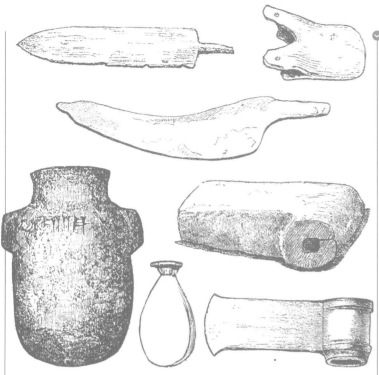

Pottery

As with other ancient civilizations, the discovery and classification of pottery is a key method of tracing the development and interactions of the peoples of Mesopotamia. Pottery has been found throughout the region dating from 6000 BC, and there is evidence for "industrial" pottery production from around the mid-6th millennium BC in the form of clusters of two-chamber kilns. Kiln temperatures of well above 1830°F (1000°C) are attested from this period.

Glassware

The Mesopotamians were skilled in glass technology from the early 2nd millennium BC, making decorative objects from faience or frit as well as producing glass proper. The earliest glass vessels were made by winding a rope of hot glass around a core of clay and then reheating it so that it fused. Different-colored glass strips were then applied and drawn into patterns with a metal rod while the glass was still plastic. Glassware seems to have been a luxury product and it is possible that the recipes for glassmaking were closely guarded.

Metalwork

The Bronze Age began in Mesopotamia around 2900 BC, before which, in common with other cultures of the period, chipped stone was used for edged tools. There were native sources of copper in Mesopotamia, although the source of the tin is uncertain. The adoption of iron after 1200 BC was relatively slow, iron technology being much more complex than that of any other ancient metal, and tools—weapons in particular—continued to be made from bronze for some centuries after iron was introduced.

See also
Work,
pages 108–9
Architecture,
pages 120–21

LEISURE

Hunting

Hunting seems to have had important symbolic value in Mesopotamia, particularly in Assyria, with dozens of depictions of the royal hunt being known to us. The triumph of the king over brute nature, and the courage that this demonstrated, added to his prestige and heroic reputation. Even allowing for the exaggeration of the reliefs, which were, after all, intended to impress visitors, tackling a lion with a bow and a spear clearly required a degree of nerve that would mark a man out as worthy to be a leader of his people.

Offering the trophies

The ceremonial aspects of the royal hunt are demonstrated by the numerous reliefs that show the king offering the animals that he has killed to the god Nergal in thanks for granting victory over the savage beast. Here the Assyrian king Assurbanipal pours a libation over a dead bull, with his vizier and musicians in attendance.

The royal hunt

The lion was the royal hunt's most prestigious prey. The king would pursue the animal in his chariot, shooting at it until the lion was brought down and then despatching it with his sword. Some reliefs show the king engaging a lion on foot, using a spear, with only one or two attendants, but we cannot know for certain if a king would expose himself to such danger.

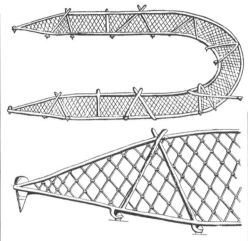

Trapping
The Assyrians used secured nets to catch game, creating a long, narrow enclosure held firmly to the ground with pegs. Dogs and beaters would drive the deer or ibex into the enclosure, where they could be readily despatched. There are also images of captured wild asses being led away with ropes.

Supplying the game

Royal lion hunts must have been epic events; one relief shows eighteen dead animals after a successful hunt. During later periods the supply of native lions seems to have been insufficient, and lions were captured and transported to the hunting field from elsewhere. This image of a lion being released from a cage forms part of a relief that shows the lion rushing at the king, who is on foot, before being caught in mid-leap by the king's arrow.

Dogs

Packs of hounds were also used for hunting deer, wild asses, and wild ibex. The dogs depicted here look something like modern mastiffs, with broad chests and big heads, and presumably they must have been used to run wounded animals to ground because they could not possibly have been fast enough to catch a healthy wild ass.

See also
Government,
pages 90–1
Work,
pages 108–9
Leisure,
pages 114–15

LEISURE

Feasting and Music

Music played an important part in rituals and religious festivals, and temples maintained orchestras. The earliest literary works of known authorship in history are hymns to be sung in praise of the moon god written by Enheduanna (*c.* 2285–2250 BC), the daughter of Sargon of Akkad and high priestess of the temple at Ur. Feasts would be held to celebrate military victories, diplomatic treaties, religious festivals and the building of new temples and palaces. When Assurnasirpal II (883–859 BC) inaugurated his new capital at Kalakh, he held a banquet that went on for ten days and entertained over sixty thousand people.

The royal feast

Representations of feasts have been found dating from the mid-3rd millennium BC, and the palaces of the Sargonid Assyrian kings are decorated with reliefs showing the king feasting. The king and queen are always centrally placed, the king raised higher than anyone else, and both are shown drinking from cups. This relief of Assurbanipal from his palace at Nineveh shows his attendant and musicians, and the head of the Elamite king, whose defeat is the occasion for the banquet, hanging from a tree on the left.

See also
Government,
pages 90–1
Leisure,
pages 112–13

Alcohol

Beer made from barley was the most common drink in Mesopotamia. Up to the time of Hammurabi, brewing was exclusively women's work, being under the protection of female divinities, and a Babylonian lexicon has an extensive list of terms relating to the activity. Date wine was also made, with wine made from grapes becoming widespread relatively late, during the 1st millennium BC.

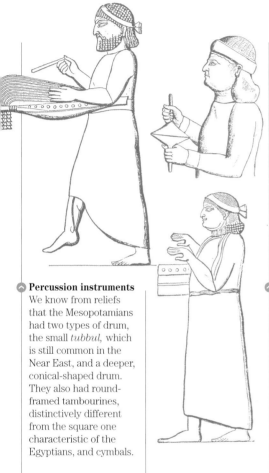

Percussion instruments

We know from reliefs that the Mesopotamians had two types of drum, the small *tubbul,* which is still common in the Near East, and a deeper, conical-shaped drum. They also had round-framed tambourines, distinctively different from the square one characteristic of the Egyptians, and cymbals.

Stringed instruments

We know of stringed instruments in Mesopotamia from at least the mid-3rd millennium BC, and they were probably in use for at least five hundred years before that. Reliefs and tablets show lutes, lyres, and harps, and the dulcimer, on which the strings were struck with a hammer rather than being plucked.

Mesopotamian music

Musicians are usually shown in groups of three or four, in varying combinations of only string players, or string players accompanied by percussionists and pipers. This relief of Assurbanipal is unusual in showing a group of eleven musicians, including string, percussion, and wind instruments. Even more unusual is that they are accompanied by singers, because it seems that vocal and instrumental music were not usually combined. All the musicians are men, and six of them are eunuchs—as indicated by the lack of beard and the rather chubby features— in fact, the majority of the musicians in the Assyrian reliefs are eunuchs.

ARCHITECTURE

The City

At the beginning of the 3rd millennium BC, there were as many as fifty urban centers in southern Mesopotamia, of which perhaps a dozen might qualify as city-states, comprising the main urban center and its associated territory and villages. The earliest city we have archaeological evidence for, Uruk, had a population of about 50,000 people by 2900 BC, and the city wall enclosed some 1,240 acres (500 hectares). The Sumerian city-states were strongly independent and jealously guarded their autonomy from any kind of central control, a characteristic that marked Mesopotamian history well into the 2nd millennium BC. This is remarkable since four of the main cities in this period—Uruk, Ur, Eridu, and Larsa—were practically within sight of one another. As Mesopotamia moved toward stronger central government, some cities became increasingly dominant, notably Babylon in the south and Nineveh in the north, and the size and grandeur of these places were representative of the power of the kings who ruled from them.

Water supply

Water was an essential commodity in Mesopotamia, and royal inscriptions throughout the history of Babylonia and Assyria record the ruler's care in building and maintaining canals, aqueducts, and other watercourses. This relief from Nineveh shows a temple with an aqueduct bringing water to irrigate the gardens below it. Sennacherib built an aqueduct of limestone blocks 985 ft (300 m) long by 79 ft (24 m) wide to carry water over the bed of a wadi—the remains can still be seen.

Gardens

The Mesopotamian kings laid out gardens and parks in their cities, and there are several possible candidates for the famous Hanging Gardens of Babylon. These were stocked with plants and trees, both native and exotic, and included ornamental ponds as well. There were even prototype safari parks, with wild animals brought back from foreign campaigns.

Housing

Beyond the temple and palace precincts there is not much evidence for town planning in the ordinary residential areas. Houses were built of mud brick, usually around a central courtyard, which might or might not be roofed. The street plan was irregular, with streets varying in width from narrow passageways up to roads 6–10 ft (2–3 m) wide. Excavation of this residential part of Ur from the beginning of the 2nd millennium BC revealed the house of a schoolmaster and a copper trader, and the presence of a restaurant with a wide window opening onto the street.

Walls

The city walls were important in terms of protecting the inhabitants from attack, but they also evidently had a symbolic function as the clearest marker of the boundary between the civilized world and the primitive. Inscriptions by victorious kings always mention the breaching and destruction of the enemy's walls, and on the flat Mesopotamian plains the walls of a city would dominate the landscape for some considerable distance.

Planning

By the 1st millennium BC, the Mesopotamian kings had begun to introduce a measure of planning to their cities. Sargon's fortified city, Dur Shurrakin, was almost exactly rectangular in plan, while Babylon as rebuilt by Nebuchadnezzar covered 2,100 acres (850 hectares) and had a rectilinear grid of main streets, including the Processional Way, a limestone-flagged roadway 650 ft (200 m) long, leading to the famous Ishtar Gate.

See also

Architecture,
pages 118–19

Architecture,
pages 120–1

ARCHITECTURE

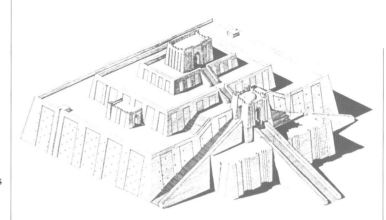

Palaces and Temples

The most important buildings in Mesopotamian cities were those related to the great institutions, the temple, and the king. As the dwelling place of the city's tutelary deity, the temple was a central symbol of the city's well-being and was generally the highest structure in the city. Kings would renew and rebuild the temples of significant cultic centers as a mark of their divine approval. Similarly, the palace was built to intimidate the outsider, and the reception rooms for ambassadors were notable for their imposing size and their decorative style, intended to impress on visitors the power of the monarch. However, there is no monumental architecture remaining to compare with that of Egypt from the same period or the subsequent Hellenic and Roman civilizations, and the most obvious traces of Mesopotamian cities are the tells, or mounds, that punctuate the landscape, marking the places where ancient settlements have been buried under centuries of sand and debris.

Dur Kurigalzu

The ziggurat, a stepped pyramid, was the most distinctive Mesopotamian building type. The remains of the ziggurat at Dur Kurigalzu, modern Aqar Quf near Baghdad, rise 187 ft (57 m) above ground level. The horizontal banding is caused by layers of reed matting and braided ropes, possibly used to bond the mud-brick layers while they were drying out. Dur Kurigalzu was probably a fortress city, built during the Kassite Period in Babylonia as a border defense against the Assyrians in the north and the Elamites to the southeast.

Reconstruction of the temple of the moon, Ur

The ziggurat is first known of from Ur, during the reign of Ur-Nammu at the end of the 3rd millennium BC. Ur was the cultic center of the moon god Sin, or Nanna, and the ziggurat was part of a temple complex enclosed by a wall that included the temple storehouse, the residence of the high priestess, and a royal palace. There was also a kitchen for preparing the god's meals. This pattern of a distinct temple precinct was repeated in later cities, perhaps so that the monumental buildings could be seen to best advantage. The ziggurat was built from baked brick and extensively restored by the Neo-Babylonian kings, aware of their responsibilities for the ancient Sumerian cultic centers.

See also
Government,
pages 90–1
Religion,
pages 104–5
Architecture,
pages 116–17
Architecture,
pages 120–1

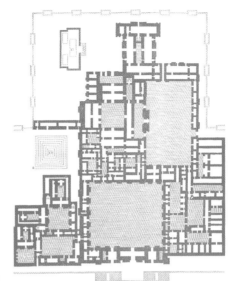

Plan of Sargon's palace
The plan view of Sargon's palace shows that it was built on the diagonal rather than symmetrically, with the main gate opening onto a large open courtyard. Another large court and several smaller ones can be seen, with the temple complex to the left of the main courtyard below the ziggurat. The king's residence is to the rear of the palace.

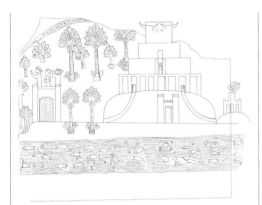

Ziggurat
This relief from the palace of Assurbanipal at Nineveh is one of very few ancient representations of a ziggurat. It shows a five-stepped building, the top section being the cella, or shrine. The building was in Elam, possibly in the city of Susa, and was known to have a temple with horns of burnished bronze, visualized here by the Victorian engraver, since the top of the stone tablet with the original representation was missing.

Sargon's palace
The palace of King Sargon II at Dur Shurrakin, in what is present-day Khorsabad, was built in 720 BC. This reconstruction shows Sargon's palace based on what is known from the excavations. The palace is built into the city walls, a common feature of Assyrian cities, giving a position of prominence to the ruler. The palace is raised on a huge mound that was faced with stone.

Palace gateway
The gateway to Sargon's palace had two crenellated towers flanking a narrow arch. This stepped cresting was the only architectural flourish, the rest of the decoration being in the form of enameled tilework. On either side of the gateway are the characteristic portal guardians, the man bulls, or *lamassu*, each carved from a single piece of stone and set into the door jambs. These colossi are sculpted in low relief with five legs so that, when seen head-on, the two front legs are visible, and from the side there are four legs shown. This gives the impression of a four-legged creature from whichever angle the sculpture is viewed.

ARCHITECTURE

Building Methods

The Babylonian architects were limited by their available resources in several ways. The mud bricks used for most construction restricted the scale of the buildings and, however well sealed against the elements, the friable nature of mud brick meant that truly permanent structures were impossible to build. The Assyrians did have sources of limestone and sandstone relatively close on hand, but seem to have preferred to retain the architectural idiom that they had learned from the Babylonians.

The apparent mania among the rulers of Mesopotamia for constantly building and rebuilding their palaces and temples can be accounted for not merely by the need for a physical demonstration of their majesty, but also by the fact that their mud-brick buildings would begin to deteriorate almost as soon as they were completed. It would often be more efficient to raze the old building to the ground and start again on the ruins than to keep up a program of repairs, which is another reason why the ancient city sites rise up above the surrounding plains, each settlement being built upon the ruins of its predecessor.

Timber

Timber for construction had to be imported, and one impulse for Assyrian expansion was to secure supplies of such raw materials. This relief from Sargon's palace at Dur Shurrakin shows the Assyrians bringing back cedarwood from Lebanon for the construction of the palace. This material dictated the design of the buildings, because in the absence of stone columns the width of a palace hall was restricted to the ceiling span of a cedar beam. Hence the state rooms of Assyrian palaces tended to be long and narrow. The Hall of the Throne in Sennacherib's palace at Nineveh was 164 ft (50 m) long but only 39 ft (12 m) wide.

See also
Technology,
pages 110–11

Architecture,
pages 116–19

Bricks

Babylonia lacks native sources of stone and timber of good enough quality for construction, but there is plenty of clay soil and so, not surprisingly, the main building material was mud bricks. These could be made in large quantities relatively easily and cheaply and were either dried in the sun or baked. The brick walls were sealed annually with a layer of plaster, which was sufficient to keep the building reasonably watertight. The brickwork of royal buildings often bore inscriptions identifying the king who had undertaken the construction. A Victorian archaeologist described being lowered down a brick-lined well and reading the name of Nebuchadnezzar on every third row of bricks.

Arches

The Mesopotamians certainly knew how to build arches, both for gateways and for drainage tunnels, although they were relatively narrow. They used a temporary timber frame to support the brickwork, but they also built vaults by slanting each arch of bricks at an angle from the perpendicular, so that the successive layers were supported by the one before and there was no need for any temporary support. Vaults of this kind have been found in excavations from the late 3rd millennium BC.

Columns

The use of columns to support structures seems to have been limited to temples or the interior doorways and windows of palaces, which had few load-bearing demands. Some stone column bases have been found, but the shafts and capitals have disappeared and the main evidence, as with many things, comes from the reliefs. Assyrian capitals bear some resemblance to the Ionic and Corinthian styles of the Greeks, but there is no evidence for extensive colonnaded temples or galleries.

Reliefs

The walls of the Mesopotamian palaces were decorated with carved stone slabs as much as 10 ft (3 m) tall. These featured scenes that redounded to the glory of the king, showing his victories over the enemies of Assyria or his prowess in hunting the lion. The reliefs in the private rooms of the palace were less propagandistic, and were more likely to show the beauties of nature. Above the wainscot of slabs the brickwork was enameled with friezes of repeating patterns of rosettes or interlacing designs or mythical creatures.

COSTUME

Clothing

It is not known when the Mesopotamians began to wear clothes. Cultic nudity was continued well into the 3rd millennium BC on the part of the priests and kings, but the Mesopotamians were certainly clad from the beginning of the period covered here. There is little physical evidence of textiles, so we are reliant for our information on documents and what visual evidence remains on reliefs and cylinders.

See also
Government,
pages 90–1
Warfare,
pages 98–9

Clothes

The earliest Mesopotamian images show the Sumerians dressed in sheepskins or goatskins. The first textiles were made from wool or sometimes linen, but cotton was not introduced into Mesopotamia until the 1st millennium BC. Leather was also used for clothes. The most common garment in the 3rd millennium BC was a skirt or kilt, with a longer woollen dress being worn by women. Toward the end of the 2nd millennium BC stitched clothing was introduced, and clothes were fitted rather than being draped. The most common garment seems to have been a belted knee-length tunic worn over a fitted undergarment.

Shoes and hats

In the earliest images everyone is shown barefoot, but from the end of the 2nd millennium BC royals and officials are shown wearing sandals, usually a thin sole with straps going over the feet. Later there are more substantial sandals that have a thicker sole and a heel piece, and at the time of Sennacherib the king and queen wear decorated shoes. The Assyrian king wears a distinctive conical hat squared off at the top, probably made of felt, which takes on a more rectilinear shape in reliefs from the beginning of the 1st millennium BC. The Babylonian king of the same period wears a similar hat of a more rounded shape, and the earlier Babylonian kings wear a close-fitting cap with a distinctive projecting rim.

Hairstyles

During the 3rd millennium BC men are frequently shown with their heads shaved, but wearing long, straight beards. From the beginning of the 2nd millennium BC, long wavy hair is more common, usually worn loose but sometimes secured with braiding or a headband. The men's beards are shown curled and luxuriant, with a squared shape. Slaves had a distinctive topknot, while doctors and priests seem to have had shaved heads throughout the period. Women also have long hair, usually gathered into a chignon or enclosed in a snood.

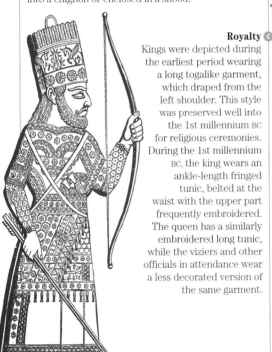

Royalty

Kings were depicted during the earliest period wearing a long togalike garment, which draped from the left shoulder. This style was preserved well into the 1st millennium BC for religious ceremonies. During the 1st millennium BC, the king wears an ankle-length fringed tunic, belted at the waist with the upper part frequently embroidered. The queen has a similarly embroidered long tunic, while the viziers and other officials in attendance wear a less decorated version of the same garment.

Priests

Priests are usually shown wearing a long fringed or layered garment called a *kanaukes*. This garment is depicted on cylinder seals from the mid-3rd millennium BC right into the 1st millennium BC, and gods are also sometimes shown wearing a similar garment. The priests wear a distinctive horned headdress.

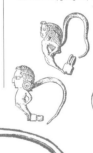

Jewelry

Jewelry was worn by both sexes and included necklaces, armlets, bracelets, and earrings. Crosses and rosettes are frequent motifs on earrings, as are crescents, but designs featuring human or mythical figures have also been found. Jewelry was made from bronze or gold, and bead necklaces were commonly made using semiprecious stones, such as lapis lazuli, carnelian, jasper, and agate. A distinctive royal collar was worn by the king as a badge of office that featured the emblems of the most important deities.

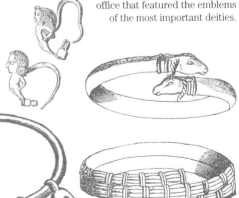

DAILY LIFE

Literature and Myth

A Mesopotamian literary tradition existed from at least the 3rd millennium BC, centered on a school of poets at Uruk, the biblical Erech, who created a number of myths and epics that are known to us from later transcriptions. It has been suggested that these myths (stories about the exploits of gods) and epics (stories relating to human heroes) reflect the economic, social, and political institutions of the time of writing and of the preceding era and, together with archaeological evidence, they have been immensely useful in helping to reconstruct the development of society in this part of Mesopotamia at the very dawn of recorded human history. It is not clear who the audience for these works would have been, because few people other than the scribes could read or write. The *enuma elish*, the best-known Mesopotamian creation myth, was recited on the fourth day of the New Year Festival in Babylon, and the battle between Marduk and Tiamat may even have been acted out, but knowledge of the other literary works that we know of may have been limited to a small intellectual elite, who preserved the stories in the *edubba* from generation to generation. The Mesopotamian scribes had a keen sense of literary heritage, and Sumerian was preserved as a literary language long after it had been displaced by Akkadian as the lingua franca of Mesopotamia.

Gilgamesh

The *Epic of Gilgamesh* has been dated to about 2200 BC in the form in which we know it, and it shows traces of at least four separate earlier Sumerian stories. It was widely known, with fragments having been found in Palestine and evidence from Turkey that it was translated into Hittite and Hurrian. It relates the adventures of Gilgamesh, the part-divine King of Uruk, and his wildman companion Enkidu. Midway through the story Gilgamesh insults the goddess Ishtar, who sends a heavenly bull to kill him. The two comrades succeed in killing the bull, but this further impiety is punished by the death of Enkidu. The remainder of the epic relates Gilgamesh's futile quest for eternal life as he fails to come to terms with the loss of his friend.

Assurbanipal's library

Assurbanipal's 7th-century BC library at Nineveh was discovered by archaeologists in 1853, and it comprises the most important cuneiform tablet collection. Assurbanipal gathered material from all over Mesopotamia for his collection, particularly from the most important scribal center at Nippur. Most of the tablets found are divinatory texts, but there are also copies of many literary works, including the *enuma elish* and the Akkadian *Epic of Gilgamesh*.

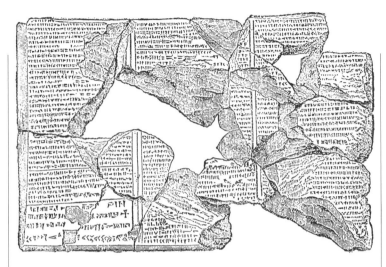

Scorpion men

Gilgamesh sets out to consult Utnapishtim, who saved the world from the Flood and was rewarded with immortality. Gilgamesh must travel to the ends of the earth, passing the scorpion men (men with scorpion tails) guarding the dwelling of Shamash, the sun god, and crossing the waters of death to the Abyss, where Utnapishtim lives eternally. He learns from Utnapishtim that human life and activity are transient; no one can avoid death. Gilgamesh is escorted to Uruk by Utnapishtim's ferryman Urshanabi, whom he takes up on to the walls to show him the splendor of the city, Gilgamesh's only consolation in the face of mortality.

The Flood

The *Epic of Gilgamesh* includes an account of the Flood, which is related to Gilgamesh by Utnapishtim, the Babylonian Noah. The story is also known from the epic *Atrahasis*, in which Enlil sends a series of natural disasters to destroy humankind, which has become too numerous and raucous. A plague and two famines are survived through the intervention of Atrahasis and the god Enki. Finally a great flood is sent, and Utnapishtim is chosen by the wise god Ea to build a ship to rescue his family and livestock and the creatures of the wild. The floods disperse, Enlil is mollified by the other gods, and humankind survives. Flooding was common in lower Mesopotamia, so a story emphasizing that divine help was on hand to help with natural adversity is not surprising.

Marduk and Tiamat

The best-known Mesopotamian creation myth is called *enuma elish*. Its central figure is Marduk, the son of Ea the all wise, who becomes involved in a civil war between the primeval gods and the younger gods. The primeval goddess Tiamat has sworn to destroy the younger gods; Marduk agrees to challenge her on condition that he is recognized as supreme in the assembly of the gods. This agreed, he goes out and defeats Tiamat, who has taken the form of a dragon, then taking up his role as supreme god he creates heaven and earth and humankind and receives the great temple complex of Esagila in Babylon as a mark of the gods' gratitude.

See also

Government,
pages 96–7

Religion,
pages 106–7

Daily life,
pages 126–9

DAILY LIFE

Death Rites

Most of the ancient tombs found in Mesopotamia are in the southern part of the region, and it may be that this was a favored place for burial as representing the most anciently settled part of the country. Bodies were usually buried in cemeteries on the outskirts of the city, although children seem to have been buried under the family home. The Mesopotamians believed that the dead became ghosts who lived miserably underground, and the proper funerary rites had to be performed otherwise the ghost would return to haunt the family. From the 3rd millennium BC, there is evidence that priests would perform funeral rites, with one king of Lagash claiming that his predecessors had allowed the priests to charge exorbitant sums for their services.

Jar coffins

Coffins of this type consisted of two deep jars into which the body was inserted. One jar had a neck narrower than the other so that it would slip inside, and the joint was then sealed with bitumen. A hole was made at one end of the coffin to enable the gases released during decomposition to escape.

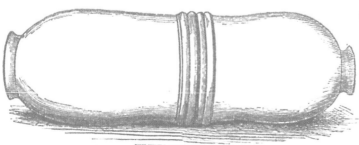

Dish-cover tombs

These clay coffins were found in great numbers at Ur. The body was laid on a flat platform of clay brick with the various utensils and provisions that would be needed for the journey after death, and then an earthenware lid was placed over the base. These lids could be up to 6 ft (2 m) long and 3 ft (1 m) high and were made as a single piece. Coffins usually contained one person, although sometimes a couple were buried together.

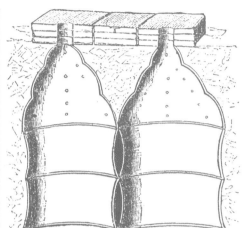

Burial mounds

The dead could be buried underground or in artificial mounds. Coffins would be laid side by side, sometimes with a layer of clay bricks to separate the levels. The top of the mound was also paved, and the whole edifice was supplied with drainage pipes running from top to bottom so that rainwater was directed away from the tombs and the bodies and other goods were preserved.

Brick vaults

More substantial arched vaults were also used for burial, possibly as family sepulchres, because they usually contain several bodies. The bodies were commonly laid on their left side with the right arm crossed over the body, and a copper or bronze bowl was sometimes placed in the left hand. The head of the deceased was supported on a clay pillow.

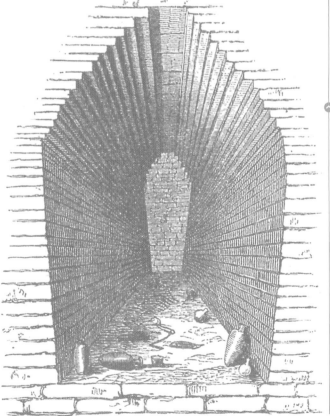

Grave goods

The items most frequently found in graves are jars and pots, with copper objects also common. Beads and cylinder seals were left with the body, and a dish of dates to sustain the ghost on his or her journey. Royal graves would contain jewelry and gold items, such as daggers, axes, and cups and bowls.

See also

Daily life,
pages 124–5

Daily life,
pages 128–9

DAILY LIFE

Art

The creative work of the Mesopotamians, like much else, was in large measure harnessed to religious and royal imperatives, art being used to serve the requirements of the king and, by extension, the city god. However, in their jewelry and in the decoration of the private rooms of palaces in the 1st millennium BC, there are indications of an aesthetic expressiveness driven by impulses other than the cultic.

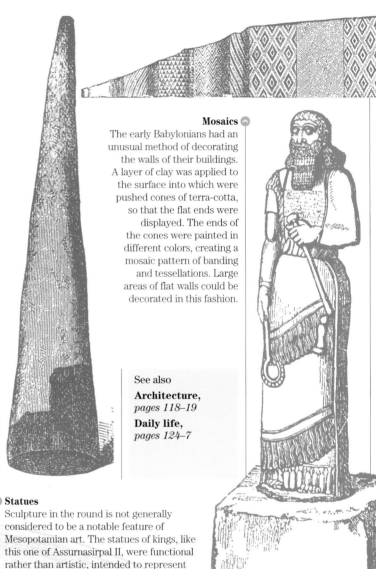

Mosaics

The early Babylonians had an unusual method of decorating the walls of their buildings. A layer of clay was applied to the surface into which were pushed cones of terra-cotta, so that the flat ends were displayed. The ends of the cones were painted in different colors, creating a mosaic pattern of banding and tessellations. Large areas of flat walls could be decorated in this fashion.

See also
Architecture,
pages 118–19
Daily life,
pages 124–7

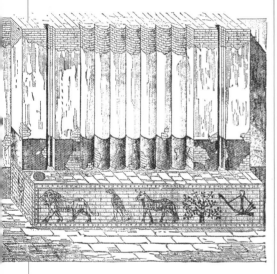

Enameled brickwork

Glazed, enameled brickwork was commonly used to ornament palaces and city gateways. Recurring patterns of sacred or royal symbols in bright colors were set against a darker background. The Ishtar Gate and Processional Way in Babylon were faced with bright-blue glazed bricks on which were molded ranks of dragons, lions, and bulls enameled in yellow and red.

Statues

Sculpture in the round is not generally considered to be a notable feature of Mesopotamian art. The statues of kings, like this one of Assurnasirpal II, were functional rather than artistic, intended to represent his presence in the temple with the city god, rather than to inspire any aesthetic response. The statue of the city god might be colossal and covered in gold, but it was an expression of religious power rather than beauty. Smaller domestic statues performed protective functions in the home and do not appear to have been valued as decoration.

Stone carving

Most of the Assyrian palaces have left examples of decorative stonework. Carpet slabs such as this, with their intricate and repetitive patterns of lotus flowers, rosettes, and tasseling, offer proof of the skill of the Mesopotamian stone carvers.

Metalwork

The Mesopotamians were skilled metalworkers, and were able to cast bronze and copper to a high standard. Examples of *repoussé* work are also common on thin metal bands used to adorn wooden gates. They also worked with gold to make jewelry, using embossing and granulating techniques to create objects of great delicacy.

Bas-reliefs

The finest expressions of Mesopotamian art are undoubtedly the limestone-and-alabaster slabs that decorated the walls of the Assyrian palaces. This is particularly true of the rendering of animals, and the scenes of the royal hunt from Assurbanipal's palace at Nineveh are among the most vivid and dramatic images from the ancient world.

GREECE

The origins of the Greeks are still not fully understood, but it is likely that they arrived in the Greek peninsula before 2000 BC. There they found a land with rivers and fertile plains, which enabled agriculture to develop; and forested mountain ranges, which provided timber for ships and buildings and marble and limestone for architects and sculptors. They may have conquered and intermarried with indigenous tribes and by 1450 BC had supplanted Minoan Crete as the dominant culture in the Aegean.

Bronze Age Greece was an era of advanced architectural techniques. The wealth of the ruling elite was immense, as evidenced by the spectacular finds in shaft graves, and trade with Egypt and the Levant brought gold and luxury goods. However, the collapse of Mycenaean civilization resulted in a less well-documented period known as the Dark Ages.

From the 7th century BC intrepid Greek traders and adventurers founded colonies throughout the Mediterranean and the Black Sea. The 5th century BC is seen as the golden age of Greek civilization when city-states, particularly Athens, reached their political, artistic, and cultural zenith. At the same time, however, wars were prevalent. Persia was a constant threat, and the struggle between Athens and Sparta during the Peloponnesian War was a tragic waste of lives and resources. In the 4th century BC the conquests of Alexander the Great changed the course of world history, spreading Greek culture and influence as far as modern Pakistan.

The power of the Greek states diminished over time, but Greek intellectual, cultural, and scientific life continued to be held in high regard and exert an influence over the new dominant power, Rome.

TIME LINE
c. 3000 BC–30 BC

3000–2000 BC

Beginning of the Bronze Age. Islanders in the Cyclades produce distinctive marble figurines and explore the Aegean Sea. Prosperous settlement at Akrotiri on the island of Thera, later called Santorini.

2000–1500 BC

Civilization of Minoan Crete with impressive palaces and villas built at Knossos and Phaistos and growth of maritime trade with Egypt and the Near East. Volcano erupts destroying most of Santorini, but houses and paintings at Akrotiri are preserved under layers of ash. Shaft graves at Mycenae display the wealth of the ruling elite.

1450 BC

Minoan supremacy ends through a combination of earthquakes and invasions from mainland Greece.

776 BC

The first Olympic Games, the date from which the ancient Greeks dated events in their history.

750 BC

Greek cities, especially Chalcis and Eretria on the island of Euboea, establish colonies in the western Mediterranean and Black Sea. The Greek trading post of Al-Mina in north Syria becomes a major emporium for goods from the east. Influenced by the Phoenicians, the Greeks devise their own alphabetic writing.

700 BC

Beginning of the Archaic Period of Greek civilization. The state of Sparta conquers its neighbor Messenia, turning its inhabitants into serfs or helots. Homer's epic poems, the *Iliad* and the *Odyssey*, are put into written form.

499–490 BC

Greek cities of Ionia revolt against the rule of Achaemenid Persia, eventually inciting King Darius to launch a naval attack on mainland Greece. A combined force of Athenians and Plataeans defeat the Persians at the Battle of Marathon.

Carved seat at the theater of Dionysus in Athens

482 BC

Athens' financial position is greatly enhanced by the discovery of silver mines at Laurion in Attica, much of the wealth being spent on triremes for its fleet.

460–446 BC

First Peloponnesian War between Athens and Sparta. After years of successes and losses, Athens and Sparta agree to the Thirty Years' Peace. Athens also attacks Egypt, then part of the Persian Empire. The attack fails and Athens makes a truce with Persia known as the "Peace of Callias."

446–433 BC

The treasury of the Delian League is transferred from Delos to Athens, in line with Athenian imperial ambitions. Art and culture flourish in Athens. Pericles becomes the leading statesman, instigating the building program that results in the splendid temples on the Acropolis.

Carving of a Spartan warrior

418 BC

As a result of Athenian machinations, fighting soon breaks out again. At the Battle of Mantinea, the Spartan hoplites are victorious over a coalition of Athenian and Argive forces, and Sparta reasserts its leadership in the Peloponnese.

415–413 BC

The prominent politician and general Alcibiades advocates the expansion of the Athenian Empire westward. The Athenian expedition, which he initially leads against the Greek colonists at Syracuse in Sicily, ends in an unmitigated disaster.

395–386 BC

Athens, Thebes, Argus, and Corinth unite against Sparta. With the help of the Persian fleet, Athens defeats the Spartan fleet at the Battle of Cnidus. However, Persia brokers a deal called the King's Peace, which leaves Sparta dominant in Greece.

382–371 BC

Sparta occupies Thebes, which is liberated after a few years. The foundation of the Second Athenian League leads to close cooperation between Athens and Thebes, which is now a strong military power. At the Battle of Leuctra, Thebes inflicts a humiliating defeat on Sparta.

336–332 BC

The son of Philip and Olympias becomes Alexander III of Macedon (Alexander the Great). After consolidating power in Greece he pursues the Persian king Darius III and wins two battles at the Granicus and Issus. He then suppresses resistance at Tyre and Gaza down the Levant coast.

Coin depicting Alexander the Great

332–330 BC

Alexander makes a short visit to Egypt and founds the city of Alexandria. He also travels deep into the desert to visit the Oracle of Zeus-Ammon in the Siwa Oasis. Back on the Persian king's trail, he wins the Battle of Gaugamela and enters Persepolis as conqueror.

1450–1250 BC

Mycenaean hegemony in the Aegean, with the expansion of fortified citadels at Tiryns, Mycenae, and major centers on Cyprus and Rhodes. Extensive trade links established between Greece, Egypt, and the Levant.

1200 BC

Upheavals in the eastern Mediterranean lead to the collapse of the Hittite Empire around 1184 BC. Destruction of the major Mycenaean citadels in mainland Greece and collapse of the Bronze Age.

1000–800 BC

Beginning of the Dark Ages and loss of Mycenaean writing. Growing use of iron for weaponry and the evolution of styles in Greek geometric pottery.

650–600 BC

The age of Tyrants in the Greek world, including at Corinth, Megara, and Miletus. At Athens, Draco draws up the first written law code and the earliest black figure pottery appears, an important artistic development.

Bust of Solon

600–500 BC

Legal reforms of Solon at Athens free the population enslaved by debts. Pisistratus rules Athens as Tyrant, but eventually Cleisthenes establishes a democracy. New techniques to produce red-figure pottery and hollow-cast bronze statues are developed.

480–479 BC

King Xerxes crosses the Hellespont with a massive army to invade Greece. The Persian forces are only briefly halted by the Spartan hoplites under Leonidas at Thermopylae, but then ravage Attica, destroying the temples on the Athenian Acropolis. Amazingly, the Greeks win both the naval battle at Salamis and the infantry engagement at Plataea. Xerxes is forced to withdraw his troops and ships from Greece.

478–467 BC

Foundation of the Delian League, under the leadership of Athens, to liberate the Greeks of Ionia, thus foreshadowing the Athenian Empire. Athenian statesman and military commander Cimon wins a decisive victory over Persia at the Battle of the Eurymedon.

431 BC

Beginning of the Second Peloponnesian War between Athens and Sparta, which is documented by the historian Thucydides.

430–426 BC

An outbreak of plague rages through Athens and Pericles dies. The Spartans capture Plataea, while the Athenians take Mytilene on the island of Lesbos.

425–421 BC

Battle of Sphacteria, an island off Pylos in the Peloponnese, ends with 292 Spartans taken as prisoners to Athens. Unable to break the Athenian Empire, Sparta agrees to the Peace of Nicias, which is meant to hold for fifty years.

413 BC–410 BC

Sparta occupies the strategic fort at Decelea in Attica, which becomes a permanent threat to the city of Athens. There is a coup of four hundred brutal oligarchs in Athens, but their unpopularity soon leads to the restoration of democracy.

405–404 BC

A Spartan victory at the Battle of Aegospotami is followed by the siege of the city of Athens, which soon capitulates, thereby ending the exhausting Peloponnesian Wars.

399 BC

Socrates, whose enquiring mind still lives today through the writings of the philosopher Plato, is put on trial on charges of impiety and corrupting the young with his controversial thoughts. He is convicted and is forced to end his life by drinking hemlock.

359 BC

Accession to the throne of Philip II of Macedon.

356 BC

Birth of Alexander the Great.

338–336 BC

Philip defeats Athens and Thebes at the Battle of Chaeronea, bringing the independence of the Greek states to an end. He forms the Corinthian League to assist in his planned war against Persia, but is murdered in Macedon.

Bust of Socrates

330–323 BC

Alexander's subsequent campaigns reach as far as modern Pakistan, stretching his troops' loyalty and stamina to the limit. He returns to Babylon, where he dies, probably from malaria, aged thirty-three.

323–30 BC

Alexander's commanders cannot control his vast Empire and it is divided into Hellenistic kingdoms. The most successful is Egypt, which falls to his general Ptolemy. Greek power is finally eclipsed when Cleopatra VII commits suicide, leaving Octavian, soon to be the Roman emperor Augustus, in control of the Mediterranean world.

GEOGRAPHY

A 19th-century rendering of the Pythia seated on her tripod

Ancient Greece

The earliest centers of power in the Greek Bronze Age were on the island of Crete. From here the Minoans sailed to trading ports in the Aegean and eastern Mediterranean. This maritime Empire was taken over by the Mycenaeans, whose major strongholds were in the Peloponnese. The royal citadels of Mycenae and Tiryns were in the east, and there was an important palace and administrative complex at Pylos on the western coast.

After the end of the Bronze Age, Greek colonists set out from the mainland and founded cities on eastern Aegean islands on the coast of Asia Minor, such as Ephesus, where the Temple of Artemis was later regarded as one of the seven wonders of the ancient world.

In the 5th century BC the Greeks defeated the armies and fleet of Persia. During the Classical Era, Athens grew into an imperial power, its wealth enhanced by the silver mines in the south of Attica. It extended its control over independent islands, such as Corcyra and Melos. Sparta became the bitter rival of Athens and, apprehensive about its growing Empire, sought to curb its power, resulting in the devastating Peloponnesian War from which Sparta emerged victorious.

In the 4th century BC the new leaders of Greece, Philip of Macedon (382–36 BC) and his son Alexander the Great (356–23 BC), came from the mountainous region of Macedonia. In his military campaigns Alexander marched through Asia Minor, the Levant, Egypt, Iraq, and Iran to defeat the Persians and briefly rule an Empire previously unsurpassed in extent.

Ancient Greece

It was partly due to their geographical setting that the ancient Greeks were a divided people. Their homeland included a mountainous mainland with hundreds of scattered islands. During the Dark Age, Greeks also settled on the islands and coasts of Asia Minor. Later, from *c.* 750–550 BC, Greeks went on to found colonies around the Black Sea and Western Mediterranean.

Delphi

The religious center of Delphi was famous for its oracle of Apollo, where the god was believed to answer questions through his priestess, the Pythia, who sat on a tripod. The oracle was consulted both by private individuals and by ambassadors from city-states, who sought advice on every major decision, from founding a new colony to declaring war.

GREECE c. 510–323 BC

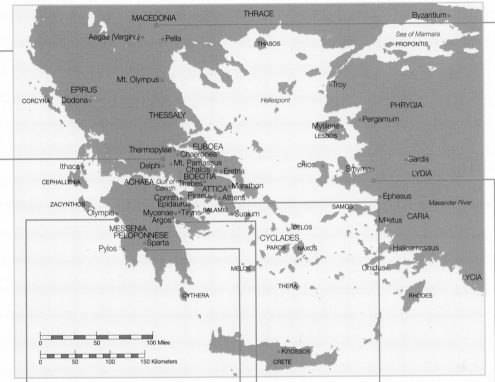

MACEDONIA
THRACE
Byzantium
Aegae (Vergina)
Pella
THASOS
Sea of Marmara
PROPONTIS
Mt. Olympus
Troy
Hellespont
EPIRUS
PHRYGIA
CORCYRA
Dodona
Pergamum
THESSALY
Mytilene
LESBOS
Thermopylae
EUBOEA
Chaeronea
Sardis
Ithaca
Delphi
Mt. Parnassus
Chalcis
Eretria
CHIOS
Smyrna
LYDIA
CEPHALLENIA
ACHAEA
Gulf of
Corinth
BOEOTIA
Thebes
Marathon
Ephesus
Maeander River
Corinth
Piraeus
ATTICA
Athens
ZACYNTHOS
Epidaurus
Miletus
CARIA
Olympia
Mycenae
Tiryns
SALAMIS
Sunium
SAMOS
Argos
MESSENIA
PELOPONNESE
DELOS
Pylos
Sparta
CYCLADES
PAROS
NAXOS
Halicarnassus
MELOS
Cnidus
LYCIA
CYTHERA
THERA
RHODES
Knossos
CRETE

0   50   100 Miles
0 50 100 150 Kilometers

Alexander in youth, debating with Diogenes

Macedon

In the late 4th century BC Macedon, in the northeast of Greece, rose as the dominant regional power. King Alexander of Macedon, also known as Alexander the Great (ruled 336–322 BC) forced the city-states to unite under his rule, then he conquered Persia. This was the beginning of the Hellenistic Age, in which Greek culture spread from Egypt to Afghanistan.

Olympic games

Every four years, athletes from all over the Greek world assembled at Olympia to take part in a great sporting festival in honor of Zeus, the king of the gods. While allowing the city-states another opportunity for competitive display, the games also reinforced their shared Greek identity.

Carving of a heroicized Spartan couple

Sparta

Sparta, in the southern Peloponnese, was unlike any other city-state. Spartan citizens were full-time soldiers, who spent their days constantly training for war. While other Greeks loved to talk, Spartans were famed for using few words. Our word "laconic" comes from Laconia, the Spartan homeland.

Mycenae

The Mycenaean civilization is named after its most important center, Mycenae, in the Peloponnese. Its people lived in kingdoms, each based on a palace. They were influenced by the Cretan Minoans' fashions and art. Yet they were more warlike, and their palaces were strongly defended with massive stone walls.

The Royal Lion Gate at Mycenae

Athens

The great rival of Sparta was Athens, the largest and wealthiest city-state in all of Greece. Athens was a leading cultural center, where theater was invented, philosophers taught, and sculptors created magnificent works of art. It was also the world's first democracy. The Athenians had ample supplies of silver, which they used to build up a formidable fleet of warships.

Ionia

The Ionic column takes its name from Ionia, the region of Asia Minor settled by Greeks. Ionians had their own Greek dialect, distinctive from Doric, spoken in the Peloponnese and Crete, and Aeolic, spoken in northern Greece. The Athenians and inhabitants of the Aegean islands were also Ionians. All Ionians believed that they were descended from a common ancestor, the legendary Ion.

GOVERNMENT

Bronze Age Kings

Forms of government in ancient Greece varied over time. Evidence from the Bronze Age citadels of Mycenae and Tiryns points to a number of states, each with a tightly organized hierarchy, at the head of which was the ruler. This is the picture reflected later in the epics of Homer that describe events in the reigns of such strong kings as Agamemnon of Mycenae and Menelaus of Sparta.

By the 7th century BC, important Greek cities were controlled by absolute rulers known as tyrants, whose autocratic rule could be benign or oppressive. It was in Athens that the democratic system emerged, enabling male citizens to have a decisive vote in the government of their city. In Sparta control was largely vested in a council of elders to whose authority even the kings were subject. In the 4th century BC, during the reigns of Philip II and his son Alexander, the northern state of Macedon became the strongest power in Greece and prominent cities, such as Athens and Thebes, were forced to acknowledge its supremacy.

See also
Government,
pages 138–41

Gold mask from Mycenae
One of the most important and splendid archaeological discoveries in Greece was made at Mycenae by Heinrich Schliemann in the late 19th century. A series of shaft tombs dating from around 1600 to 1450 BC—known as Grave Circle A—had been incorporated behind the later citadel walls. The gold mask here, from one of the burials of the ruling warrior elite, conveys a sense of majesty and confidence in the exercise of power.

Lion Gate
The entrance to the palace and acropolis of the Mycenaean rulers was finally completed about 1250 BC. It consisted of a fortified ramp and an impressive gateway, today cleared down to ground level. Blocks of limestone, each over 19¾ tons (20 tonnes), make up the threshold, two jambs, and the lintel. To give an idea of the supreme power of the rulers of Mycenae, a triangular slab of limestone was inserted above the lintel carved with the heraldic device of two lions, now headless, on either side of a column, perhaps signifying the royal palace or ritual monument.

Mycenaean warriors

Dating from toward the end of the Mycenaean hegemony, this *krater*, or mixing bowl for wine, was discovered in a large house near the citadel wall. The design shows the warriors, wearing distinctive horned helmets, whom the ruler could deploy in battle and upon whom he depended for guarding his position as *wanax*, or king.

Oedipus and the sphinx

The city of Thebes in Boeotia had a troubled tradition of power struggles for the throne. According to myth, Oedipus became ruler when he solved the riddle of the destructive sphinx who was wreaking havoc on its citizens. The sphinx asked what creature goes on four legs in the morning, two legs at noon, and three legs in the evening. Oedipus answered that it was a man: he crawled as a child, walked upright in the prime of life, and needed a stick in old age. Unknowingly, prior to this, Oedipus had killed his father Laius in a quarrel on the way to Thebes. He then married Jocasta, Laius' queen and his own mother. The discovery of his deeds caused him to blind himself and go into exile.

Theseus killing the king of the centaurs

There were a number of legendary kings who ruled Athens and who were commemorated in historical times. The most famous was Theseus, whose exploits before becoming king included freeing Athens from a tribute in which children were sent to Crete every nine years to be devoured by the Minotaur. In this relief from the Parthenon, Theseus is depicted killing the king of the centaurs who had led an attack on a wedding banquet. Theseus was credited with making Athens the most prominent city in Attica.

Cypselus of Corinth

Tyrants in Greece usually came to power through a violent coup, supported either by aristocrats or the people. Around 655 BC Cypselus overthrew the ruling family of Corinth and became tyrant of the city. This bronze plaque reflects some of the gold and ivory designs on the cedarwood chest in which he had allegedly been smuggled past enemies when he was a baby, dedicated in the Temple of Hera at Olympia. It shows heraldic winged quadrupeds, a centaur, and a goddess taming wild lions. During the reigns of Cypselus and his son Periander, Corinth became very wealthy and founded colonies in Sicily and Italy.

The tyrant slayers

In the 6th century BC Athens was ruled by the tyrant Pisistratus, who used mercenaries to keep a hold on power. He was succeeded by his sons, Hippias and Hipparchus, who ruled Athens even more harshly. Two aristocrats, Harmodius and Aristogiton, plotted to murder them, but managed to slay only Hipparchus before they themselves were killed. However, with the fall of Hippias soon afterward, the Athenians saw the tyrant slayers as catalysts in the transition to democracy and honored them with statues in the *agora* (market place).

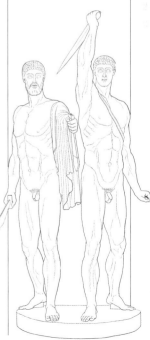

GOVERNMENT

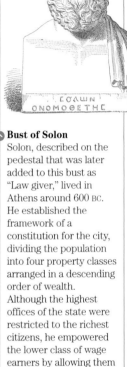

Athenian Democracy and Sparta

Athenian democracy owed its final form to a number of personalities and measures introduced through the 6th and 5th centuries BC, both to meet concerns of privilege and as solutions to practical problems. In the reforms of Solon (*c.* 638–558 BC), who was *archon* or chief magistrate, an attempt was made to reserve the highest positions in the state for a wealthy oligarchy, but also to allow other citizens to participate in government, although with restricted powers. After the fall of the tyrants, Cleisthenes gained popular support with a program of reforms. These included the reorganization of the citizens into 139 local groups called *demes*, which then were the basis for ten tribes upon which the political machinery of Athens and Attica was based. It was Cleisthenes who, ostensibly to prevent a monopoly on power, brought in the system of ostracism by which, if enough people voted against a particular politician or general, he could be banished from Athens for ten years. In contrast, the organs of government in Sparta were more rigid, with all energies concentrated on securing the continuing supremacy of a military elite.

Bust of Pericles
This marble bust of the Athenian statesman and general (hence his war helmet) Pericles (*c.* 495–429 BC) is a Roman copy of an original Greek sculpture dating to the 5th century BC. Pericles' influence over the Athenian Assembly was immense. Through his persuasive speeches he instigated payment for men on jury service and restricted Athenian citizenship to children of parents who were both already citizens of Athens. Once the war with Sparta began, he directed the Athenian military strategy. A funeral oration by Pericles for the soldiers who had died in the first year of the Peloponnesian War, as rewritten by Thucydides (*c.* 460–395 BC), is the most eloquent testimony to the privilege of being an Athenian. It was Pericles' vision that led to Athens becoming embellished with outstanding architecture. His death from the plague in 429 BC robbed Athens of its most perceptive and powerful leader.

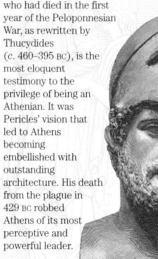

Bust of Solon
Solon, described on the pedestal that was later added to this bust as "Law giver," lived in Athens around 600 BC. He established the framework of a constitution for the city, dividing the population into four property classes arranged in a descending order of wealth. Although the highest offices of the state were restricted to the richest citizens, he empowered the lower class of wage earners by allowing them to become members of the *ekklesia*, or political assembly, of citizens. His most immediately effective reform, the *seisachtheia* ("shaking off of burdens"), was to prohibit the practice of enslaving the poor through debts.

Coin of Lycurgus
The constitution of Sparta was supposedly devised by the legislator Lycurgus. His historical existence has been disputed, but his association with Spartan laws and customs was often referred to by ancient Greek writers. In particular, by tradition he devised the system of government by the *gerousia* (council of elders) of twenty-eight men over the age of sixty. This council operated in tandem with two hereditary kings from royal families. In addition, five *ephors* (guardians), elected by the citizen assembly, exercised a strict scrutiny over the behavior of the kings, with powers to prosecute them.

Spartan warrior
Military training was highly prized by the Spartans, and warriors, such as the one depicted here, were regarded as protectors of the state. Each year the government symbolically declared war on the serf population, or helots, so that young soldiers could legitimately kill a quota as a deterrent to those perhaps contemplating revolt. However, this state-run homicide was offset by granting freedom to those helots who distinguished themselves in battle.

Heroicized couple
In Sparta the state encouraged moral values that cemented the austere discipline of society. By this pressure, the council, kings, and *ephors* controlled the lives of the citizens in a way unthinkable in Athens. The couple seen on this sculpture are shown after death as being heroicized and receiving gifts, by virtue of having lived their lives according to accepted Spartan ideals of fighting with valor and bearing fine children.

See also
Government,
pages 136–41

Spartan women/youth
Lycurgus was credited with inventing the state-approved rigorous physical exercise regime for girls that was designed to toughen them up for childbirth and ensure that their offspring would be sturdy Spartans. Consequently, girls were expected to run, wrestle, and throw the javelin. On occasions they paraded naked in a display of pride in their physical prowess, praising or criticizing onlooking young men in front of the kings and elders. Possibly the young woman here is showing an athletic injury to her male companions.

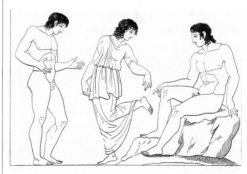

Athenian knights
The knights of the Athenian cavalry were ranked as the second property class in the city. They numbered around a thousand and were an auxiliary unit in times of war, because most of the action would be left to the infantry. The status of the knights in government reflected a sort of aristocracy wealthy enough to own horses. This relief from the Parthenon shows knights galloping along the Sacred Way to the Acropolis during the festival of the goddess Athene.

Athenian Treasury and the Suppression of Democracy

The rise of Athens in the Classical Era was driven by Pericles, who persuaded the democratic organs of government to make their city preeminent throughout Greece. During the war with Persia a fund, kept on the sacred island of Delos, had been established to liberate Ionia. After the Persian defeat in 479 BC, the Acropolis was left as a ruin for many years, as a reminder of the havoc wreaked by the Persians. As Athens grew in power, the states that had been its allies in the war increasingly resembled an Athenian Empire. In 454 BC the Treasury was transferred from Delos to Athens. The Acropolis was restored and the Treasury housed in the Parthenon. The disastrous war with Sparta saw an erosion of effective democracy, and with the rise of Macedon in the 4th century BC some Athenians warned of the threat to liberty. However, the accession to the Macedonian throne of Alexander the Great was to change the political fortunes not only of Athens but of the entire Mediterranean.

ACROPOLE D'ATHENES — FACE OVEST RESTAVRATION

The Acropolis

The center of the city of Athens was dominated by a huge crag of rock known as the Acropolis. It had been occupied in the Bronze Age, and in the Classical Era became the site of major temples, in particular to the goddess Athene. The Acropolis was the also last place of refuge for those citizens who stayed in Athens during the invasion of the Persian King Xerxes (reigned 485–465 BC). The Parthenon, in addition to being the religious center of the complex, also housed the treasury. It stands on the southern side of the rock, approached through the Propylaea, or ceremonial gateway. The colossal 29½-ft (9-m) bronze statue to the north representing Athene as a war-champion was erected to commemorate an Athenian victory over Boeotia and Chalcis.

Plan of the Acropolis

This plan of the Acropolis shows the major buildings of the Classical Era. The Propylaea led through to the Parthenon, which was entered from the east, giving access to the gold-and-ivory statue of Athene. The earlier temple of Athene to the north survives only in its foundations because it was destroyed by the Persian Army in 480 BC. A monument called the Erechtheum had associations with Poseidon, god of the sea and earthquakes. At the foot of the rock of the Acropolis, a wealthy patron of the arts named Herodes Atticus, who lived in the 2nd century AD, commissioned an *odeion* for concerts. Nearby was the Theater of Dionysus, where performances of tragedies by the great Greek playwrights—including Aeschylus (*c.* 525–456 BC), Sophocles (*c.* 496–406 BC), and Euripides (*c.* 480–406 BC)—were staged.

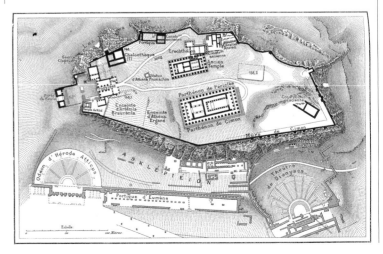

Coins of Alexander

Most coins showing the head of Alexander were issued after his early death in Babylon in 323 BC. They commemorate his bloodline and link him to mythical heroes and the historical events of his remarkable campaigns. The decadrachm depicts him wearing a lion skin in honor of his legendary ancestor Heracles, the son of Zeus, king of the gods, who is shown on the reverse holding his sacred bird, the eagle. On the tetradrachm Alexander is crowned with the head of an elephant, a reference to his defeat of the Indian King Porus, whose army included a formidable force of war elephants.

Bust of Socrates

Socrates (*c.* 469–399 BC) had one of the most questioning minds in Classical Greece. He devoted his life to searching for the answers to what constituted an upright life. His philosophy survives in the dialogues of Plato (*c.* 428–347 BC), who refined and embellished the arguments into literary masterpieces. His questioning of other people's claims to wisdom won him enemies and, in 399 BC, he was put on trial on false charges of impiety and corrupting the minds of young Athenians, and he was condemned to death by the jury. Socrates drank hemlock while in prison, and Plato has left a moving account of his last hours.

Decadrachm

Tetradrachm

Didrachme

Drachme

Triobole

Obole

Obole

Alexander and Diogenes

Alexander's education had been guided by the philosopher and scientist Aristotle, and he developed a keen intellect. He was also ruthless in exercising power and was ready to destroy any enemy who defied him. However, there is a story that the Cynic philosopher Diogenes, who famously lived in a large pottery jar, was not overawed by Alexander, who visited him on one occasion, enquiring if he could benefit him in any way. Diogenes requested that Alexander stop blocking his sunlight. Alexander took it in good humor, asserting that he himself would not mind being Diogenes.

See also

Government,
pages 136–9

Architecture,
pages 186–7

SOCIETY

Citizens

Men and women in the upper echelons of Greek society had responsibilities that governed their lives. In Athens, many of the wealthy, established families provided the statesmen and generals even under a democratic system. Similarly, daughters of eminent parents could expect to get the most prestigious offices in temple rituals and festivals. But in general, while men had unlimited freedom to get out of the house, for women such spontaneous opportunities were few and far between. Pericles even asserted that the highest accolade a woman could receive was never to be talked about by men, favorably or otherwise. In the home the activities of women, assisted by slaves, included working wool, weaving, and preparing meals. Social gatherings outside the house would, for the most part, be a male preserve, especially when undertaken for commercial or political reasons.

Mansions
Rich citizens lived in houses that centered, as in this exaggerated imaginary scene, on a rectangular courtyard, perhaps with a small pool, open to the sky for light and air. Activities could take place in the sheltered passages and side rooms. Men would gather in the *andron*, where there were dining couches, while women supposedly had their own spaces, perhaps on an upper story. Hospitality offered to guests, as here, could include a slave washing a visitor's feet. The peacock and the musician by the pillar suggest an ostentatious display of wealth.

Social gatherings in Athens
Athens had public spaces where people could gather to relax or discuss social or political topics. The Agora, a market and civic center below the rock of the Acropolis, had stones known as *horoi* marking its boundaries. During the day, there would be the bustle of stallholders, traveling merchants, and money changers, so that the tranquillity evinced by this scene would be rare. Groups of citizens such as those shown here would also meet in the vicinity of the law courts and the Council meeting house, which were prime centers of gossip.

See also
Society,
pages 144–7
Work,
pages 168–9

Man and his dog

This grave stela from Naxos shows a Greek man looking down at his dog. The love of Greek men for their dogs, used for hunting and guarding the home, is first mentioned in Homer. When Odysseus finally returns home to Ithaca, he is recognized by his faithful dog Argus, who wags his tail but no longer has the strength to approach him: "The doom of dark death closed over Argus when, after nineteen years had gone by, he had seen Odysseus."

Women

The role of women in the *oikos,* or household, was straightforward and limited in scope. Women and their slaves had the responsibility for providing clothes and textiles. Weaving on wooden looms of the sort illustrated in this scene produced garments and bedclothes. The skill of the seated woman in the center is symbolically rewarded by a victor's garland. The ritual robes for statues of goddesses would also be woven by designated groups of women.

Libation

There were specific occasions when religious or funerary ceremonies required women to make libations. This young Spartan woman, graceful and solemn, pours the libation from her jar into the more elaborate vase of an honored dead relative. In fact, such everyday chores as going to the water fountain provided an escape for women and slave girls from the confines of the house.

SOCIETY

Love and Marriage

The purpose of marriage in ancient Greece was for legal control over a woman to pass from her father or guardian to her husband. She was then expected to have children, and failure to do so could be grounds for divorce. Once married, a man could still enjoy the company of courtesans and take a concubine, although any children from such a liaison would not be considered legitimate. In both Athens and Sparta a chronically sick child or one considered to be physically not conforming to the standards of the time might be abandoned and left to die. Girls spent their early years learning domestic skills, such as spinning and weaving—although Athenian girls had the chance to spend a short, carefree period before marriage in the Temple of Artemis at Brauron. Education for young boys was the responsibility of a tutor at home, and later they might study under professional teachers, learning reading, writing, music, and athletics.

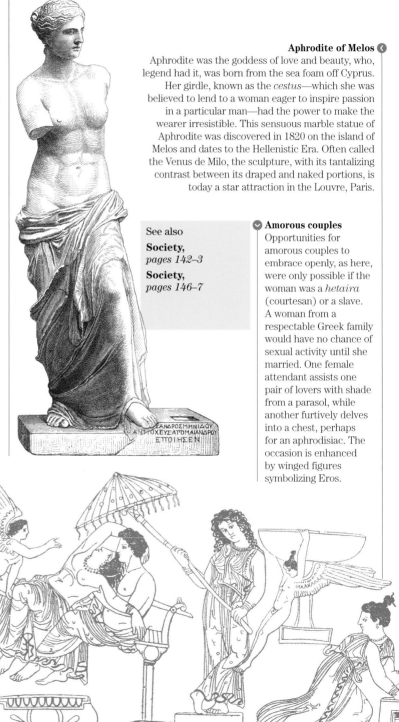

Aphrodite of Melos

Aphrodite was the goddess of love and beauty, who, legend had it, was born from the sea foam off Cyprus. Her girdle, known as the *cestus*—which she was believed to lend to a woman eager to inspire passion in a particular man—had the power to make the wearer irresistible. This sensuous marble statue of Aphrodite was discovered in 1820 on the island of Melos and dates to the Hellenistic Era. Often called the Venus de Milo, the sculpture, with its tantalizing contrast between its draped and naked portions, is today a star attraction in the Louvre, Paris.

See also
Society,
pages 142–3
Society,
pages 146–7

Amorous couples

Opportunities for amorous couples to embrace openly, as here, were only possible if the woman was a *hetaira* (courtesan) or a slave. A woman from a respectable Greek family would have no chance of sexual activity until she married. One female attendant assists one pair of lovers with shade from a parasol, while another furtively delves into a chest, perhaps for an aphrodisiac. The occasion is enhanced by winged figures symbolizing Eros.

⌃ Wedding procession

Wedding processions are shown on Athenian vases, providing a panorama of the ceremonies that accompanied a bride as she traveled to her new home. The journey took place at night with female relatives of the couple carrying torches, like the two women here. The bride walks along solemnly with her head modestly inclined, with a winged figure of Eros flying toward her. The procession is accompanied by flute players and singers and by a woman carrying a large amphora decorated with nuptial celebrations for the bride to keep as a souvenir of the occasion.

⌄ Unveiling the bride

After her nuptial bath, a bride normally dressed in lavish robes and covered her face so that, in a preliminary ceremony to the ensuing wedding night, the groom would remove her veil. In this terra-cotta statuette the couple are on a bed. The groom, all but undressed except for a cloak, has tenderly unveiled his bride. Although he is shown as a youth, in reality he would probably be around thirty years old, while his bride would often be much younger.

⌄ Women and children

The overriding purpose of marriage was for the woman to bear children, preferably sons. If a family was well off, there would be wet nurses and slaves to help care for the youngest children, some of whom might, as here, be tucked up in wickerwork cribs. This left Athenian matrons with more time to supervise the running of the household. There were a variety of games for children to play, and a particularly popular toy for young boys was a small wooden cart.

SOCIETY

Death and Funerary Rights

From the Bronze Age to the Classical Era, funerary rituals exhibited great diversity. At Mycenae gold masks were placed over the faces of the dead elite, who were buried in shaft graves, while the slain heroes of Homer's epics were burned on funerary pyres. In Athens the archaeological evidence left by gravestones, sarcophagi, and painted vases gives a full picture of burial rites, from the laying out of the corpse to the cortege to the tomb. Literary references add to our knowledge of the importance of funerary rituals, a prime example of which can be found in Sophocles' tragedy *Antigone*. The tyrant Creon instructed that Antigone's brother remain unburied because he had attacked his native city of Thebes. However, because of the significance of these rites, she performed them in defiance of the order even though it meant her own death.

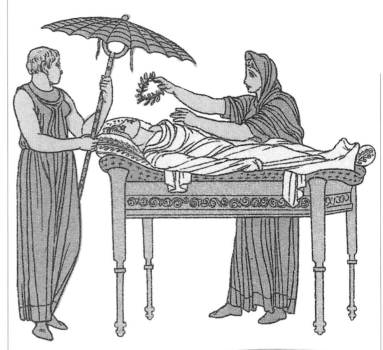

Deceased on a bier
One of the duties carried out by Greek women was to prepare for burial the body of any family member who died. This laying out was called "prothesis" and was considered a subject suitable for painting on vases. The corpse was washed before being wrapped in a funerary shroud and placed on a bier. Here, under the shade of a parasol, a woman adds a garland to the head of the deceased.

Warrior leaving his wife
There were frequent occasions when soldiers had to say good-bye to their wives as they left to go to war. On this Athenian vase there is a deep sense of poignancy surrounding the warrior's imminent departure to a conflict from which he might never return. His wife, looking inconsolably sad, has poured a farewell drink for him into the bowl that he raises to his lips, while his parents watch with foreboding. In contrast, in Sparta women viewed a brave death in battle as a cause for rejoicing.

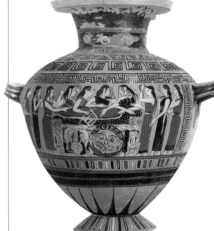

Mourners over the corpse of Achilles
Tearing at their hair and displaying extreme grief, female mourners, one of whom holds a lyre, perhaps to accompany a dirge, embrace the corpse laid out on the elaborate funerary bier. Against it rests a shield with the motif of a gorgon's head. The scene actually portrays the funeral rites for Achilles, killed by the arrow of the Trojan prince Paris. According to legend, his body was then burned on a pyre and his bones gathered in a golden casket.

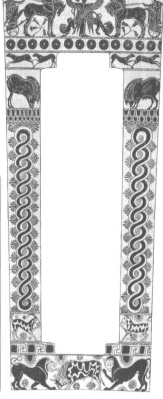

Mourners

Extravagant gestures of grief are customary in Greek scenes of mourning the deceased, hence the upraised arm to the top of the head in the case of the man and woman shown here. Funerary rituals were essential, and no family would neglect all the requisites of a proper burial. At the climax of Homer's *Iliad*, Priam, King of Troy, after much effort and humiliation, eventually persuades Achilles to release the body of his son Hector for a funeral worthy of a hero.

Funerary cortege

An integral part of the funerary arrangements, following a due period allowed for private grief was the *ekphora*, or cortege, transporting the body to the tomb. Traditionally, as here, the corpse was carried on a cart to the cemetery accompanied by mourning relatives. In Classical Athens by law inhumations took place outside the city boundaries, particularly at Kerameikos, where archaeologists have discovered the most prestigious burial sites.

Hermes

Greek ideas of the afterlife were influenced by Homer, who described Odysseus summoning the spirits of the dead. The spirit was thought to be transported across the River Styx to Hades via the ferryboat of Charon. By necromancy, Odysseus was able to communicate with souls in Hades, but the image conjured up is of ghosts living in a pointless world. The god Hermes was thought to be a guide and intermediary between the underworld and the land of the living. On this vase, in his role as god of herdsmen, he carries a ram and holds the caduceus, a powerful golden wand.

Decorated sarcophagus

Burial customs varied over the millennia of Greek civilization. Cremated remains, particularly of warriors, would be placed in chests made of precious metal—an exquisite gold casket was found in a tomb at Vergina in Macedon that may contain the bones of Philip II, father of Alexander the Great. Another practice was to place the body in a stone sarcophagus, a Greek word meaning "flesh-eater." The decorations on the sarcophagus might symbolically emphasize the prowess of the deceased—here the tomb's occupant is shown hunting lions, bulls, and wild boars.

See also
Society,
pages 142–5
Religion,
pages 150–1

WARFARE

The Age of Heroes

The Greeks glorified the battles of the Age of Heroes, particularly those of the Trojan War, traditionally dated to around 1200 BC. Archaeological discoveries from the Mycenaean Period have revealed helmets made of boar's tusks and bronze corselets. There are also frescoes from palaces showing warriors in battle. In the epics of Homer there are memories of Bronze Age military equipment, such as the tall shield of the Greek warrior Ajax. Later, however, on Classical Greek vases, artists naturally showed the kind of weapons and armor that were in use at that time. The value of armor meant that there would be struggles on the battlefield to strip a dead enemy of his equipment. The visual evidence on the vases also reflected the exotic and—to the Greek mind—unmanly costumes worn by their enemies in the vast Persian Empire.

Greeks and Trojans

In reality, the armor that would have been worn at the time of the Trojan War would be different from that worn by soldiers of the Classical Era, but painters—who frequently represented this theme on vases—depicted contemporary weapons and equipment. In this battle both the Greek and Trojan combatants are similarly armed with crested Attic-style helmets and circular shields. The attempt to rescue the body of a fallen comrade shown in the thick of the fighting recalls episodes in the *Iliad*.

Hector and Menelaus

This splendid plate was made at Kameiros on the island of Rhodes. The accomplished painter has surrounded the warriors with elaborate palmettes and rosettes. In addition to crested helmets and painted shields, the soldiers wear metal cuirasses and bronze greaves. The scene can be linked to a specific point in the war at Troy, as described by Homer, because the names of the warriors are on the plate. Menelaus, King of Sparta (left), confronts Hector in a struggle over the body and armor of the Trojan Euphorbus.

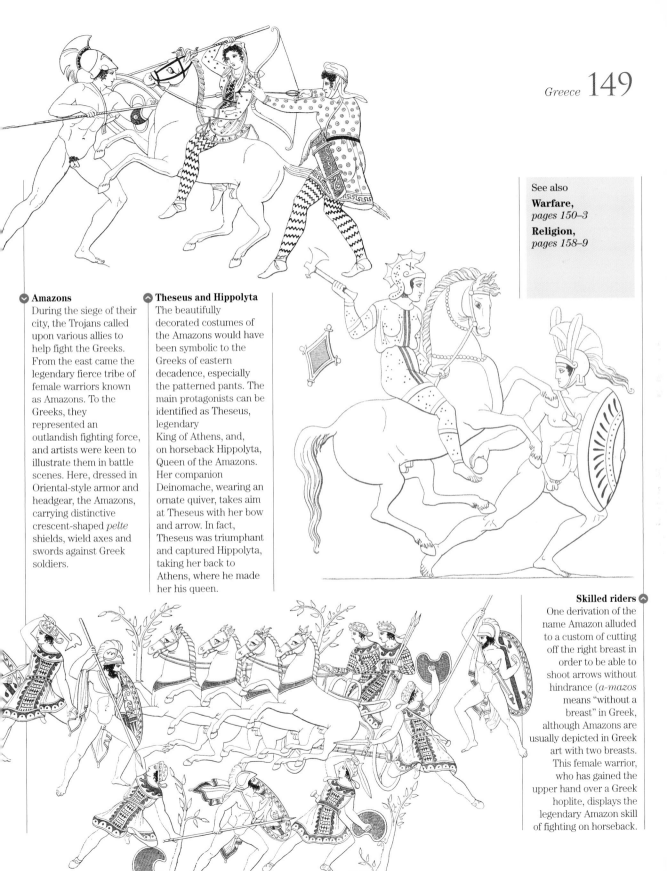

See also
Warfare,
pages 150–3
Religion,
pages 158–9

Amazons
During the siege of their city, the Trojans called upon various allies to help fight the Greeks. From the east came the legendary fierce tribe of female warriors known as Amazons. To the Greeks, they represented an outlandish fighting force, and artists were keen to illustrate them in battle scenes. Here, dressed in Oriental-style armor and headgear, the Amazons, carrying distinctive crescent-shaped *pelte* shields, wield axes and swords against Greek soldiers.

Theseus and Hippolyta
The beautifully decorated costumes of the Amazons would have been symbolic to the Greeks of eastern decadence, especially the patterned pants. The main protagonists can be identified as Theseus, legendary King of Athens, and, on horseback Hippolyta, Queen of the Amazons. Her companion Deinomache, wearing an ornate quiver, takes aim at Theseus with her bow and arrow. In fact, Theseus was triumphant and captured Hippolyta, taking her back to Athens, where he made her his queen.

Skilled riders
One derivation of the name Amazon alluded to a custom of cutting off the right breast in order to be able to shoot arrows without hindrance (*a-mazos* means "without a breast" in Greek, although Amazons are usually depicted in Greek art with two breasts. This female warrior, who has gained the upper hand over a Greek hoplite, displays the legendary Amazon skill of fighting on horseback.

WARFARE

Warriors and Armor

Greek armies consisted of a number of contingents that are extensively illustrated on vases and described by ancient poets and historians. Crucial to Greek military success was the discipline of the heavy infantry—and no state trained these troops harder than Sparta. The light infantry was made up of soldiers who carried only basic arms, such as a sword, a spear or a club, and wore only tunics to avoid impeding their speed as skirmishers. In addition, slingers, particularly from Rhodes, could cause serious casualties with their shots of stone or lead. In the Classical Era, cavalry played a minor role in warfare. Instead of making mass charges, they acted as scouts and skirmishers, and pursued the fleeing enemy.

Archer

Archers did not make up an important element in the Greek military, whereas they figured prominently in the Persian forces, as seen at the Battle of Thermopylae against the Spartans in 480 BC. Archers wore leather corselets and normally their quivers were elaborately decorated. The best archers came from Crete or Scythia and were hired by the Greeks as mercenaries.

Peltast

Peltasts were soldiers who got their name from the small crescent-shaped, wicker shield, or *pelte*, which they carried. Their main weapon was a light throwing spear. They were originally mercenaries from Thrace, whose skill was to act as skirmishers harassing the enemy with swift attacks. Their methods of warfare were successfully adopted by Greek armies.

General

This general, or *strategos*, in command of Greek troops wears a full panoply of armor. His plumed helmet has a feather added on each side. His cuirass is made of flexible material or leather to which metal has been attached. In addition, leather strips weighted with metal plates, known as pteruges, hang down from his shoulders and from his waist. Although soldiers were often barefooted below their greaves, he wears sandals.

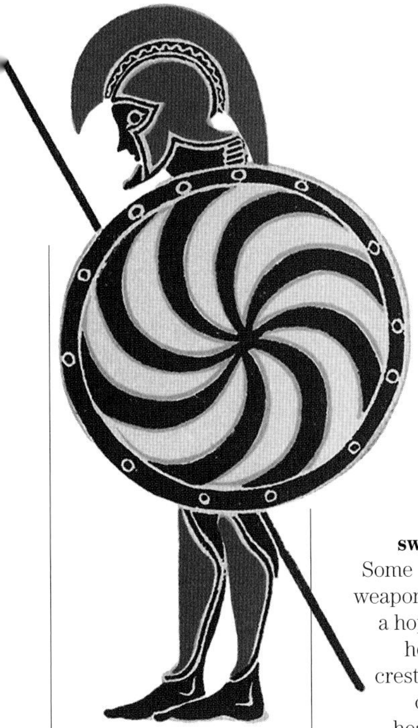

Hoplite shields

In battle formation the hoplites were tough, disciplined fighters. Their large, round shields were the most distinctive part of their weaponry, and in a line of troops advancing toward the enemy, the hoplite held his shield in a way that protected half his body and overlapped half of the exposed body of the soldier on his left.

Hoplite with sword and shield

Some of the essential weapons and armor of a hoplite are shown here. He wears a crested helmet with cheek guards, a heavy bell-shaped cuirass over the upper part of his tunic, and bronze shin protectors. His large, round shield was called a *hoplon*, and his hand grips a short thrusting sword.

Hoplite

The valor of hoplites, Greek infantry soldiers, in battle is very well documented, and many were proud of their deeds. The playwright Aeschylus, renowned among the Athenians for his tragedies, requested that his gravestone only commemorate his service as a hoplite at the Battle of Marathon in 490 BC. In complete contrast, the lyric poet Archilochus (*c.* 680– *c.* 645 BC) had no qualms about abandoning his shield and running away to save his life, remarking that he could easily find another of the same roundness and quality.

See also
Warfare,
pages 148–9
Warfare,
pages 152–3
Technology,
pages 170–1

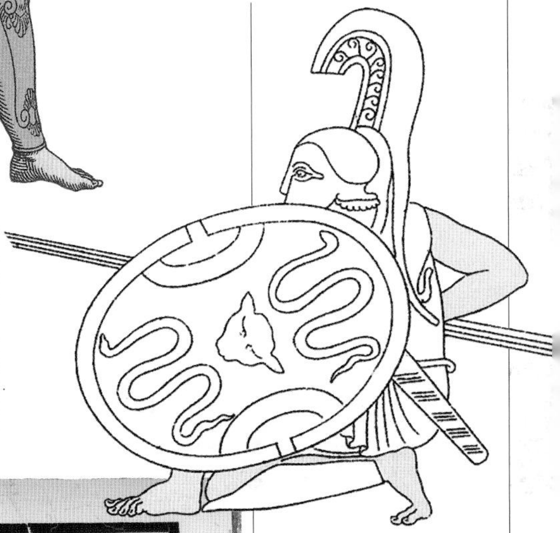

Helmeted hoplite

This hoplite kneels, spear in hand behind his shield. The shield boss is decorated with the head of a panther and snakes, dangerous creatures that were meant to unnerve an opponent. The interior of such shields had a supporting armband and hand grip. Holding a long-shafted spear, he is about to spring forward as part of the formation charge.

Helmeted warrior with shield

This hoplite's shield is decorated with a satyr, a monstrously ugly mythical creature with a horse's tail. His helmet sports a crest made out of horsehair. The hoplite is clearly running forward with his spear poised, a tactic that was a decisive factor at the Battle of Marathon, when Greek hoplites rushed the Persian front line at the double to avoid the hail of arrows.

WARFARE

Into Battle

Ancient historians have recorded the battle tactics used by Greek commanders on many occasions. For example, at the Battle of Marathon in 490 BC a Greek trumpeter sounded the signal to advance, with the aim of forcing the Persians toward the marshes or the sea—successfully as it turned out. Other battles were more closely fought, such as that at Plataea in 479 BC, where the Greek infantry had a hard struggle against the Persian cavalry before driving the enemy out of Greece. Some of the most detailed accounts of warfare concern the campaigns of Alexander the Great against the Persian Empire. His successes depended heavily on the employment of the Macedonian infantry phalanx, his brigade of hypaspists (guards), and his squadrons of cavalry.

See also
Warfare,
pages 148–51

Facing the enemy
These massed ranks of hoplites confront each other on this vase fragment, which clearly shows how their shields protected the exposed side of the soldier beside them. One shield displays the terrifying face of the gorgon. These troops are in the "killing zone," where spears will soon inflict lethal or agonizingly incapacitating wounds. As hoplites marched into battle, they would be accompanied by an *aulos* (flute) player, whose music kept them in step or, as here, by a pipe player, who played an intimidating martial tune.

Warrior throwing a rock
As a provocation to the enemy troops, this hoplite hurls a rock toward their front line. Below his helmet, locks of long hair fall onto his shoulders. Spartan soldiers astounded the Persians when they saw them calmly combing their hair before the Battle of Thermopylae. From the hoplite's round shield, with its blazon of a scorpion, there hangs down a textile or leather protector used to deflect weapons aimed at the legs.

Alexander the Great and Darius III
In 333 BC Alexander the Great's forces defeated the Persian Army at the Battle of Issus. Some historians believe that the turning point of that battle is captured brilliantly in a famous mosaic surviving from Pompeii (reproduced in this engraving).
The figure on the left is thought to be Alexander on his indomitable horse, Bucephalus, riding toward the Persian king Darius III, shown in his chariot looking terrified and who, moments later, fled the battlefield.

Pikemen
One reason for Alexander the Great's military successes was the infantry phalanx of Macedonian soldiers, each armed with a 20-ft (6-m) pike known as a *sarissa*. The approach of rows of pikes with such an extended reach was a formidable sight, and the effect on enemy soldiers and cavalry was devastating. In this illustration of a pitched battle against the Persians, the phalanx of pikemen have stood their ground so that a Greek cavalry charge from the flank can now inflict heavy losses on the enemy.

RELIGION

Triumph of the Gods of Olympus

The Greeks believed that in the earliest times the kingship of the world was held by the sky god Ouranos, but power was wrested from him by his son Cronus. Cronus devoured his own children as they were born so that he could not be usurped in his turn, but his son Zeus was hidden from him on the island of Crete, and he challenged Cronus and eventually beat him. Zeus became the supreme ruler on Mount Olympus, and his new dynasty of gods and goddesses each had a responsibility for one or more aspect of life on earth. For example, Ares was the brooding and violent god of war, while Hermes had various duties as a divine messenger and ambassador as well as guiding the souls of the dead into the underworld. Greek heroes such as Cadmus, founder of Thebes, had the pattern of their lives dictated by the often fickle will of the gods.

Athene and Alcyoneus
One of the leading giants in the battle against the gods was Alcyoneus, son of Gaia, the earth. Alcyoneus fought against Heracles, who repeatedly knocked him to the ground, but on contact with the earth his mother gave him new strength. This detail from the Altar of Pergamum shows Alcyoneus being wrenched away from his mother by the goddess Athene so that Heracles can kill him. Nike, the goddess of victory, flies into the scene from the right.

See also
Warfare,
pages 148–9
Religion,
pages 156–65

War against the giants
The offspring of Ouranos, the sky god, and Gaia, the earth goddess, were the giants, who could cause such disastrous natural phenomena as earthquakes. The battle for supremacy between the gods and giants was a very popular artistic motif and had undertones of the Greek victory over the Persians. The finest representations of the battle were carved in the 2nd century BC on the Altar of Pergamum.

Dionysus on a panther

By tradition, Dionysus was a god from the east, the son of Zeus and the Phoenician princess Semele. He is often depicted in a chariot drawn by exotic animals, such as lions and tigers, or, as here from a Greek a vase, riding on the back of a panther. He introduced mankind to the pleasures of wine, traveling over the Mediterranean world planting vines in the company of wild companions, such as the satyr behind him. Both Dionysus and the satyr are holding masks worn at festivals held in his honour.

Dionysus and his entourage

Dionysus is holding a *krater* (mixing bowl). An important ritual object in the worship of Dionysus was the *thyrsos*—a stick with pinecones and ivy leaves at one end—which he also carries here. In front of him, also holding a *thyrsos*, is the personification of comedy, indicating the crucial role that Dionysus played in the development of Greek theater. Leading the procession is the satyr Marsyas, who possessed pipes discarded by the goddess Athene and with which he produced sublime music.

Cadmus and the dragon

Cadmus was sent by his father, the King of Phoenicia, to find his sister Europa, whom Zeus had abducted. It was a fruitless task, and instead he took the advice of the Delphic Oracle to found a new city, Thebes. To celebrate this event, he sent his followers to fetch water for a libation from a nearby spring, unaware that it was guarded by a fierce dragon. The dragon killed his retainers, so Cadmus attacked the creature, eventually despatching it with a spear. He extracted its teeth, sowed them in the ground, and they grew into armed warriors, five of whom, with Cadmus, were believed to be the ancestors of the Theban nobility.

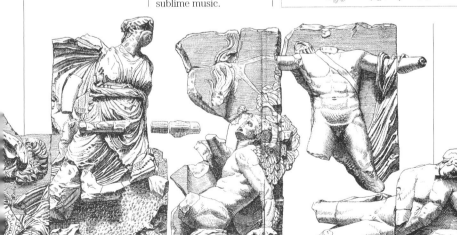

RELIGION

Myths, Legends, and the Labors of Heracles

Greek literature and art is full of myths and legends. The behavior of the gods was not always exemplary, especially when it came to the voracious sexual appetite of Zeus. He frequently aroused the wrath of his wife Hera, who could cause untold miseries for his lovers—the Phoenician princess Semele, for example, was tricked by Hera into looking at Zeus in his true splendor and was burned to ashes by his divine fiery presence. His techniques of seduction were highly imaginative, and he often won women over by taking on various disguises, including a satyr, a swan, a bull, and a shower of gold. The great heroes of Greek legend, such as Perseus and Heracles, often had divine blood. Heracles was the son of Zeus and a Mycenaean princess Alkmene, and he incurred the mortal hatred of Hera from the day he was born, even having to strangle giant snakes that she sent into his cradle. She blighted his marriage and was the cause of the Twelve Labors he was obliged to undertake.

Perseus and Medusa

Perseus was the son of Zeus by Danae, a princess of Argus. His quest to kill Medusa, one of the three gorgons, is one of the most exciting Greek myths. The gorgons were hideous, having writhing snakes on their heads, boar's tusks, and hands of bronze, and one glance at them would turn a mortal into stone. Perseus had supernatural help in the form of winged sandals and a cap that made him invisible, both clearly shown in this relief from one of the temples at Selinunte in Sicily. Here, beside the protective figure of Athene, he cuts off the head of Medusa, whose deadly eyes he has avoided by looking in the reflection of his shield. From the blood that spurted from Medusa's neck, the winged horse Pegasus was born, seen here rearing up beside her.

Leda and the swan

Zeus had taken Hera as his principal wife, and she was honored as the Queen of Heaven on Mount Olympus. He also had love affairs with six other goddesses and with a number of mortal women. Leda was a princess in Aetolia in central Greece, whose beauty had caught the eye of Zeus. He courted her in the form of a swan, a story that became a favorite theme for artists. Her children from this union, one of whom was Helen of Troy, hatched from eggs and were semidivine.

See also
Religion,
pages 154–5
Religion,
pages 158–65

Heracles and Busiris

As a punishment for killing his wife and children in a fit of madness, Heracles was set a series of arduous and sometimes life-threatening tasks. This episode occurred during his lengthy travels to find the golden apples of the Hesperides. Heracles had to journey through Egypt, which was ruled over by Busiris, whose custom was to sacrifice strangers on the altar of Zeus. The strength of Heracles is dramatically portrayed as he tramples on, hurls in the air or strangles the Egyptians who had attempted to seize him. Busiris is quivering with fear on the altar, soon to be killed, along with his son, by Heracles.

Heracles and the Cretan Bull

Heracles' Seventh Labor was to capture the Cretan Bull. King Minos had tried to deceive Poseidon by avoiding sacrificing a magnificent bull sent by the god of the sea. Consequently, Poseidon drove the bull mad, so that it raged throughout the land of Crete causing havoc. Heracles is shown wrestling the bull under the gaze of Athene, and he not only captured it but tamed it, too, riding on its back across the sea to Mycenae. Nike, the goddess of victory, hovers above him.

Heracles and Cerberus

The last of the Twelve Labors was to bring Cerberus, guardian dog of the underworld, up to the world of the living. As seen here, Cerberus was a monstrous, three-headed hound with venomous snakes growing out of his body. Wearing his protective lion skin and armed with his cudgel, Heracles, by sheer brute force, dragged Cerberus into the world to confront Eurystheus, King of Mycenae, who had devised all the labors. Here Eurystheus takes refuge in a cauldron to avoid Cerberus' jaws.

Laocoön

The ruthlessness of the gods toward humans was well exemplified by the fate of Laocoön, a priest of Apollo at Troy. The reaction of some Trojans to the fateful gift of the Wooden Horse from the Greeks was favorable, but Laocoön warned that it was a treacherous device and stabbed it with a spear. He then went outside the city with his two sons to perform a sacrifice. Suddenly, two gigantic serpents sent by the gods rose from the sea and devoured Laocoön and his sons at the altar, their agonizing death captured here in a sculpture that is today in the Vatican Museum, Rome. Such was Athene's punishment of him for his years of pious devotion to (Trojan) Apollo.

RELIGION

Trojan War and its Aftermath

There is no archaeological evidence for a historical war fought by the Greeks at Troy, although there were upheavals in the eastern Mediterranean around 1200 BC, in which Mycenaeans could have been involved. Nevertheless, to historians such as Thucydides, and the epic poets, such as Homer, the Trojan War was an integral part of Greek history. Homer's *Iliad* and *Odyssey* were written down about 700 BC, but had been recited in an oral tradition for hundreds of years. The epics were a great source of material for artists and writers, and the fortunes of the Greek warriors in the aftermath of the Trojan War gave Athenian tragedians scope to elaborate on concepts of justice and fate.

Judgment of Paris

Before being recognized as a son of King Priam of Troy, Paris lived as a shepherd. Here Paris, labeled by his other name of Alexander, is seated playing the *kythara* among a herd of goats. He is approached by Hermes, who leads in three goddesses: Athene, Hera, and Aphrodite. The reason for this visit is that Eris, the goddess of strife, had thrown to the goddesses an apple inscribed with the words "for the fairest," and Paris had been chosen to make the award. Spurning the gifts of power and supremacy in war offered by Hera and Athene, Paris opted for the hand of the most beautiful woman in the world, promised to him by Aphrodite. This woman was Helen, already married to Menelaus of Sparta. This choice was the mythical cause of the Trojan War as the Greeks, in support of Menelaus, pursued Paris and Helen to Troy.

Achilles and Hector

This scene depicts the combat between Achilles, the Greek champion, and Hector, son of King Priam of Troy. The vase painter has labeled all the participants, and here Achilles, urged on by Athene, rushes forward in triumph toward Hector, who is already severely wounded and sinking to the ground. In a masterly psychological touch, the painter shows the god Apollo, a staunch supporter of the Trojans, leaving the scene to avoid the contagion of human death, but, as he doies so, looking back to Achilles and holding up an arrow. This is a portent of the fate that Achilles himself is doomed to suffer when Paris fires an arrow into his heel, the only vulnerable spot on his body.

See also
Warfare,
pages 148–9
Religion,
pages 154–7
Religion,
pages 160–5

Weighing the souls of warriors

In the war at Troy, the fate of heroes on the battlefield was not decided by the gods, but by golden
scales in which the souls of the slain, depicted here
as winged figures, were weighed. Even Zeus and Hera
are powerless to intervene. Zeus had to let his son
Sarpedon, leader of a contingent of troops from
Lycia fighting on the side of the Trojans, die in battle.
Here the mother of the fatally wounded warrior is
distraught with grief as her son's soul weighs down
the balance of the scales.

Sack of Troy

Once the Greek warriors had got into the city of Troy
in the Wooden Horse, they showed no mercy. Here,
clinging to the statue of Athene and hoping for
sanctuary, Princess Cassandra is grabbed by the
Greek warrior Ajax, who then rapes her. On the altar
of Zeus, Achilles' son Neoptolemus slaughters King
Priam. The young boy across Priam's knees is Hector's
son Astyanax, soon to be hurled from the battlements.
One Trojan prince escaped, however, Aeneas, son of
Aphrodite, seen here carrying his aged father.

Orestes and Electra

After the sack of Troy, the victorious Greeks returned
to their kingdoms. At Mycenae, Clytemnestra,
Agamemnon's queen, had taken a lover called
Aegisthus. She hated Agamemnon, who had
sacrificed their daughter Iphigenia in order to obtain
a fair wind for the fleet to sail to Troy, and she
murdered him in his bathtub. Here his tomb is
surmounted by a crested helmet, and sitting brooding
beside its column is his daughter Electra, planning
vengeance for his death. It was her brother Orestes,
shown approaching her with his faithful companion
Pylades behind him, who was to kill their mother.

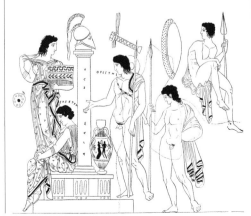

Achilles and the Queen of the Amazons

The Amazons were allies
of the Trojans and were
led to the war from
their distant homeland
in the east by Queen
Penthesileia, daughter
of the war god Ares.
Penthesileia challenged
the Greek champion
Achilles to single
combat, vowing to
avenge Hector's death.
In the contest she fought
furiously and Achilles
had to kill her to save
his own life, but he had
nothing but respect for
her, possibly even falling
in love with her as he
dealt the lethal blow.
Here Penthesileia, in
oriental dress with her
battleaxe and crescent
shield, is transported
from the battlefield by
Achilles, who then
returned her body to her
Amazon and Trojan
comrades.

RELIGION

Rituals

In a temple the focal point for worshippers was the cult statue of the deity. This could range in size from the archaic image known as a *xoanon* to an impressive colossal image. Although philosophers warned against confusing the statue with the real god, worshippers clearly used these statues as a means of direct communication with the deity. Some priests were full time, but often a magistrate or member of an elite family entitled to a hereditary priesthood could carry out essential rituals. The priest's dress normally consisted of a garland or headband around his long hair and expensive purple or white robes. Among the privileges a priest might expect was a seat of honor at the theater. In conducting sacrifices the priest ensured that the gods received their due portions of burned bones and fat—the entrails and meat went to himself and the participants at the ritual.

Sanctuary of the goddess with worshippers
The scene here is complex, but is clearly centered on the anthropomorphic cult image of a deity within a stylized *naos*, or sanctuary. The statue could be made of clay or metal, but the oldest and most revered images were carved from wood. Around this statue are female suppliants rather casually seated. On more formal occasions they would address the statue with prayers, which was the main reason for entering a temple. There are also links here to the worship of Dionysus, with the contemplative seated man holding a *thyrsos* and others holding vine branches.

Dancing for the gods
Greek religious rituals often included music and dance. Every year, during the Festival of Artemis, goddess of the hunt, wild animals and fertility, Spartan maidens performed a chain dance for the goddess, as depicted on this vase. There was also the wild *oreibasia* (mountain dance) by frenzied women in honour of Dionysus, god of ecstasy. The Greeks did not share the Roman belief that respectable women should not dance.

Women worshippers

Greek women played a greater public role in religious worship than their Roman counterparts. Goddesses were always served by priestesses rather than priests, and ordinary women took part in religious processions and dances. Melanippe, the heroine of a fragmentary tragedy by the playwright Euripides (*c.* 480–406 BC) argued that: "As to religion, we women play the most important role ... Women conduct rites for the goddesses which would be unholy for men to perform." Here a female worshipper is shown garlanding a bull that is to be sacrificed.

Athene's birthday

The most important religious festival in Athens was the Panathenaea, the birthday celebrations of Athene, patron goddess of the city. The festival included musical competitions and sporting events and climaxed in a great procession, in which a new yellow *peplos* (dress) was presented to the ancient wooden statue of the goddess as a birthday present. The procession is depicted on the Parthenon frieze, now in the British Museum. This scene shows the handing over of the folded *peplos*.

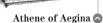

Athene of Aegina

A splendid marble statue of Athene once graced a temple on the island of Aegina in the Saronic Gulf, dedicated to her and to a local goddess called Aphaia. It was surrounded by a wooden balustrade, so worshippers climbed stairs to view it from a gallery. Also from Aegina is this statue of Athene as warrior goddess presiding over success in battle. Her statues would be honored in anticipation of the fortune that the state might accrue from victory in war.

See also

Warfare,
pages 154–9

Religion,
pages 162–5

Priest at an altar

The most expensive cult ritual involved the sacrifice of animals. The usual victims were oxen, goats, or piglets. Sometimes the slaughter was on a lavish scale, such as when hundreds of heifers and sheep were sacrificed in the festival that celebrated the birthday of Athene. Here, to the accompaniment of a pipe player, the priest places incense on the flames of the sacrificial altar while an attendant roasts meat on a spit.

RELIGION

Mysteries and Oracles

The exact activities during celebrations in honor of Demeter at Eleusis near Athens were classed as mysteries, the disclosure of which could incur the death penalty, although there are some hints as to the nature of the secret ceremonies that took place by torchlight in the darkness of the Hall of Mysteries. The annual procession from Athens to Eleusis took all day and attracted people from all over the Mediterranean world. At Eleusis, objects sacred to the cult of Demeter and her daughter Persephone were revealed to the initiates. The best known oracle was that in the Temple of Apollo at Delphi. The interpretation of the oracle's pronouncements was not always easy, as when the Athenians, under threat of the Persian advance, received the response to rely on their "wooden walls." Those who believed it meant to abandon the city and take to the ships were saved, while the citizens who barricaded themselves behind wooden planks on the Acropolis were slaughtered by the Persians.

Demeter and Persephone
The goddess Demeter (right) presided over grain and fertility and also epitomized the idea of protective motherhood. Her daughter by Zeus was Persephone, sometimes called Kore, who stands opposite holding a torch brand. When Persephone was snatched away by Hades, god of the underworld, Demeter's grief was so extreme that eventually Hades was forced to restore her to her mother for eight months every year. The young figure between the goddesses is Triptolemus, who was sent by Demeter to spread the knowledge of growing corn across the earth. This relief was discovered at Eleusis, where Demeter's temple was the center of the mysteries that drew initiates from all over the Greek world.

Gifts for Delphi
The magnificent Temple of Apollo at Delphi stands against the dramatic background of Mount Parnassus. Here an important delegation has come to consult Apollo's oracle, and out of courtesy brings the god costly gifts such as vases of precious metal. Because of the fundamental importance of the oracle in the minds of politicians and rulers, the Temple of Apollo became one of the wealthiest in Greece.

See also
Religion,
pages 154–61
Religion,
pages 164–5

Croesus on the pyre

The ambiguity of the oracle at Delphi meant that it could not often be proved wrong. King Croesus of Lydia (595–*c.* 547 BC) gave costly gifts to the oracle, including a golden statue of a lion. He wanted to expand his territory into Persia, so he enquired of the oracle how successful his plan might be. The response was that if he attacked Persia, he would destroy a great Empire, which satisfied him. However, he was defeated by Cyrus the Great (*c.* 600 or 576–*c.* 530 BC) and lost his own Empire to Persia. On this vase Croesus is seen on the pyre on which Cyrus intended to burn him alive but at the last minute took pity on him and saved him.

Pythia on her tripod

The priestess who gave the answers to questions put to Apollo's oracle at Delphi was called the Pythia, shown here seated on her tripod. She spent her life at Delphi, where she would bathe in the sacred Castalian spring. To receive the words of Apollo, her tripod is set over a chasm from which vapours emerge. The Pythia then shakes the branch of bay leaves that she holds in her left hand and falls into a trance. Her utterances are refined by the priests into elaborate lines of poetry.

Orestes and the oracle

The tripod of the Pythia at the center is surrounded by images relating to the flight of Orestes from Mycenae after he killed his mother Clytemnestra. Orestes, kneeling in a structure by the tripod over which the Pythia strangely leans, with serpents around her, sought sanctuary at Delphi from the Furies. His request was denied, but Athene, splendidly dressed with all her emblems, brought him safely to Athens. In this scene Apollo is turned toward the personification of the Python, the dragon who had guarded the site of Delphi before he killed it.

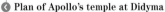

Plan of Apollo's temple at Didyma

Other oracles included the oracle of Zeus at Dodona and Apollo's oracle in his temple at Didyma on the western coast of modern Turkey. The Temple of Didyma was architecturally impressive. On the plan here a vast number of marble columns enclose an open court—it was uncovered because it was too big to build a roof to cover it—and there is a monumental staircase. Somewhere in this temple, but now lost, was the sacred spring in which the priestess paddled to breathe in its vapors and achieve a state of ecstasy.

RELIGION

Zeus and Olympia

Zeus was the supreme god of the Greek pantheon. His attributes included the thunderbolt, symbolizing his destructive power, and the eagle, his splendor. The Greeks built magnificent monuments in his honor, of which the most outstanding was his temple at Olympia. Near by was a huge altar, now vanished, which was made from the ashes of animals burned in sacrifice to him. Visitors to Olympia could enter his temple and ascend a platform to view Phidias's incredible gold-and-ivory statue of the god. Its splendor was so overwhelming that one poet wrote that either Phidias had ascended to heaven to see Zeus or the god himself had come down to Olympia. Not only was the temple a sacred edifice to marvel at, but every four years crowds flocked here to the stadium in their thousands to celebrate the Olympic Games.

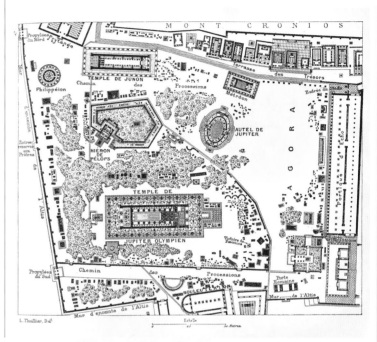

Zeus and the eagle Zeus was primarily a sky deity. On this bowl he is enveloped in a richly decorated robe. Flying toward him is an eagle, the majestic and mighty bird that became a symbol of his authority. His earliest known temple was in the north, at Dodona in Epirus, where the god was thought to speak to his priests through the rustling leaves of a gigantic oak tree.

Plan of Olympia Olympia was in the Peloponnese, and it grew to become the principal sanctuary of Zeus in the whole of Greece. This plan shows the major monuments, the earliest of which date to the 6th century BC, such as the Temple of Hera, whose name is given here in its Roman form of Juno. Other important structures are the Treasuries at the foot of Mount Kronos. The Temple of Zeus, here called Zeus Olympios, measured about 88½ by 210 ft (27 m by 64 m).

See also

Religion, *pages 154–63*

Architecture, *pages 190–1*

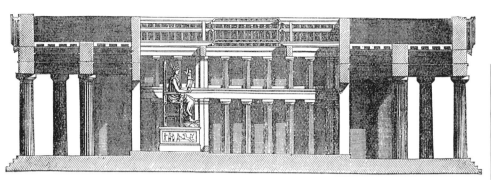

Temple of Zeus
When it was built, in around 450 BC, the Temple of Zeus was the largest temple in the Peloponnese. Visitors could climb up to the wooden gallery, supported by a row of Doric columns, and gaze at the statue of Zeus, which was housed in the interior, from shoulder height. One visitor, Strabo (*c.* 63 BC–*c.* AD 24), said that, although magnificent, the statue was too big for the temple. He complained that Phidias: "has depicted Zeus seated, but with the head almost touching the ceiling, so that we have the impression that if Zeus moved to stand up he would unroof the temple."

Zeus of Phidias
The statue of Zeus was one of the Seven Wonders of the Ancient World. This colossal statue was over 39 ft (12 m) high and had been made by the master sculptor Phidias, using gold and ivory over a wooden frame. The statue was destroyed in antiquity, but there are descriptions of it by classical authors. In this illustration the artist has diminished the height of the statue, which showed Zeus enthroned with a winged figure of Nike, goddess of victory, on his hand. In front of the statue was a pool of olive oil, which was supposed to minimize any damage to the ivory that might be caused by damp.

Image of divinity
While working on his statue, Phidias was asked what model he was using for Zeus. He answered with lines from Homer's *Iliad*: "He spoke, the son of Cronus, and nodded his dark brow, and the ambrosial locks swept down from his immortal head, and all Olympus quaked." Inspired by Homer, Phidias created an awe-inspiring image of divinity, which even outlasted his statue's destruction. His bearded Zeus, ruling in majesty, is thought to have influenced the depiction of Christ Pantocrator (Ruler of All) in Byzantine churches.

WORK

Rural Life

Agriculture and domesticated animals are well-documented essentials of Greek life from the Bronze Age onward. Major cities depended on supplies of crops and meat from the countryside. Rural living conditions could be harsh, especially in winter, something vividly captured by the early poet Hesiod (probably 8th century BC). Oxen would only be kept by wealthier farmers, so plowing would mostly be done by hand. The diet for ordinary agricultural workers (besides coarse bread) included beans, onions, garlic, and fish. There is a long history of viticulture in Greece, and wine became a vital commodity in daily life and in state and temple rituals. Similarly, olive oil was essential in food preparation and a valuable export.

Trapping wild bulls
These gold cups from a burial site at Vapheio near Sparta date from the 15th century BC, and they are skillfully decorated with scenes of trapping wild bulls. The upper image shows hunters trying to capture the bulls with nets, with one man being trampled beneath a bull's hooves while another runs safely away. On the other cup there is less turmoil. A hunter has secured a rope around the hind leg of one animal, while another has been distracted by the presence of a cow.

See also
Work,
pages 168–9
Food,
pages 192–3

Country scenes
In Greece the basic diet was based on cereals—shown being harvested here—vegetables, oil, and wine. Wheat and barley were sown in the fall and were used both to make bread and to produce a kind of porridge. The oxen pulling the cart would have been used in the sowing season to drag the wooden plows and break up the ground. Olives from the trees in the background provided the fats necessary for making the cereals more palatable.

Grape harvest

Wine had an important role in Bronze Age Greek society, and archeological discoveries of amphorae with residue show that wine impregnated with resin was probably being produced for export even then. On this pottery fragment a man collects grapes from a vine tendril. Greek wines were rated according to where the grapes were grown, and wines from the islands of Samos, Thasos, Chios, and Rhodes were considered among the best.

Making wine

On this amphora the painter presents a realistic scene of work in a vineyard. Techniques of training and pruning vines were well known, even the more complicated methods, as shown here, of growing the grapes up trees. Once the grapes were trodden and pressed, the juice was poured into jars and left to ferment for nine days, after which the jars were sealed and inspected regularly to check when the wine would be ready for consumption.

Collecting olives

Olive were a staple dietary item and an important export. Olive trees can take over ten years to reach maturity, but are sturdy and need little attention. The really laborious job, however, was harvest time. Olives had to be picked from the branches or beaten down with sticks. Once pressed, the oil, in addition to its everyday uses, was sometimes bottled in elaborate amphorae and awarded as prizes in competitions; for example, to victors at the Panathenaic Games in Athens.

Satyrs

Satyrs, the wild and unruly companions of Dionysus, god of wine, are shown here eagerly plucking grapes from the vines, treading them in a bowl, and pouring the juice into a large amphora. The Greeks had the choice of white, brown, or red wine, which was always mixed with water. It was drunk socially, but also formed a crucial element in religious libations.

WORK

Making Vases and Weaving

The rich legacy of painted vases from ancient Greece indicates a flourishing industry employing manual workers, skilled artisans and gifted painters. There was the backbreaking task of cutting the raw clay from pits and then transporting it to the urban workshops, where potters shaped vases and placed in kilns. They worked in blistering heat, stacking the vases for the three different phases of oxidizing required for firing. The painting of pottery led to distinctive styles across the Greek world, with patterns and rows of real or imaginary animals predominating in the Archaic Period, giving way to exciting scenes of gods, heroes, and daily life in the Classical Era. Centers noted for the production of fine vases included Corinth and Athens.

Although few textiles survive, literary and visual evidence show women responsible for making clothes from the first stages of spinning fibers to the final woven garment.

Potter's workshop
The district of Athens where the greatest concentration of potters and vase painters worked was near an important cemetery that took its name, Kerameikos, from the ceramics (*keramos*) industry. In this vase painting a potter attends to the kiln, where temperatures could reach up to 1742°F (950°C) to fire the vases that had previously been air-dried.

Finished vase
The shapes and decorations on Greek vases varied considerably over the centuries, and changes in styles and motifs help us to date them. Here is a good example of an early design used by potters in the 7th century BC, the so-called "Orientalizing" Period, when influences from the Near East are evident. The surface has horizontal bands of grazing wild goats, while at the top, below the interlocking spirals, is a fine example of the mythical winged griffin.

Men extracting clay
These men are digging and mining for clay in a pit. The regions around Athens produced a clay of exceptionally good quality, containing the iron oxides that gave it a light red color when fired. Once these workmen had extracted the clay and hoisted it out of the pit in leather buckets, they would then need to remove pebbles and other impurities.

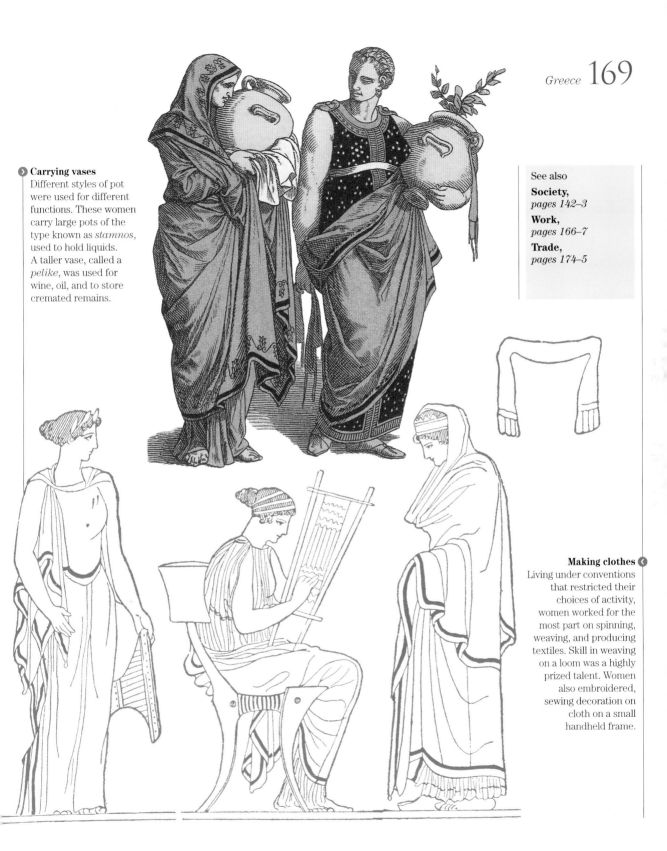

Carrying vases
Different styles of pot were used for different functions. These women carry large pots of the type known as *stamnos*, used to hold liquids. A taller vase, called a *pelike*, was used for wine, oil, and to store cremated remains.

See also
Society,
pages 142–3
Work,
pages 166–7
Trade,
pages 174–5

Making clothes
Living under conventions that restricted their choices of activity, women worked for the most part on spinning, weaving, and producing textiles. Skill in weaving on a loom was a highly prized talent. Women also embroidered, sewing decoration on cloth on a small handheld frame.

TECHNOLOGY

Metallurgy and Military Devices

The metalworkers of Mycenaean Greece left a proud legacy in the shaft graves of their rulers, notably dagger blades with intricately inlaid miniature scenes of wild animals and hunters. A memory of their expertise is found in Homer's description of the decoration of the shield of Achilles. In Classical Greece few people could afford vases of metal as opposed to ceramic, but there is plenty of evidence of the technology available for their manufacture. There was also a thriving industry for manufacturing bronze votive figurines.

Military technology advanced over time, and catapults and other projectile weapons were developed. Heavily fortified siege machines were constructed to inflict the maximum damage to enemy strongholds.

Metal vases

This metalworker is probably turning bronze sheets on a lathe to form a vessel. Other finished vases are hanging up. Mold-cast spouts and handles would be attached to the body of the vase with rivets.

Armor for Achilles

One of most interesting passages in Homer's *Iliad* describes the armor that the god Hephaestus made for Achilles once he decided to return to fighting the Trojans. Thetis, mother of Achilles, transports the helmet, body armor, shield, and greaves from Olympus to the Greek camp. The massive shield is described in great detail as being lavishly decorated with numerous scenes and emblems, which were gilded or inlaid with silver.

Metalworkers in a forge

Greek metalworkers are seen here in their forge in a scene realistically portrayed by a vase painter. On the left a man uses tongs to place a piece of metal just removed from the furnace on an anvil, where another worker is about to begin hammering it into shape. The wall in the background is hung with the tools of their trade, including mallets, chisels, and a saw. The owner of the workshop points a metal vase out to a prospective client.

Mycenaean dagger

The techniques used in the manufacture of metal objects in the Bronze Age resulted in some of the finest examples of decorated weapons in the ancient world. Justly admired is this dagger inlaid with gold and niello—a black, metallic alloy—to portray a scene of men hunting lions. The hunters hold massive shields behind which an archer hides, and one man lies on the ground below the front paws of the attacking lion.

See also
Warfare,
pages 150–1
Technology,
pages 172–3

Votive bronzes

Bronze statuettes were manufactured for dedication to the gods at temples and sacred sites. The two figurines here are of the goddess Athene and a pipe player, and they were found in the sanctuary of the Oracle of Zeus at Dodona in northern Greece. Votive bronzes were made either by using stone open-face molds or clay molds.

Catapults and siege engines

Engineering advances at the time of Philip II of Macedon and his successor Alexander the Great led to the construction of huge siege towers that were used to devastating effect in battering the walls of Tyre and Gaza. Slightly later, during the siege of Rhodes (305–304 BC) by Demetrius the Besieger (337–283 BC), a nine-story machine was employed that ran on eight wheels clad with iron plates. Various types of catapult were also invented to fire sharp, pointed missiles at the enemy, with the more devastating torsion catapult coming into use in the Hellenistic Period.

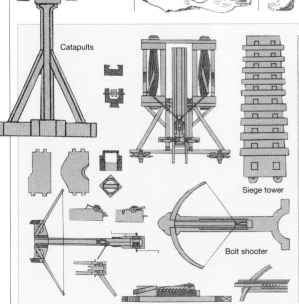

Catapults

Siege tower

Bolt shooter

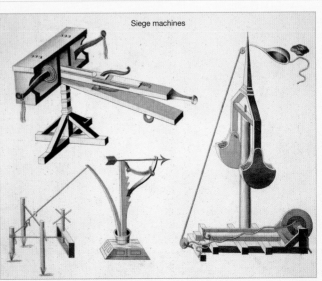

Siege machines

TECHNOLOGY

Ships

The Greeks were a maritime people from the earliest times, and their settlements were rarely far from the sea. Oared galleys, first described by Homer, played a key role in Greek history. From *c*. 750 BC oared galleys carried Greek colonists from their homelands to found new settlements around the Mediterranean and Black Seas. The most famous oared galley was the *trieres*, more familiar by its Roman name, trireme. The trireme had a highly trained crew of 170 oarsmen, rowing on three levels. With a light hull built for speed and a bronze battering ram, it functioned like a guided missile, smashing into the sides of enemy ships. It was thanks to the use of the trireme that, in 480 BC, a small Athenian fleet was able to defeat a much larger invading Persian navy at the Battle of Salamis. Using its fleet of triremes, Athens went on to become the dominant naval power in Greece.

Odysseus' ship
From an early date the Greeks painted eyes on the prows of their ships, believing that these helped a vessel find its way safely through danger. This 5th-century BC vase painting shows Odysseus' ship passing the Sirens, deadly birdwomen whose songs lured men to their doom. Wishing to hear the song yet survive, Odysseus and had himself tied to the mast and his men's ears filled with wax.

Pentecontor
The standard early warship was the pentecontor, which had fifty oarsmen rowing on a single level, as in this vase painting. The next development was the bireme, a Phoenician invention, with two levels of oarsmen. Doubling the levels allowed the Greeks and Phoenicians to build shorter, more maneuverable ships, which were much more efficient at ramming.

Horned ships
In the *Iliad*, written down in the 8th century BC, Homer describes the "black ships" that carry the invading Greeks to Troy. Attic vases, dating from Homer's own time, show warships with long ornamental horns curving back from the prows. This curious feature is mentioned by Homer, who tells us that Achilles has "ships of upright horns." The ships used a single square sail, shown on the upper fragment, for long sea passages. In battle, however, they were rowed.

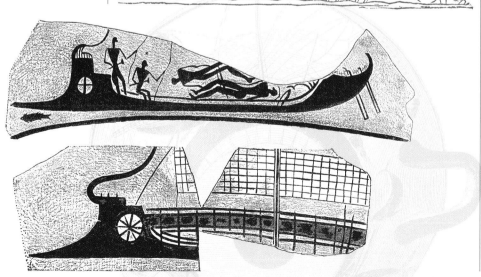

Trireme rowers

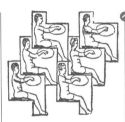

Many attempts have been made to work out the relative positions of the three levels of oarsmen. Because of the outward curve of the ship's hull, it is likely that the upper rowers were not directly on top of those below them, but to their side. The *thranites* at the top would be nearest to the edge of the ship, while the *thalamites* were closest to the center.

See also

Technology,
pages 170–1

Trade,
pages 174–5

Trireme
According to Thucydides, the first triremes were built in Corinth in the 7th century BC. With 170 oarsmen on three levels, a trireme was much faster than a bireme and soon became the standard Greek warship. The size of the Athenian ship sheds at Piraeus reveals that a trireme was 121 ft (37 m) long, and 19 ft (5.9 m) at its widest. On this plan the longest oars are those of the sixty-two *thranites*, or top-level oarsmen. The shorter oars belong to the fifty-four *zygites*, on the middle level, and the fifty-four *thalamites*, on the lowest level.

The Lenormant relief
The most important evidence for how a trireme was rowed comes from the Lenormant relief, discovered in Athens. The *thranites* at the top, who are naked, are shown rowing through an outrigger—a wooden frame projecting from the side of the hull. The *thranites* had the hardest task, for their oars were longer and hit the water at a sharper angle than those of the lower oarsmen. They rowed in time to the music of a pipe player.

Helmsman
The *kybernetes*, or helmsman, controlled the navigation of the ship, whether it was rowed or under sail. In battle, it was the helmsman's skill that enabled a trireme to ram an enemy vessel amidships or disable it by sheering off its oars. A cup painted by the Athenian artist Nicosthenes (flourishing *c.* 545–510 BC) in around 530 BC shows two Greek warships under sail, steered by helmsmen. The bronze rams are shaped like boars' heads.

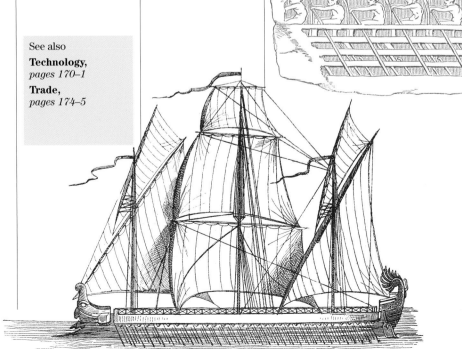

Victorian trireme
This fanciful Victorian engraving shows a trireme with three tall masts, rigged like a 19th-century sailing ship. In fact, for a trireme to bear so much sail, it would need a massive, heavy hull, which would be impossible to row at any speed. In the 1860s the French emperor Napoleon III had a reconstructed trireme built on a similar massive scale. It proved so unseaworthy and slow that it ended up being used by the navy for target practice.

TRADE

Vases for Export and the Trading Colony at Naucratis

The Greeks had flourishing trading links right across the Mediterranean, and high-quality painted vases have been discovered at sites from Spain to the Black Sea. Greeks who prospered in the cities of southern Italy had an insatiable thirst for pottery decorated by fashionable artists in Athens (although they did produce pottery for export themselves, notably Apulian ware from Taras). Some vase painters incorporated themes in their exported designs that aimed to appeal to communities abroad and were rarely used in the home market. Shipping products could be hazardous, but the trade was too lucrative to give up despite cargoes being lost to storms or pirates. The Greek trading post set up at Naucratis in Egypt was important because it gave access to products, such as papyrus for writing materials, ropes for the rigging of ships, and flax for linen clothes and sails. In return, the Egyptians purchased valued commodities, such as olive oil and wine, from the Greek merchants.

Vase painter

The individual styles of the most talented vase painters can be recognized. Experts on Greek pottery have, in a number of cases, been able to identify individual painters by their style of work and favorite subjects, so that when vases or fragments are found, often in different parts of the Mediterranean, it is sometimes possible to name the painter—usually an Athenian, such as the young man decorating a wine cup here. One exquisite *krater*, or wine-mixing bowl, discovered in an Etruscan tomb, was painted in Athens by an exceptionally talented artist called Kleitias (flourished 580–550 BC).

Potter's workshop

Some of the finest vases made in Greece were for export, and these were sent to locations across the Mediterranean. In this scene of a potter's workshop, the goddess Athene, holding a crowning garland as if in acknowledgment of the economic importance of the this trade, approaches a painter who is adding details to a wine cup. To cater for the high overseas demand, apprentice potters are also seen at work here, and a woman is painting the handle of a large vase of the kind used to mix water and wine.

See also
Work,
pages 168–9
Technology,
pages 172–3
Trade,
pages 176–9

Shapes of vases

Greek vases came in a variety of shapes, some basic and others intricate. The Greeks needed prestigious vessels on social occasions for all stages of serving wine, from mixing to pouring, and examples of such vases are shown here. In the top register, at the left end, is an *oinochoe*, which was used as a ladle for pouring wine. In the lower register are two drinking cups known as a rhytons. These were often in the shape of animals' heads, in these examples a dog and a griffin.

Krater from Naucratis

This *krater*, discovered at Naucratis, is painted with an eye-catching design of deer, a panther, and two cockerels on either side of a coiled serpent. The site of Naucratis today shows little indication of the layout of the trading post, but there have been finds of pottery, mainly shards, and some stone statuettes. However, the Greek historian Herodotus visited Naucratis and left valuable information on how it was organized and the buildings it contained. He also mentioned that it had a reputation for being the home of some of the most famous courtesans of his time—after all, it was a busy port.

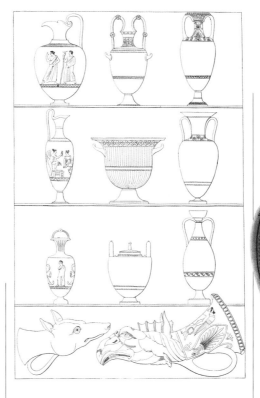

Bowl from Naucratis

Naucratis was a very important Greek *emporion* (trading post) in Egypt. It was allowed a degree of autonomy by the Egyptians, which meant that temples could be built for the worship of Greek gods and goddesses, and it was also granted privileges that gave it the right to collect taxes from all ships sailing into the Nile Delta. The bowl here, decorated with grazing goats, was made on the island of Chios and was dedicated to Aphrodite at her sanctuary at Naucratis by a Greek called Sostratos. Around the rim of the bowl are heads of the goddess.

Panathenaic amphora

One highly sought-after amphora was an impressively large type that featured an image of the warrior goddess Athene. These vases contained olive oil, which was always an important export, but was especially valuable in these jars because the oil came from the Sacred Grove of Athene. However, the vase itself also became a valued collectors' item because it had traditionally been awarded to victors in the Panathenaic Games, held in honor of the goddess's birthday.

Since one winner alone was awarded 140 Panathenaic vases, some jars would certainly have been traded on.

TRADE

Libyan Silphium, Perfume Jars, and Precious Metals

The domestic demand for luxury goods was the impetus for intrepid journeys undertaken by Greek merchants. They traded frankincense with the Egyptians and Phoenicians and brought lapis lazuli from a region now in modern Afghanistan, while ivory could be obtained from the tusks of African or Syrian elephants. Greek traders in the colony of Cyrene in modern Libya thrived, with caravans bringing exotic goods along the trade routes of the Sahara. They also produced silphium from the silphium plant that grew there and exported it. Other portable luxuries, such as costly oils and perfumes, were kept in small, elaborately decorated jars. In earlier times gold was the preserve of rulers and their immediate entourage, but it later became more widely available, and this has meant that today there is a dazzling legacy of gold items from the Greek world.

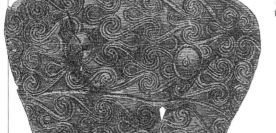

Gold cups from Mycenae

In the Bronze Age gold was often a royal present or diplomatic gift. Later the trade in gold became more widely spread as the Greeks explored diverse sources of precious metals, ranging from Africa to the Black Sea. These gold cups, some exquisitely decorated with spirals or rosettes, were part of Heinrich Schliemann's finds in the shaft graves at Mycenae where, in around 1500 BC, the ruling elite were buried with prestigious grave goods. One such cup has two handles fashioned as birds; it is reminiscent of the goblet described in the *Iliad* as being used by Nestor, King of Pylos.

Bowl of Arcesilaus

In 630 BC the Greeks established a colony at Cyrene in eastern Libya. A plant unique to that region was silphium, a wild thistlelike vegetable now extinct. The sap of silphium was thought to possess medicinal properties, and its root could be pickled to eat. The merchants of Cyrene exported it throughout the Mediterranean, and it became so vital a part of the economy that the plant was depicted on its coins. Here, King Arcesilaus of Cyrene, seated on a ship, supervises the weighing of silphium on a huge pair of scales.

See also
Trade,
pages 174–5
Trade,
pages 178–9

Gold diadem

The purpose of acquiring such luxury materials as gold, ivory, or lapis lazuli—often carried vast distances along arduous trade routes—was to raise the status of the elite ruling families, enabling them to wear jewelry or costumes that clearly set them apart from less wealthy citizens. This gold diadem, decorated in repoussé, was found on a woman at Mycenae in a grave with other gold ornaments that were originally attached to long-perished textiles.

Animal-headed jars

Exotic perfumes and expensive oils, often obtained from the Levant, were transported in small jars, such as this one, with the lion's head, made in Corinth in around 640 BC. This kind of oil bottle was called a *lekythos* or an *aryballos* and was shaped so that its neck restricted the flow of the precious oil to a thin stream. Many *lekythoi* were dedicated as gifts in tombs. On this jar, one of the finest to survive, there are three registers showing hoplites in battle, a horse race, and a hare hunt. The pitcher with the head of a griffin was probably made on the island of Paros in the Cyclades, but was then traded on to the island of Aegina near Athens. It shows consummate skill in its decoration, with a horse and a lion on the back of a stag above guilloche and meander patterns.

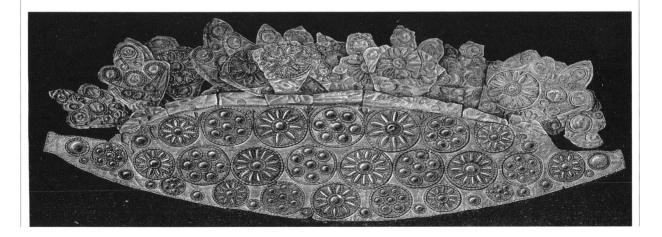

TRADE

Money and Measures

Greek trading practices are well documented. There was a need for precision in purchasing goods and commodities, and formal means for establishing measures were developed. One system consisted of a measuring table set up in the market with hollowed-out bowls of officially sanctioned units.

One theory concerning the origin of coinage was that it may first have been produced to pay mercenaries with portable tokens of an intrinsic monetary value. Lydia in Asia Minor is credited with minting the first coin, but the enterprising Greeks adopted the system, and coins became the medium of commerce. Mints sprang up across the Greek world, producing coins that portrayed emblems or legends proclaiming the identity of the issuing city.

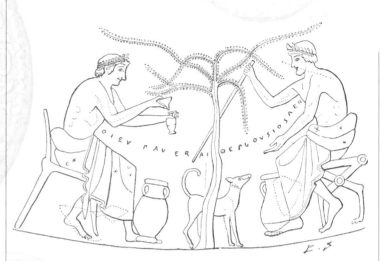

Measuring olive oil

For trading purposes, exact measurements were necessary. This scene shows a man meticulously pouring olive oil scooped from a large amphora into a small pitcher. The text on this vase has the man hoping Zeus will make him rich, and his companion opposite observing that a full measure has been poured.

Weighing goods

Here heavy sacks are being weighed so that their value can be ascertained. It seems one has already been assigned a value, and now the other sacks are being weighed against it. Before coinage was introduced into the Greek world, goods would be put on scales against an accepted standard weight; in the Bronze Age these might be cylinders of stone or metal marked with circles to indicate the denomination, although some were shaped like a bull's head. In the Classical Period weights were normally made of lead.

Measuring bowls

This marble table found at Gythion, which was the port for Sparta, has official measures of capacity hollowed in its top surface. The large hollow in the center is marked around its rim as a *chous*, a unit of liquid measurement, twelve of which equaled the contents of a large amphora.

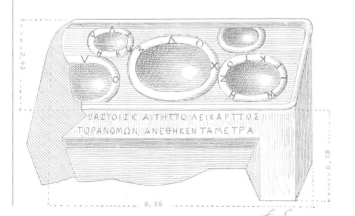

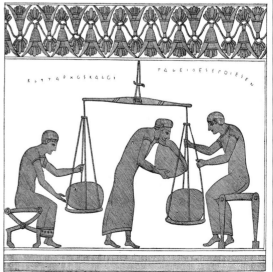

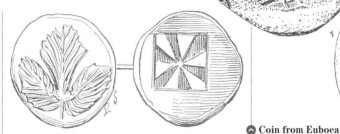

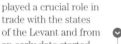

Coin from Euboea

The island of Euboea played a crucial role in trade with the states of the Levant and from an early date started producing coins to facilitate commerce. The first metals used for this were gold and silver and an alloy of the two called electrum. This coin has the image of a cockerel on one side backed with a cow licking its calf.

Coin from Cyprus

Cyprus lies on the trade routes between Greece and Asia Minor and the Near East. It was believed to have been the birthplace of Aphrodite, and on this coin there is a representation of the Temple of Aphrodite at Paphos—a welcome source for scholars because the monument was destroyed in antiquity. Aphrodite's sacred bird, the dove, is shown in the foreground.

Coin stamp

Coins were minted in numerous Greek cities, and each displayed its own emblem on its coinage. Coins were made by stamping the metal blank of the required weight between two die stamps, such as those pictured here.

Coins from Greek Sicily

The Greek colonies in Sicily were prosperous mercantile communities, and they issued a variety of coins, such as the ones shown here. The parsley-leaf design associates the silver coin with the town of Selinous; the human-headed bull personifies the river near the town of Gela; and an impressive coin with the legend "Akragas," modern Agrigento, displays motifs of eagles tearing at the body of a hare backed with the founding hero of the city. In the 5th century BC the Greeks in southern Italy and Sicily were also the first to make coins in bronze.

See also

Trade,
pages 174–7

LEISURE

Banqueting and Music

The Greek love of wine-fueled social occasions meant banquets and drinking parties were a choice topic for vase painters. Lavish banquets thrown by wealthy citizens would mean hiring musicians and dancers to entertain the guests. However, married women took no part in this revelry, but probably enjoyed music and dancing in their own private spaces of the house. The celebrations for the men were held in the *andron*, which was equipped with couches, tables, and large wine mixers and a supply of painted cups. The pottery itself might be decorated with scenes of partying, sometimes showing outrageously explicit behavior by the guests. The symposium was a particularly popular event where the drinking might accompany elevated conversation between the guests, but also with the valued and educated courtesans who were an accepted part of high society.

Couple on a couch
The man holding a rhyton reclines sensuously on decorated cushions. However, the woman opposite is not his wife because respectable married Athenian women would never be portrayed in a partying context. She is a *hetaira*, or high-class courtesan. Hetairas were trained to be socially accomplished and exciting company at banquets.

See also
Society,
pages 142–3
Leisure,
pages 182–5

Drinking vessels
Three of the men reclining on couches at this party hold up empty pottery wine cups of the type known as a *kylix*. One man holds a rhyton with the terminal shaped like an eagle's head. The presence of Eros might indicate that the wine drinking is a prelude to sexual activity.

At the banquet
Here a feast is well under way. Fruit lies on a table as courtesans—one playing the pipes—entertain the banqueters. Courtesans could become wealthy through gifts from their male lovers. One *hetaira*, Aspasia, who came to Athens from the Ionian city of Miletus, mixed with the political elite, becoming the mistress of the Greek leader Pericles.

Music

Music was integral to Greek social occasions. This man is probably on his way to a party where he has been hired to perform. With his lyre slung across a pole, he walks along playing the *aulos*, commonly translated as a flute, but which specialists insist had a reed mouthpiece, thus making it more like a modern oboe.

Symposium

An integral part of social life in ancient Greece was the symposium, a drinking party held in the men's quarters of the house. Prayers to the gods were said at the beginning and end of the event. Banqueters reclined on couches covered with cushions, talking and listening to musicians and singers and then, as shown here, engaging in sexual activities.

Men and women

Here a *hetaira* stands on a stool to kiss and embrace one of the young revelers. Men also had other chances for sexual encounters with street prostitutes and household slaves. The bearded man may well have taken the youth leaning on him as his lover, a relationship that would not have been a problem in Greek society.

Woman playing a lyre

This woman holds a *kythara*, an elaborate box lyre that was the instrument of choice for formal musical recitals. It had a wooden sound box and the strings were made of gut or sinew. Unlike this example, most had seven or more strings, which were either plucked with the fingers or with a plectrum.

Musical instruments

Here revelers processing at night with the aid of torches include a female musician playing the *aulos* and a man thumping a tambourine. The tambourine provided rhythm and was used to raise the atmosphere to feverish intensity during celebrations in honor of the god Dionysus.

Lyric Poetry and Theater

Lyric poetry was one of the refinements of
leisure time, and there are surviving poems,
often fragmentary, which present diverse
reflections on life, ranging from the
perilous existence of a mercenary soldier
and political concepts to fables and the
torments of desire. The lyric poets lived
mainly in the 6th century BC, both on the
mainland and on the eastern islands. In the
following century cultural life in Greece,
particularly in Athens, was exceptionally
vibrant, especially the development of
drama, both tragedy and comedy, which
was performed in the awe-inspiring
Theater of Dionysus.

Sappho and Alcaeus

Reading and listening to lyric poetry was part of
cultural life in the Greek world. Some of the surviving
poems are intense and poignant love songs that
would have been accompanied by sweeps of the lyre.
Greatly admired was Sappho (between *c.* 630 and
612–*c.* 570 BC), shown here, who lived on the island
of Lesbos and addressed her poems about the pangs
of love and heartbreak to her circle of female friends.
Opposite is another noted lyric poet of Lesbos called
Alcaeus (*c.* 620–6th century BC), an aristocrat who
expressed his political views in verse.

Theater relief with masks

One of the lasting
legacies of Athenian
culture is the rich
corpus of tragedies and
comedies that survive,
although the majority
have been lost. Drama
evolved from sung
hymns performed in
honor of the god
Dionysus and during
which the participants
wore masks. These
grotesque, garlanded
masks—which represent
Silenus, an aging satyr
prominent in processions
of Dionysos—were
carved in marble.

Seat at the Theater of Dionysus

There was an important annual festival
held in the Theater of Dionysus beneath
the Acropolis in Athens, at which the most
eminent writers of tragedies competed for a
prize. This marble seat is in a prime position
in the theater, and it has fine carvings of vine
tendrils and winged lions. As the inscription
informs us, it was the seat reserved for
Eleuthereos, priest of Dionysus.

At the theater
This is an unusual scene, showing three women and a man in a theater or perhaps in an *odeion*, a smaller venue for recitals and concerts. The sexes would not normally mix at theatrical events, so perhaps these are visitors. The stylized column surmounted by an image of a temple might be part of the stage scenery.

Comedy scene on vase
On this *krater* the actors are labeled with the names of their characters, including the centaur Cheiron. Comedies were performed at the City Dionysia, an annual festival in honor of Dionysus. The best-known surviving examples are the plays of Aristophanes, full of biting satire and sexual innuendo. Later plays featured hilarious but believable situations and human foibles.

Comedy scene
Comic actors wore hilarious or grotesque masks, as in this scene. The artist has also given a good idea of the stage building and entrance door. Their costumes are padded to exaggerate their pot bellies, and a standard accoutrement was a prominent artificial phallus attached to a belt. The story for this episode is not known, but it seems to involve an old man with his stick entrapped by two youths, a scenario that fits perfectly into the kinds of plots found in New Comedy (*c.* 350–*c.* 320 BC) texts.

See also
Leisure,
pages 180–1
Leisure,
pages 184–5

Tragedies
The works of Homer and other early Greek epics were ideal sources upon which tragedians could draw for their plays. Aeschylus wrote a trilogy for the annual festival centered on the story of Agamemnon. This scene represents the murder of Agamemnon, who has recently returned from Troy, by his wife Clytemnestra. The vase painter is able to show the killing, but dramatists conjured up in brilliant verses the horror of events such as this because the action always took place offstage.

LEISURE

Games

The Greeks admired athletic prowess, and most cities had their own games, such as the Panathenaic Games in Athens. The most famous, at Olympia, were the earliest all-Greek games to be instituted, in 776 BC. The events included running, jumping, wrestling, boxing, discus and javelin throwing, and prestigious equestrian competitions. The *pankration* was a particularly brutal combination of boxing and wrestling, with only biting and eye-gouging prohibited. Because of the cost of stabling, chariot racing and horse riding were extremely expensive activities, but the events were supported financially by powerful politicians and kings. In equestrian contests the victory honors went to the owners, not the riders.

Athlete throwing javelin
What is known of the techniques of javelin throwing is borne out by the decoration on this vase. The wooden javelin was wrapped in the middle by a leather thong known as an *ankyle,* with a loop at the end through which the athlete put two fingers, keeping it taut until the throw.

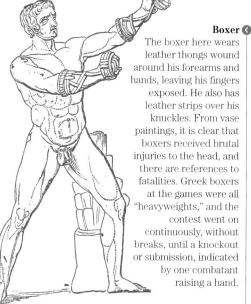

Boxer
The boxer here wears leather thongs wound around his forearms and hands, leaving his fingers exposed. He also has leather strips over his knuckles. From vase paintings, it is clear that boxers received brutal injuries to the head, and there are references to fatalities. Greek boxers at the games were all "heavyweights," and the contest went on continuously, without breaks, until a knockout or submission, indicated by one combatant raising a hand.

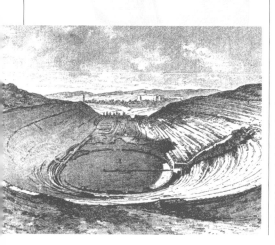

Athenian stadium
Ancient Greek athletes had opportunities to participate in a circuit of games that took them to Olympia, Delphi, Corinth, and Nemea. In Athens the Panathenaic Games were held to celebrate the birthday of the goddess Athene. The stadium was originally built southeast of the city across the river Ilissus, which required a huge landscaping operation in a ravine between two hills. It was renovated with marble by the great benefactor Herodes Atticus (*c.* AD 101–70) in the 2nd century AD and took its final form in 1896 for the first modern Olympics.

Statue of a discus thrower
An event unique to the Greek games was discus throwing, as seen in this Roman statue after an original by the sculptor Myron (flourished 480–440 BC). The discus was made of stone or bronze, and the average weight was just over 4½ lb (2 kg). It is still a matter of debate as to whether the athlete threw the discus with just a slight twist of his body or made a full spin.

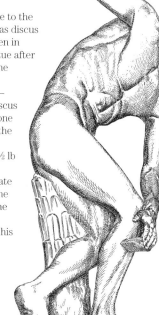

⟩ Wrestling

Greeks regularly practiced wrestling in an open courtyard with surrounding rooms known as a *palaistra*. The wrestling contest at the games focused on using technical skill to throw an opponent off balance so that his back or hip touched the ground—one of the wrestlers in this sculpture is trying to avoid it happening. Three pin downs, and the match was over.

⟩ Chariot racing and horse riding

Both chariot racing and horse-riding figure in all the major games. Chariots could be two-horse vehicles, called the *synoris*, or a four-horse version, the *tethrippon*. The courses were between 6–8 miles (10–13 km) long. For a brief period mule-cart racing, popular among Greeks from the western Mediterranean, was in vogue. There was also an event for bareback riding called the *keles*, which involved just one circuit of the racetrack.

⌄ Chariot rider with Nike

The winged image of Nike, goddess of victory, is crowning the winner of the two-horse chariot event as he passes the Ionic column marking the finishing post. Charioteers were normally depicted wearing white robes, in contrast to the other contestants at the games, who competed naked.

⌃ Victor and ribbon

This winner in an equestrian event receives a ribbon symbolizing victory from a richly attired woman. It is not now known for sure whether women could attend the Olympic Games, but, if so, given the logistics of travel from other states, any women spectators would be likely to be local.

See also
Leisure,
pages 180–3

ARCHITECTURE

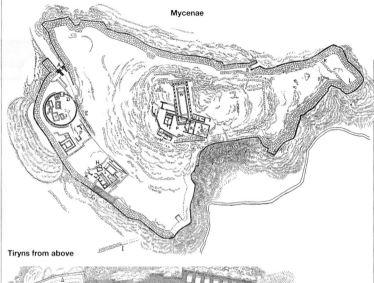

Mycenae

Athens, Citadels, and Orders

In contrast to the relatively low-key defenses of palaces on Minoan Crete, the citadels of Bronze Age Greece were heavily fortified. The walls were constructed with massive stone blocks, in a style dubbed Cyclopaean masonry, because it was believed that only the Cyclops would have been strong enough to move them.

Over time architectural techniques advanced, and by the end of the 7th century BC the Ionic and Doric orders were being used extensively. The Classical Period saw Athenian architects grappling with problems of combining practicalities with aesthetics, because there was a huge drive to make the monuments of the city the envy of the rest of Greece.

Archaeologists have discovered evidence that Greek monuments were lavishly painted, creating a different architectural impression from the austere marble we see today.

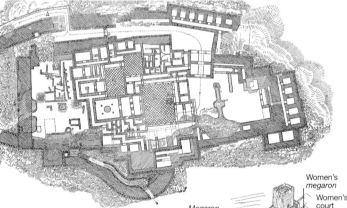

Tiryns from above

See also
Government,
pages 140–1
Architecture,
pages 188–91

◗ **Citadel of Tiryns**
The architectural hallmark of Mycenaean Greece is the fortified citadel. Mycenae itself is the grandest, but the citadel of Tiryns boasts some intricate defensive features. Its proximity to the sea was the probable reason that it was the first of the Mycenaean palaces to be heavily fortified. The limestone walls seen today date from the third building phase in the 13th century BC. One of the great feats of military architecture here is the construction of corbeled galleries within the exceptionally wide walls. On top of the citadel, beyond a number of gateways and courtyards, was the *megaron*, a large hall where the royal throne rested on a raised platform.

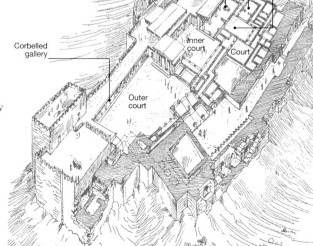

Tiryns from the south

Women's *megaron*

Women's court

Megaron

Corbelled gallery

Inner court

Court

Outer court

Column capitals

The three main architectural orders of columns in Classical monuments are shown here. The Doric column (A), developed from prototypes in wood, has a very solid appearance. At the top, its fluted shaft widens into the circular column capital. The Ionic column (B) is more graceful and slender and terminates at its capital in a coils of a double spiral known as volutes. In the case of the later Corinthian column (C), the shaft ends in an ornate cluster of acanthus leaves.

The Acropolis at Athens

The city of Athens is dominated by the Acropolis, which was enriched architecturally under the leadership of Pericles. In the left foreground is the spectacular Hephaesteum, which is the best preserved temple in Greece today. Dedicated to Hephaestus, god of the forge, the temple is a fine example of architecture using the Doric order. Its reliefs above the columns include scenes from the life of the Athenian hero Theseus— hence the monument is popularly, but incorrectly, called the Theseion. The boundary of the city is marked by the walls and gateway at the bottom of the picture.

Temple Styles

The huge number of temples throughout the Greek mainland and islands bears witness to the pride that the various states took in honoring both local and Olympian deities. The citizens of the island of Aegina, for example, accommodated the major cults of Apollo and Athene, but still found room for their minor goddess Aphaia.
In Athens the Temple of Hephaestus proclaimed, in a magnificent building, the importance of this god of forges and metalworkers. The richness of Greek temple architecture is complemented by the varied repertoire of the sculptors, who carved monumental statues to be set high up in the pediments. In Doric architecture the reliefs of the metopes, which lie below the pediment, would commemorate events in the lives of heroes or mythical battles. In Ionic buildings there would be frieze in the same position.

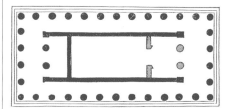

Hephaesteum
The Hephaesteum is the marble temple built to the west of the Athenian Agora. It is a fine example of a Doric temple, with six columns across the front and thirteen along the sides. Hephaestus, the blacksmith god, was worshipped in this temple together with Athene and their cult statues stood inside. Above the capitals of the columns are, at intervals, three vertical bars called triglyphs, which divide the sculptured metopes, with their themes of the Labors of Heracles and Theseus.

Temple of Aphaea on Aegina
In its present state the Temple of Aphaea—later shared with Athene—on the island of Aegina is remarkably well preserved. However, the pediment sculptures and metopes are no longer in situ, having been lost, destroyed, or removed to museums abroad. The eastern pediment is above the temple entrance, and it was decorated with sculptures depicting the sack of Troy, over which Athene is shown presiding.

See also
Architecture,
pages 186–7
Architecture,
pages 190–1

Caryatid ◀
The six statues supporting the roof of the south porch of the Erechtheum are caryatids—sculpted female figures used in place of columns. Although it is not known for sure who or what they represent, one suggestion is that they were somehow concerned with the cult of the mythical Athenian king Cecrops. Because of pollution damage to the marble, all the original statues at the Erechtheum have been replaced by casts.

Erechtheum doorway

Erechtheum decoration

Ionic Temple of Athene Nike

Plan of Erechtheum Temple

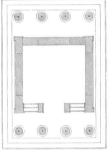

Plan of Temple of Athene Nike

Erechtheum Temple

Ionic temples ◀
In Athens, both the temple of Athene Nike and the Erechtheum were built in the Ionic style. The Erechtheum is a complex and unusual temple dedicated to a number of deities, principally Athene as protector of the city of Athens, but also to the god Poseidon and to Erechtheus, one of the mythical kings of Athens. The pavement of the Erechtheum north porch marks where Poseidon struck the ground with his trident during his contest with Athene over the right to become protector of Athens.

ARCHITECTURE

Sculpture

The Greeks were the most influential sculptors of the ancient world. Their art was brought west by the Romans, and most of the sculptors of the Roman era whose names we know were Greek. Hellenistic sculpture was also taken east by Alexander the Great, where it influenced depictions of the Buddha from India to Japan. Our notion of Greek sculpture is informed by the white marble figures that fill our museums, but originally these were brightly painted, and marble was just one of the materials used. Cult statues were carved from wood and made from chryselephantine (gold and ivory), and temple sanctuaries were also filled with bronzes. Sculptors also cast bronze in sections to make huge statues, famously the 112-ft (34-m) high Colossus of Rhodes. Only a few Greek bronze statues have survived, however, mostly from shipwrecks.

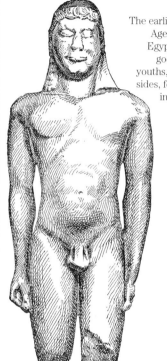

Egyptian influence
The earliest surviving Greek statues, from the Archaic Age (*c.* 600–480 BC), were strongly influenced by Egyptian freestanding sculptures of pharaohs and gods. Like the Egyptian works, Greek statues of youths, *korai*, had their arms firmly pressed to their sides, for ease of carving, and their left leg advanced in front of the right. Unlike Egyptian pharaohs, the youths were depicted naked.

Parthenon marbles
The most famous Greek sculptor of the 5th century BC was the Athenian Phidias (*c.* 490–432 BC), who was responsible for the sculptural decoration of the Parthenon. These are the goddesses Demeter and Kore from the temple's east pediment, their bodies shaped to fit the triangular space. Phidias was regarded as the greatest interpreter of gods, shown here in serene poses with flowing drapery.

Chryselephantine Athene
This is a marble copy, made for tourists, of Pheidias' 39-ft (12-m) statue of Athene, which stood in the Parthenon. The original was of chryselephantine, with the goddess's white skin made from hundreds of tiny strips of elephant ivory imported from Egypt, while her dress comprised 220 lb (100 kg) of gold, and the statue cost more the whole Parthenon. Only a few fragments of chryselephantine statues survive, the white skin now turned black.

Centaur metope

No Greek temple had more sculptural decoration than the Parthenon. Apart from the pediment statues and a long frieze depicting a religious procession, Phidias created ninety-two relief panels, called metopes, that lined the temple's architrave. These showed scenes of single combat in which gods fought giants and Greek heroes fought foreign enemies—Trojans, Amazons, and centaurs. These reminded the Greeks of their victory over the barbarian Persians.

Farnese Heracles

The Farnese Heracles is a marble copy of a lost Greek bronze. It was discovered in AD 1450 in the Baths of Caracalla in Rome. The original was made by Lysippus of Sicyon (active *c*. 370–315 BC) or one of his circle. Lysippus was Alexander the Great's favorite sculptor and a founder of the new Hellenistic style, which depicted the body in striking and unusual poses. Here the sculptor chose to depict the mythical strongman as exhausted, following his Labors.

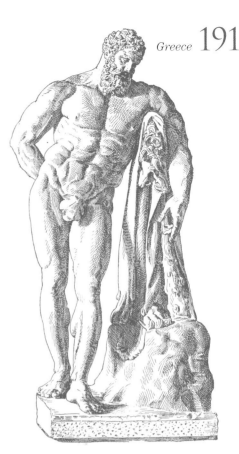

Winged victory of Sampthrace

This winged victory goddess, Nike, is another Hellenistic sculpture, dating from the 2nd century BC. It was discovered on Samothrace in 1863 by Charles Champoiseau, the French consul and amateur archaeologist, and now stands in the Louvre, Paris. Since its discovery it has been admired for its beautiful rendering of the draped garments and the sense of movement created by the sculptor.

Drunken satyr

The Hellenistic taste for striking poses is clearly shown in the Barberini Faun, also called the Drunken Satyr, a marble work by an unknown sculptor of the late 3rd or early 2nd century BC. It depicts a sprawling, naked satyr and places the focus on the figure's genitals. The statue was discovered in the 1620s in Hadrian's Mausoleum in Rome.

See also
Religion,
pages 164–5
Architecture,
pages 186–9

FOOD

Hunting Game and Preparing Food

Early Greek society set great store by the bravery of hunters and their hounds. In a fresco from the Bronze Age citadel of Tiryns, hunting dogs are shown ferociously attacking a wild boar whose tusks could inflict crippling injuries or death. From vases archaeologists understand many facets of Greek food preparation, and there is also the evidence from discarded household kitchenware, including cooking pots, pottery ovens, and storage jars. The diet was simple and was based on cereals, but there were also vegetables and legumes ,such as lentils and chickpeas. To brighten up the staple fare, accompanying dishes might include cheese and pickled fish.

⌃ Hunters and hunting dog with wild boar
Wild boar are exceptionally dangerous animals and required a great deal of bravery and expertise to corner and kill. There is a vivid account in Homer's *Odyssey* where Odysseus rushes a boar in a dense thicket, but is gouged by its tusk before spearing it in its shoulder. Here three hunters carry a dead boar home, where their reward will be to share in the meat roasted on a spit. Dogs were essential in tracking the boar for the hunters to pursue.

⌃ Hunter with his kill
Myths and epics have many references to heroes as hunters, displaying courage against lethally dangerous wild animals. In reality, hunting was a way to supplement a dependable but tedious diet. The hunter shown here belongs to the Heroic Age, his status proclaimed by his richly decorated tunic. The hunter's kill hanging from the pole includes wild boar and deer.

⌃ Bringing home the kill
This somewhat strange scene shows a young hunter dragging a bleeding boar into the house, while a woman with a box of perfume phials looks admiringly at him. He also holds some fruit in a bowl. Whatever the story, it is clear the couple are going to dine well.

⌄ Butchering an ox

Here an ox is butchered, destined for the tables of those in the higher echelons of society. Even for such elevated people, however, this would only be during religious festivals or special occasions. The domestic context of the scene is emphasized by the *krater* and pouring jug.

See also
Work,
pages 166–7
Leisure,
pages 180–1

Women grinding corn ⌃

Here two fairly well-dressed women are grinding corn with large pestles in a coarse pottery mortar. Grain provided the staple diet in ancient Greece, and women would make a porridge or coarse bread from barley and oats. High-quality wheat was a luxury, but when available it could be ground to make a loaf that, with the addition of honey or cheese, would be nutritious.

Satyr carrying a krater ⌃

This satyr carries a large *krater*. Wine was available at all levels of Greek society, but the quality of the vintage would vary considerably between the cups served to rich banqueters and the jars drank by less well-off citizens.

Woman with honeycomb ⌃

Honey was the principal sweetener used in ancient Greece, and bees were kept in terra-cotta hives. The woman here carries a honeycomb on a dish, which might be used to flavor cakes or to be eaten with fruit, such as figs, grapes, or apples.

COSTUME

Men's Dress

Unlike modern clothing, Greek dress was not tailored to fit the body. Instead, it was made of rectangles of wool or linen that were worn in various ways. For men, the simplest garment was the tunic, made from two rectangles of cloth. This came in two varieties: the *exomis*, fastened only on the left shoulder, which was worn by manual workers and slaves; and the *chiton*, fastened on both shoulders, which anyone might wear. Middle- and upper-class men also wore a large mantle called a *himation*, which might be wrapped in various ways around the body and could be worn on top of the tunic or over the naked body. It was the Greek belief that close-fitting garments, such as pants and shirts with sleeves, were fit only for barbarians.

Chiton

This man, an Athenian soldier, is wearing a *chiton*. It was formed by two rectangles of linen cloth, fastened at the shoulders with the sides sewn together. It was often worn with a belt around the waist. The image comes from an Athenian urn depicting a soldier taking leave of his wife and child.

See also
Work,
pages 168–9
Costume,
pages 198–9

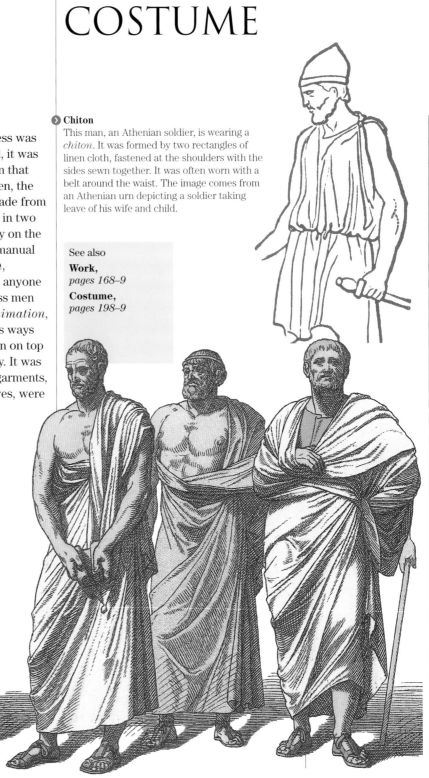

Himation

The Greek *himation* measured approximately 9 by 6 ft (2.8 by 1.75 m). It resembled a toga, although, unlike the Roman garment, it was rectangular rather than semicircular and could be worn in many different ways. It might cover the left shoulder or completely cover both arms. It was usually made of unbleached or white wool, although a darker himation was worn for mourning. The ability to move gracefully while wearing the garment was seen as a sign of good breeding.

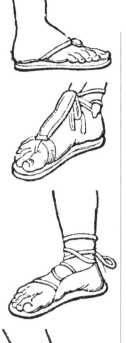

Hats

The *petasos*, shown at the bottom, was just one of several types of hat worn by Greek men. At the top there is a round cap worn by a metalworker in a vase painting. In the *Odyssey*, Homer describes a similar hat made of goatskin, which is worn by an elderly peasant. The tall hat in the center, called a *pilos*, was popular with sailors and merchants. In vase paintings Odysseus is often shown wearing one of these.

Traveling clothes

The *chlamys* was a woollen cloak, sometimes with a decorative stripe along its bottom edge, worn by travelers, especially horsemen and heralds, and often paired with a wide hat called a *petasos*. It is thought to have originated in Thessaly, an area famed for its horsemen. Hermes, the messenger of the gods, is frequently shown in art wearing the chlamys and *petasos*.

Party clothes

This vase painting shows a Greek symposium, or drinking party. The male guests wear garlands of flowers in their hair and have their himations informally dropped to waist level. The men are clean shaven, evidence that this painting is from the Hellenistic Period.

Footwear

Greeks wore a variety of leather sandals and also leather or felt boots for riding. This selection of footwear comes from statues. Vase paintings often show both men and women barefoot, although it is unclear how far this was a reflection of actual custom or an artistic convention. Used to exercising naked, Greek men would certainly have toughened the soles of their feet.

COSTUME

Women's Dress

There were two basic styles of Greek women's dress: Doric, from the mainland, and Ionic, from Ionia. As with the architectural orders, Doric dress was simpler than Ionic. Its earliest form was the Doric *peplos*, a close-fitting sleeveless woollen dress with an overfold, fastened at the shoulders. In the 6th century BC the lighter Ionic chiton, which was made of linen and had wide sleeves and pleats, came into fashion. In the early 5th century BC there was a revival of the Doric sleeveless dress, although the garment was now made of linen and called a chiton rather than a *peplos*. For outdoor wear women, like men, covered themselves in a himation, a warm woollen mantle. Traces of paint on statues suggest that women's clothes were often colorful and richly embroidered.

Ionic chiton
The Ionic chiton was wider than the Doric *peplos*, and its extra width was used to form sleeves, with the top edges sewn together. Unlike the woollen *peplos*, it was made of light linen, which was usually pleated and hung close to the body. It is not surprising that this fashion spread, for it was more flattering and comfortable to wear than the earlier Doric style.

Doric dress
Doric clothing was formed by a wide rectangle of woollen cloth, which was substantially taller than the woman who wore it. The top edge was folded over until it reached the waist, and the whole garment was then wrapped around the body and fastened at the shoulders with brooches. The simplest way to recognize Doric dress is by its overfold and absence of sleeves.

Doric chiton
The two seated women shown here gazing into mirrors are wearing the linen Doric chiton, which came into fashion in the 5th century BC. One theory is that the Doric style was revived as a patriotic statement following the Greek victory over the Persians. The chiton was looser and more comfortable than the earlier *peplos*, which is always shown as a close-fitting garment in vase paintings.

Medea ◁
This vase painting
from southern Italy
depicts Medea,
mythical enchantress
and wife of Jason.
A Greek would instantly
recognize her clothing,
with its tailored sleeves
and unusual headdress,
as that of a barbarian.
Medea came from
Colchis in what is now
Georgia. The richly
decorated clothes
she wears are based on
those worn in Phrygia
in western Anatolia.

Storing clothes ◁
One advantage of clothing made from rectangles
of cloth was that they were easy to fold and store.
This vase painting shows two women wearing Ionic
chitons folding a garment decorated with stars before
placing it in a chest. Other clothes can be seen piled
on a chair or suspended from the wall behind. This is
a scene of daily life in the gynaikonitis, the secluded
women's area of a Greek house.

See also
Work,
pages 168–9
Costume,
pages 194–5
Costume,
pages 198–9

▷ **Women's himations**
When they went
out Greek women
wrapped themselves
in a himation, which
was similar to those
worn by men but
usually more colorful.
These terra-cotta
statuettes, dating from
the late 4th century
BC, show different
ways in which women
wore their himations.
The statuettes are
called Tanagra
figurines, after a site in
Boeotia where many
of them were found.

⌄ **Making clothes**
Apart from childcare, the main occupation of
all Greek women was making textiles, and even
goddesses were believed to spin and weave. In this
vase painting a woman in an Ionic chiton winds wool
from a *kalathos* (wool basket) around a distaff prior
to spinning it into thread. She would then weave it
into cloth, using an upright, warp-weighted loom.

COSTUME

Hairstyles and Jewelry

The evidence of vase paintings and statues enables us to trace the changing fashions in Greek hairstyles from the Archaic Age, when both men and women grew long hair, through the Classical Age, when shorter hair came into fashion, down into Hellenistic times, when men began to shave their beards. Greek women wore beautiful and elaborate jewelry, and many exquisite earrings, necklaces and bracelets have been found in tombs. In a fragment from his lost play, *Thesmophoriazusae*, Aristophanes (*c*. 455–386 BC) joked about the variety of ornaments and cosmetics used by women: "A veil, some rouge, two necklaces, some eye paint … earrings, a pendant, more earrings—a lot, pins, necklet, armlet, bangles—It's past man's power to tell you all the things."

Long hair
In the *Iliad* Homer often describes his Greek heroes as the "long-haired Achaeans." The style is depicted in this scene from a vase painting, in which a young man, decorating a helmet, has long hair falling in ringlets over his shoulders. He wears a fillet around his hair.

Long-haired warrior
The conservative Spartans continued the male fashion for long hair. Spartan law giver Lycurgus reputedly said that long hair made a good-looking man appear more handsome and an ugly man fiercer. Before battle Spartan men combed and garlanded their hair with flowers.

Beards
Until the late 4th century BC, all adult Greek men grew beards. Vase paintings reveal that, in the Archaic Age, the beard was long and pointed. This illustration shows a more rounded, shorter beard, which came into fashion during the Classical Age. Beards later went out of fashion because of Alexander the Great, who was clean shaven himself and who ordered his men to follow his example. He said that this prevented enemies from seizing soldiers by their beards in battle.

Ephebe
This short-haired ephebe, a young man in his late teens, is wearing a chlamys and petasus. Ephebes were clean-shaven and did not grow a beard until they reached their twenties. To the Greeks, this was an important stage on the path to adulthood, a time when youths received their military and social training from their elders.

Archaic hair
During early times, Greek women, like men, grew their hair long and wore it over their shoulders. This color illustration is based on an early *kore*, or statue of a maiden. *Korai* served a commemorative function or acted as votives in temples, where they were supposed to serve the deity on behalf of the worshipper.

Hairstyles

In the Classical Age Greek women continued to grow their hair long, but usually wore it gathered together, tied up in a bun, sometimes with short ringlets falling behind or in front of the ears. These drawings show a variety of hairstyles, along with fillets and diadems worn over the hair. Such hairstyles were revived in Europe in the late 18th century.

See also
Costume,
pages 194–7

Earrings

Women wore many types of ear ornament, from simple earrings to elaborate pendants made of gold, silver, and precious stones. Here are three examples found in graves. The two on the left, a pendant in the form of a siren and an earring decorated with the heads of a lion and a snake, were both found in Ithaca. The example on the right comprising a garnet with two pendants shaped like clubs, comes from Thrace.

Gold wreath

This magnificent gold wreath, dating from the 4th century BC, was discovered in a Greek tomb at Armento in southern Italy. It combines intertwined flowers and leaves of narcissus, convolvulus, ivy, roses, and myrtle with winged goddesses at the top. It reflects the increasing use of ostentatious jewelry during the Hellenistic Age.

Jewelry

Wealthy women wore elaborate jewelry, which was often buried with them as grave goods. This section of a gold necklace is decorated with pendants in the form of pine cones and heads. Pinecones—a symbol of fertility—were sacred to Dionysus, who carried a staff called a thyrsos, which was tipped with one.

Brooch pins

The Doric *peplos* was fastened at the shoulders by two brooch pins. Herodotus (*c.* 484–*c.* 425 BC) has a grisly tale about brooch pins. At some unnamed date, Athens was said to have suffered a terrible defeat by the people of Aegina. On his homecoming, the sole survivor was killed by the furious Athenian womenfolk, who stabbed him with their brooch pins. The Athenians were so shocked by this that they ordered their women to stop wearing brooches and adopt the Ionian chiton. The story is likely to be an aetiological myth, invented to explain the change in fashion.

ROME

The last and most influential ancient civilization of the Old World was Rome. By the 1st century BC, the Romans had united all the lands around the Mediterranean in one state. Unlike the Greeks, the Romans welcomed outsiders, and under the Emperor Caracalla (ruled AD 211–217), citizenship was offered to every free inhabitant of the Empire. Many emperors were not even from Italy. The Romans won loyalty by offering a high standard of living to the upper classes in conquered territories. In the 2nd century AD the Greek orator Aelius Aristides summed up the benefits of Roman rule: "The coasts and interiors have been filled with cities …For security it is enough to be a Roman citizen, or rather one of those united under your rule … You have accustomed all areas to a settled and orderly way of life."

The Western Roman Empire fell in the 5th century AD, but its influence is still felt. We use the Roman calendar, with months named after Roman gods (March from Mars) and rulers (August from Augustus). The Romance languages are derived from Latin. English, although Germanic, incorporates thousands of originally Latin words. The Roman alphabet is the most widely used writing system in the world. Political and legal systems of many Western countries—including modern republics such as the United States—are also influenced by Rome. Europeans live in cities founded by the Romans and travel along roads first laid out by them. The world's two billion Christians are followers of a late-Roman religion, and the Pope wears Roman robes and is called the Pontifex Maximus, the title of Rome's chief priest.

TIME LINE
753 BC–AD 476

A murmillo gladiator

753 BC

Traditional date for the founding of Rome by Romulus, son of the war god Mars.

73–71 BC

The gladiator Spartacus leads a great slave rebellion against Rome. After winning several victories, he is defeated in southern Italy.

A dramatic 19th-century rendering of the death of Caesar

510–509 BC

The Romans drive out their last king and establish a republic.

67–62 BC

Gnaeus Pompeius Magnus (Pompey the Great) clears the eastern Mediterranean of pirates. He then defeats King Mithridates of Pontus, makes Syria a Roman province and reorganizes the government of Judaea.

44 BC

Caesar, who has declared himself dictator for life, is assassinated by a group of sixty republican senators, led by Brutus and Cassius.

AD 14–37

After the death of Augustus, his stepson, Tiberius, rules as the second emperor.

C. AD 30

Crucifixion of Jesus Christ in Jerusalem.

343–290 BC

Rome fights and wins three wars against the Samnites of central Italy.

Lictors, bodyguards of the senior magistrates who governed Rome

AD 69–79

Vespasian, final victor in the civil wars, founds the Flavian Dynasty. He begins the construction of the Flavian amphitheater, later known as the Colosseum.

The Colosseum, begun during the reign of Vespasian

AD 193–211

Rule of Septimius Severus, the north African emperor and founder of the Severan Dynasty.

AD 235–84

Troubled period, with civil wars and emperors ruling for short periods. The Empire comes under attack from all sides.

AD 284–305

Diocletian establishes the tetrarchy, splitting the Empire into western and eastern halves, with a senior and junior emperor in each.

AD 324

Constantine wins a civil war against the eastern emperor, Licinius, and reunites the Empire.

AD 330

In the east, Constantine founds a new Christian capital, Constantinople.

AD 376–8

The Visigoths invade the Roman Empire, defeating and killing Emperor Valens at the Battle of Adrianople in AD 378.

AD 391

Emperor Theodosius closes pagan temples and bans sacrifices.

264–41 BC

First Punic War, in which Rome fights Carthage for the control of Sicily. The Romans win the war, conquer Sicily, and become a great naval power.

218–1 BC

Second Punic War, in which the Carthaginian general Hannibal crosses the Alps to invade Italy from the north. He is unable to capture Rome. Romans invade Spain.

146 BC

Rome fights and wins the Third Punic War and also a war against a league of Greek cities. Roman armies sack Carthage and Corinth.

90–88 BC

Social War: Rome's Italian allies revolt, and are defeated but granted Roman citizenship.

58–49 BC

Julius Caesar conquers Gaul and leads two expeditions to Britain, in 55 and 54 BC.

Coins celebrating Octavian's rule and his victory over Egypt

49–48 BC

Julius Caesar marches on Rome, starting a civil war with the Senate, whose champion is Pompey. Caesar defeats Pompey at the Battle of Pharsalus.

42 BC

Mark Antony and Octavian defeat Brutus and Cassius at Philippi and divide the Empire between them, Octavian taking the west and Antony the east.

33–30 BC

A new civil war between Octavian and Antony, ending in the latter's defeat at the Battle of Actium. With Antony's suicide, Octavian is sole ruler of the Empire.

27 BC

Octavian becomes Rome's first emperor, taking the new name Augustus (revered one).

AD 37–41

Rule of the mentally unbalanced Caligula, who demands to be worshipped as a god.

AD 41–54

Reign of Claudius, who organizes the conquest of Britain in AD 43.

AD 54–68

Rule of Nero, the last emperor of the Julio-Claudian Dynasty.

AD 66–70

First Jewish revolt against Roman rule. Destruction of the Temple by Titus.

AD 68

Following a revolt, Nero kills himself, civil war breaks out, and Rome is ruled by four emperors in one year.

Courtyard garden, Pompeii

AD 79

The volcano Vesuvius erupts, burying Pompeii and Herculaneum.

AD 98–117

Rule of Trajan, who conquers Dacia and Mesopotamia, extending the Empire to its greatest size.

AD 117–38

Rule of Hadrian, who gives up some of Trajan's conquests. He constructs new frontier defenses, including Hadrian's Wall across northern Britain. He also builds the magnificent Pantheon temple in Rome, and a huge pleasure villa at Tivoli.

AD 312

Following his victory over Maxentius, Constantine, the first Christian emperor, wins power in the west.

The Pantheon

AD 410

The Visigoths, led by King Alaric, invade Italy and sack Rome.

AD 476

The last western emperor, Romulus Augustus, is overthrown by Odoacer, a Germanic chieftain, who makes himself King of Italy.

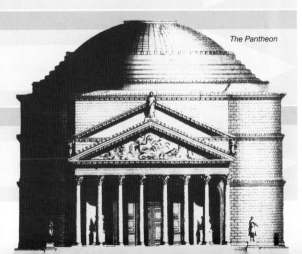

GEOGRAPHY

Ancient Superpower

The Roman Empire reached its greatest extent under Emperor Trajan (ruled AD 98–117), stretching for 2,300 miles (3,700 km) north to south and 2,500 miles (4,000 km) east to west. Within this vast area, people of many races shared a similar way of life, following Roman fashions, using the same coins and worshipping common gods. The Romans believed that it was their destiny to rule other peoples, an attitude summed up by the poet Virgil: "Romans, these are your arts: to bear dominion over the nations, to impose the ways of peace, to spare the conquered and subdue the proud."

Center of the Mediterranean world

Rome occupied a central position in Italy, which was itself in the middle of the Mediterranean. The Romans' geographical position gave them a great strategic advantage in their unification of the peninsula and later conquests. Italy was also much easier to unite than Greece, with its mountainous interior and scattered islands. This map shows the Roman Empire at its height in AD 117.

Celtic tribes

Much of western Europe was home to Celtic tribes, speaking languages related to modern Welsh. The Celts of Gaul, Spain, and much of Britain were conquered by the Romans. Only Ireland and northern Britain remained outside the Empire.

Celtic warrior

THE ROMAN EMPIRE *c.* AD 117

Public provinces
Imperial provinces
Client states

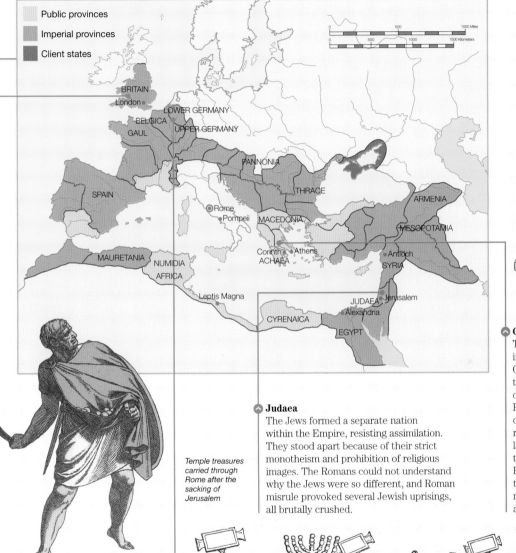

BRITAIN
London
LOWER GERMANY
BELGICA
GAUL
UPPER GERMANY
PANNONIA
SPAIN
THRACE
ARMENIA
Rome
Pompeii
MACEDONIA
MESOPOTAMIA
Corinth Athens
ACHAEA
Antioch
SYRIA
MAURETANIA
NUMIDIA
AFRICA
Leptis Magna
JUDAEA Jerusalem
Alexandria
CYRENAICA
EGYPT

*Venus, goddess
of love*

Greeks
The Romans had much in common with the Greeks, worshipping the same gods under different names. The Romans admired Greek culture, and Greek remained the common language spoken in the eastern half of the Empire. Like the Greeks, the Romans referred to most foreign peoples as "barbarians."

Judaea
The Jews formed a separate nation within the Empire, resisting assimilation. They stood apart because of their strict monotheism and prohibition of religious images. The Romans could not understand why the Jews were so different, and Roman misrule provoked several Jewish uprisings, all brutally crushed.

*Temple treasures
carried through
Rome after the
sacking of
Jerusalem*

*A slinger, specialist
auxiliary soldier*

The Rhine and Danube frontiers
Although the Romans made several attempts to conquer the Germanic tribes, their conquests beyond the Rhine and the Danube were limited to Upper Germany and Dacia. These great rivers provided easily defended frontiers for the Empire in central Europe.

GOVERNMENT

Republic

Until the end of the 6th century BC, Rome was ruled by kings, but in 510 BC the Romans drove out their last king and in 509 BC established a republic. Rome was now governed by annually elected magistrates, the most important being the two consuls, who were joint heads of state. They governed with the advice of the Senate, an assembly of serving and ex-magistrates, and in theory the Senate's role was to advise the magistrates. However, in practice, such was the prestige of its members, who served for life, that Rome was essentially an oligarchy. Magistrates were unpaid, and only the richest Romans could afford to stand for office. The Senate drew its members from a small number of wealthy families. However, the people elected all magistrates, voted on all laws, and had tribunes of the people to champion them.

Cursus honorum
For Rome's nobility, public service followed a career path called the *cursus honorum* (path of honors), which provided wide experience in law and military matters. At eighteen, aspiring politicians joined the army, where they served for several years. After this they became lawyers, for skill at public speaking and an understanding of the law was essential for a public career.

See also
Government,
pages 208–11

> **Magistrates**
At the age of thirty a Roman could stand for his first magistracy, as one of the twenty quaestors who over-saw state finances. Then there was the option to stand for the aedileship. There were four aediles, who oversaw markets, religious festivals, and public order. Aediles were also responsible for public entertainment, and staging lavish games was an excellent way to win votes for the next magistracy, the praetorship.

Senior magistrates
At the age of forty a Roman was eligible to become a praetor, one of up to eight (Republic) to twelve (Empire) judges. At forty-three he could stand for the consulship. In a crisis the Senate might also appoint a dictator, who had absolute power, for a limited period. These senior magistrates originally had the power to whip and execute citizens. Their *imperium* (power) was symbolized by the *fasces*, the bundle of rods and axes carried by their attendants, called lictors.

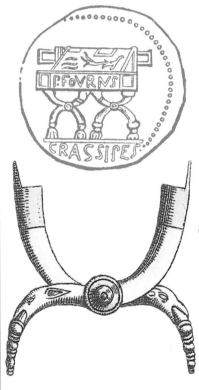

Lictor

The lictors were the bodyguards and attendants of senior magistrates, and they accompanied them wherever they went, clearing a path through crowded streets, and standing beside them when they made speeches. While a praetor had six lictors, a consul had twelve and a dictator twenty-four.

Curule chair

Magistrates were entitled to sit on a folding stool made of, or inlaid with, ivory, called a curule chair, so the chair became a symbol of political power. The silver denarius above was minted in 84 BC by the aedile Publius Furius Crassipes, whose name appears beside two curule chairs.

Duumvir

Every Roman town had its own annually elected magistrates. The most important were the duumvirs, literally "two men," responsible for the administration of justice. There were also two aediles overseeing public works and markets. Below is an example of election graffiti from a wall in Pompeii. It declares that "the fruit-sellers unanimously, together with Helvius Vestalis, ask your vote for M. Holconius Priscus for duumvir."

M HOLCONIVM
PRISCVM II VIR I D POMARI UNIVERSI
CVM HELVIO VESTALE ROG

GOVERNMENT

Republic to Empire

In the 1st century BC, the republican system broke down as a series of ambitious generals used their armies to seek power more lasting than the consulship. In 49 BC, Julius Caesar (100–44 BC), conqueror of Gaul, quarreled with Gnaeus Pompey (106–48 BC), who dominated the Senate. When Pompey ordered him to surrender his command and return to Rome, Caesar instead invaded Italy. After winning a crushing victory over Pompey, in 44 BC, Caesar declared himself dictator for life, becoming king in all but name. A month later he was assassinated by a group of sixty senators who hoped to restore the republic. Caesar's death did not save the republic, however, but led to more years of civil war. The final victor was Caesar's great-nephew and adopted heir Octavian (63–14 BC), who became Rome's first emperor, Augustus.

Octavian

Caesar's murder was avenged by Octavian and Mark Antony, who defeated Brutus and Cassius in 42 BC at Philippi in Macedonia. They then divided the Empire between them. However, they, too, argued and went to war. This coin celebrates Octavian's victory over Antony and his mistress, Queen Cleopatra of Egypt, at the Battle of Actium in 31 BC.

Pax Augusta

The final victory of Octavian, renamed Augustus (the revered one), brought peace after years of civil war. In 27 BC he announced he was restoring the republic and giving power back to the Senate and people. He claimed he was only the *princeps* (first citizen), but really his power was total, because he controlled the armies and chose the senators. This coin celebrates the Pax Augusta (peace of Augustus).

From Augustus to Tiberius

Augustus learned from Caesar's mistakes and treated the Senate with respect. Consuls continued to be elected, although the position now held prestige rather than real power. Augustus governed Rome for more than forty years, and the Romans grew accustomed to the idea of rule by one man. On his death in AD 14 he was succeeded by his stepson Tiberius (43 BC–AD 37), who had him deified, just as Caesar had been. This coin, issued by Tiberius, shows both Augustus and his wife Livia as divine.

The ides of March

Caesar deeply offended republican sensibilities by his autocratic behavior and insulting treatment of the Senate. On the ides, or fifteenth day, of March 44 BC, sixty senators, led by Brutus and Cassius, stabbed him to death in the Theater of Pompey. He fell dead at the foot of the statue of his old rival.

Recovery of Armenia

Augustus used his coins as miniature newspapers. While one side carried his portrait, the reverse celebrated an achievement. Coin texts include "He restored the laws and rights of the Roman people" and "Roads have been built." This coin celebrates his recovery of Armenia from the Parthians. Although he lived to be seventy-six, Augustus' portraits always showed him as a handsome young man.

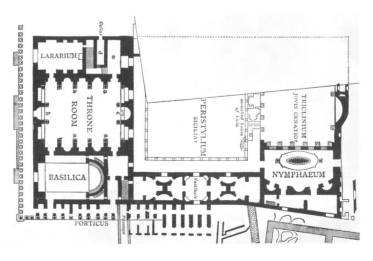

The palace

Augustus lived relatively simply in the Domus Augustiana, a large house on the Palatine Hill, Rome's most aristocratic district. To its northwest, his successor Tiberius constructed the first large purpose-built palace, the Domus Tiberiana. Later emperors continued to enlarge the palace until it covered most of the Palatine Hill. Consequently, the word "palace" is derived from Palatine.

See also
Government,
pages 206–7
Government,
pages 210–11

Gemma Augustaea

The Gemma Augustaea is an onyx cameo depicting the divine Augustus surrounded by his fellow gods. Augustus sits on a throne beside Roma, the personification of the city. He is being crowned with a *corona civica* (civic crown) of oak leaves, an award for saving the lives of Roman citizens. Below, Roman soldiers erect a trophy, or victory monument. The victorious general riding in the chariot on the left is thought to be Tiberius.

Domitian's Palace

The emperors who followed Augustus departed increasingly from republican traditions. Domitian (AD 81–96), who was openly autocratic, built a vast palace on the Palatine. It was described thus by the poet Statius: "Awesome and vast is the edifice, distinguished not by a hundred columns but by as many as could shoulder the gods and the sky if Atlas was let off."

GOVERNMENT

The Emperor's Role

A Roman emperor performed multiple demanding roles. As Pontifex Maximus he was chief priest, spending much of his time overseeing sacrifices. He was also the commander in chief of the armies, and many emperors campaigned in the field in person. He stood at the head of the legal system and acted as the final court of appeal for Roman citizens. His image, on coins and statues, carefully controlled for propaganda purposes, was familiar to everybody. The hardest-working emperor was Hadrian (AD 117–138), who spent much of his reign on journeys, visiting almost every part of the Empire. The historian Cassius Dio relates of Hadrian that "once when a woman made a request of him as he passed by on a journey, he said to her, 'I haven't time.' She replied, 'Then stop being emperor!' He turned about and granted her a hearing."

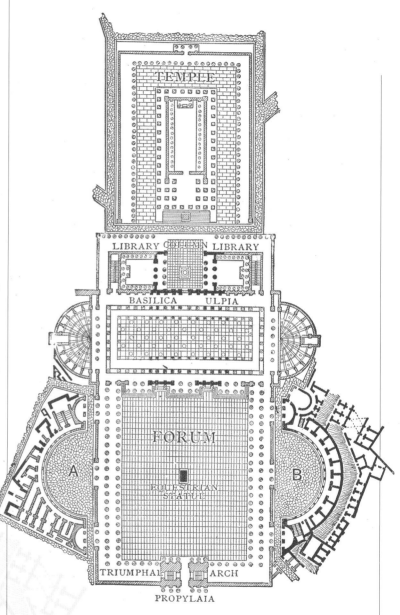

Adlocutio
Coins show emperors performing various official activities, and they were intended to show people how hard-working and conscientious their emperors were. This coin of Nero (AD 54–68) shows him addressing the troops. This was a formal act, called an *adlocutio*. Other coins show emperors dispensing justice and performing sacrifices.

Trajan's Forum
Between AD 107 and 112 Trajan (AD 98–117) used the spoils from his Dacian wars to build a vast new forum in Rome, measuring 656 by 328 ft (200 by 100 m), which was dominated by a colossal, gilded equestrian statue of the emperor. Beyond it lay a basilica and two libraries, on either side of a 130-ft (98.83-m) tall column, carved with reliefs showing Trajan's wars.

See also
Government,
pages 206–9
Religion,
pages 230–1

Trajan's congiarium

This coin of AD 107 shows Trajan performing a *congiarium*, a periodic distribution of cash to Roman citizens. Trajan sits on a tribunal while imperial slaves or freedmen, called *dispensatores*, distribute money to an approaching citizen. This was Trajan's third *congiarium*, and it was made possible by booty from his Dacian wars.

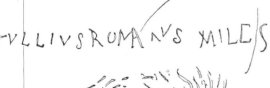

Caricature of Nero

Since emperors carefully controlled their public images, we seldom discover how they were seen by ordinary people. This caricature of Nero, with his distinctive bull neck, was found in 1876 in the substructure of the imperial residence on the Palatine. It is signed Tullius Romanus *miles* (soldier) and some have speculated that it may have been the work of one of Nero's Teutonic bodyguards.

Conquest and clemency

This relief shows the soldier-emperor Marcus Aurelius (AD 161–80) on horseback, being approached by two defeated barbarians, who kneel at his feet. The emperor's hand is outstretched, offering them mercy. A famous surviving equestrian statue at Rome of the emperor shows him making the same stylized gesture, demonstrating both power and clemency.

SOCIETY

Status in Roman Society

There were several varieties of status division in Roman society. The main division was between citizens and noncitizens (*peregrini*). Male citizens had the right to vote and to serve as magistrates and were offered greater legal protection than noncitizens. Within the citizen body there was an archaic division, based on birth, between patricians, the ancient aristocratic families of Rome, and the plebeians, or commoners. Over time the patricians lost power, and, between the 5th and the 1st centuries BC, the number of their clans shrank from fifty to just fourteen. More important was the aristocracy of wealth, divided into two orders: the politically active senatorial order, whose income came mainly from the land, and the much larger equestrian order, who gained an increased political importance under the Empire as imperial officials.

Citizenship

Unlike ancient Greece, where each *polis* jealously guarded its own citizenship, Roman citizenship was sometimes open to outsiders. Foreigners were allowed to become Romans as a reward for loyalty. One way for a foreigner to earn citizenship was to serve in the Roman Army as an auxiliary. This is a tomb carving of an auxiliary cavalryman. On his discharge, after serving twenty-five years, he would be given a grant of citizenship and the right to wear a toga.

See also
Society,
pages 214–15
Costume,
pages 262–3

The senatorial order

This toga wearer is a member of the senatorial order, distinguished by the broad purple *clavus*, or band, on the front of his tunic. Membership of the order required ownership of property valued at a million sesterces or more. The equestrians, who were much more numerous, needed only 400,000 sesterces. An equestrian showed his status with a narrower purple clavus on his tunic. Admission to both orders was controlled by the emperor.

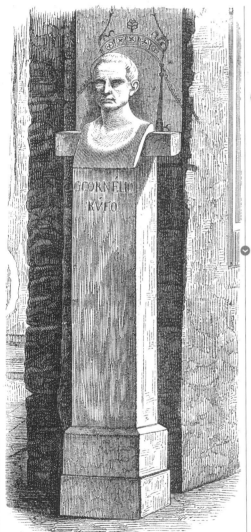

Women

Although Roman society was dominated by men, women had greater rights and independence than in the Greek world. They could not vote or stand in elections, but they could own property and run their own businesses. This is a statue of Eumachia, one of the richest citizens of Pompeii. A patroness of the guild of fullers, she used her wealth to construct an impressive public building by the forum in Pompeii.

Priesthoods

Although the patricians lost their political power, they retained control of the most important priesthoods in Rome. This picture shows two of the twelve *salii*, a body of priests who played a leading role in the Festival of Mars. Only patricians could be *salii*.

Patricians

The patricians were a group of aristocratic *gentes*, or clans, which, in early times, had a monopoly on political power. In the 4th century BC they were forced to share their power with the leading plebeian families. One of the most influential clans was the Cornelii, which provided many Roman consuls. This is a bust of C. Cornelius Rufus, a member of the clan.

SOCIETY

Slavery

Like most ancient societies, Romans viewed slavery as a fact of life. The expansion of the Empire in the 2nd and 1st centuries BC brought vast numbers of captives to Italy. Slaves were also bred from slave mothers or bought from beyond the Empire through trade. Conditions of slavery varied greatly, from slaves in chain gangs, in mines, and on some estates, to trusted household slaves, who were considered part of the family. Household slaves could save money and buy their freedom or be freed as a reward for loyal service. They would then take their former owner's name, as his or her freedman or freedwoman. Wealthy Romans often set up their freedmen with businesses, and the former slaves would then themselves become slave owners. In 8 BC one of Augustus' freedmen, Caecilius Isidorus, left 4,116 slaves in his will.

Slave collar
A runaway slave was regarded as a thief, for he had stolen his master's property. Runaways were hunted down by professional slave catchers, called *fugitivarii*. Recaptured slaves might be branded on the forehead with an F, for *fugitivus* (runaway), or forced to wear a metal collar around their neck. This collar's Latin inscription reads, "I am the slave of Scholasticus, a gentleman of importance. Catch me lest I flee from home."

See also
Society,
pages 212–13
Leisure,
pages 246–7

Captives of war
A relief from the column of Marcus Aurelius shows Roman soldiers raiding a Germanic village on the Danube in the late 2nd century AD. The soldiers are shown taking captives, including a woman and child. The captives would be sold as slaves to traders, who always followed Roman armies on campaign.

10

Flagellum

This is a *flagellum*, a whip made from ox-hide thongs, knotted with small bones. It was used to whip slaves on their bare backs, a punishment that sometimes proved fatal. In one of his Satires, the poet Horace warns against using the "horrible *flagellum*," when the offender only deserved to be beaten with a *scutica*, a whip of twisted leather strips.

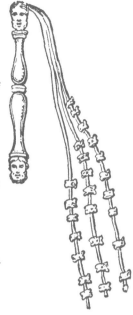

Household slaves

Rich families owned dozens of household slaves, who performed the same specialized functions as servants in a Victorian stately home. There were cooks, nurses, tutors, ushers, secretaries, and slaves whose sole role was to carry their owners through the streets in a *lectica*, or litter. *Lecticarii* (litter bearers) were selected for their height, strength, and handsome appearance.

Treadwheel

Slaves were often used in treadwheels, which had a variety of functions, including pumping water out of mines and lifting stones in building projects. A relief from Capua shows a building scene where two slaves turn a treadwheel to raise a column. To the right stands Minerva, goddess of crafts and commerce.

WARFARE

The Roman Army

By the time of the emperors, the Roman Army was one of the most efficient and best-trained military forces in history. There were around thirty legions, each made up of 5,500 citizen-soldiers. Legionaries were full-time professionals, who served for twenty-five or more years. A legion was divided into ten cohorts, each subdivided into units of eighty men, called centuries. Attached to each legion was a cavalry unit of 120 men, who acted as scouts and messengers and pursued fleeing enemies. Alongside the legions were cohorts of noncitizen soldiers, called auxiliaries, often armed in specialist ways. The legions' main purpose was to conquer new territory or put down rebellions. The defense of frontiers, such as the Rhine in Germany, was left to the auxiliaries.

Centurion
The centurion, who commanded each century, carried a long staff, called a *vitus*, made of twisted vine, which he used to strike soldiers during inspections. Harsh disciplinarians, centurions were often hated and feared by their men. They received at least five times the pay of an ordinary legionary.

Standard-bearer
Individual centuries had their own standard, the *signum*, which carried up to six bronze disks. The number of disks identified the particular century within each cohort. Standard-bearers, called *signiferii*, wore the skins of animals, such as wolves and bears, over their helmets.

See also
Warfare,
pages 218–21

Commander in chief
The commander in chief of the whole army was the emperor, shown here carrying a baton of command and wearing a full military cloak called a *paludamentum*. The emperor appointed the generals, who commanded the legions and governed the provinces. Generals, called legates, were senators, who might spend three to four years as military commanders as part of their career path.

Legionary
The best trained soldiers in the army were the legionaries. Their main weapons were javelins, for throwing, and a short sword for stabbing at close quarters. They carried rectangular curved shields, decorated with Jupiter's thunderbolts and eagle wings. Early legionaries wore heavy mail shirts. From the middle of the 1st century AD, they adopted articulated plate armor, called lorica segmentata.

The eagle

Roman military standards were both rallying points in battle and sacred objects. The most important was the eagle, which represented the whole legion, a bird chosen because of its close association with Jupiter. The eagle was kept in a shrine in the legion's headquarters and only left a camp or fort when the whole legion set off on a campaign. The loss of the eagle in battle was viewed as a terrible disgrace.

Cavalry

This tomb carving shows Flavius Bassus, a Thracian auxiliary cavalryman, trampling a fallen enemy. Flavius Bassus served on the Rhine frontier in the 1st century AD. Roman cavalrymen had to be expert riders for they had no stirrups to give them a firm seat on their horses. They learned to control their mounts using only their legs and knees, leaving their hands free for a shield, sword, and spear.

Auxiliary

Fighting alongside the legions were units of auxiliaries, noncitizen soldiers from all over the Empire. They could be distinguished from legionaries by their oval shields. They served for twenty-five years, and on retirement they were awarded Roman citizenship.

Slinger

Auxiliaries were often specialist fighters, who used the traditional fighting techniques of their homelands. Germans, Thracians, and Gauls were celebrated as cavalrymen; Syrians served as archers. This slinger may have come from the Balaeric Isles. Such lightly armored auxiliaries gave the legions mobility in battle.

Parade helmets

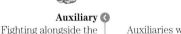

Cavalrymen performed exercises wearing gleaming parade helmets with masks showing idealized faces. Such masks had a depersonalizing effect and must have added to the impressive spectacle of cavalry drill. A surviving cavalry manual describes the exercises, which included leaping onto a running horse and throwing spears at targets from horseback.

WARFARE

The Army on the Move

Everything that the Roman Army did, from marching to pitching camp and fighting, was done in an orderly way. Roman soldiers were highly disciplined and trained to adopt different formations in response to trumpet signals. New recruits were drilled twice a day until they had learned the signals. They were taught to swim, to vault onto a horse in full armor, to use swords and javelins, and to fire catapults. Much of their time was spent marching, up to 19 miles (30 km) a day, carrying full equipment. They were also kept busy in construction projects, quarrying stone and building roads, frontier defenses, and forts. Roman roads were built for military purposes, as a deterrent to rebellion or foreign invasions. Thanks to their roads and their ability to march quickly, the army could reach any trouble spot in a couple of days.

On the march

When marching, legionaries wore full armor and carried their equipment slung from a pole over their shoulders. Their kit, weighing around 40 lb (18 kg), included weapons, tools, three days' rations and a bronze container. For every eight men there was a mule, which carried their shared tent and two mill stones for grinding corn. These legionaries are crossing a river on a bridge of boats, led by their century *signifer*.

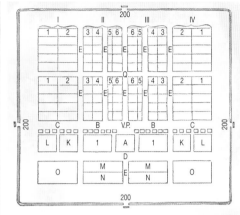

I: Left wing of the Allies
II: 2nd Roman Legion
III: 1st Roman Legion
IV: Right wing of the Allies
A: Praetorium
B: Tents of Tribunes
C: Praefecti Soclorum tents
D: Street 100 ft (30 m) wide
E: Streets 50 ft (15 m) wide
L: Select Foot and Volunteers
K: Select Horse and Volunteers
M: Extraordinary Horse of the Allies
N: Extraordinary Foot of the Allies
O: Reserved for Occasional Auxiliaries
Q: The street called Quintaua, 50 ft (15 m) wide
V.P.: Via Principalis, 100 ft (30 m) wide

Setting up camp

At the end of each day's march the legionaries built a square camp, surrounded by an earth rampart and ditch. Roman camps always had the same plan, with straight streets and a market. This made the task of pitching camp quicker and meant that the soldiers always knew where they were, even if attacked at night. The Greek historian Polybius (*c.* 203–120 BC) wrote that when a Roman army pitched camp it was as if it had returned home.

Tortoise formation

When approaching enemy walls or ramparts, legionaries raised their shields over their heads, locking them together in the *testudo* (tortoise) formation. Shields were placed around the sides to make a box. According to the Roman historian Cassius Dio (*c.* AD 155–*c.* 229), the *testudo* was so strong that horses and vehicles could be driven across it.

See also
Warfare, *pages 216–17*
Warfare, *pages 220–1*

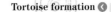

Catapults

Each legion had sixty catapults; some were for throwing stones, while others, such as this example, were for shooting metal-tipped bolts. Both were powered by animal sinews, which were twisted, forming torsion springs. Catapults were a Greek invention adopted by the Romans.

Rock thrower

The largest catapults could hurl rocks up to 100 lb (45 kg) in weight, which were capable of smashing stone walls. This example has a long central arm, holding the stone, which was winched down, building up torsion in twisted sinews at the base. The arm, released by a catch, flung forward, hurling the missile with great force.

WARFARE

Rewards and Punishments

The Romans maintained military discipline through a system of rewards and harsh punishments. Soldiers who fell asleep on duty or deserted their posts were stoned or beaten to death by their fellow troops, the men whose lives they had risked. Mutiny or mass desertion was punished by decimation—the execution of every tenth man, selected by lot. By contrast, there were rewards in the form of various medals and decorations. Soldiers also hoped to gain booty through warfare, and a successful campaign might be followed by a triumphal procession through Rome, the purpose of which was to give thanks to Jupiter for the victory. Religion played a central role in maintaining morale, for soldiers believed that their very lives depended on the good will of the gods.

Medals
Here an officer, called a tribune, is wearing a set of large disks, called *phalerae*, awarded as medals. *Phalerae* were made of bronze coated with silver or gold and decorated with images of gods and mythological animals. These were worn with pride during parades. Tombstones of soldiers often show them wearing their *phalerae*.

Crowns
There were various crowns awarded for particular achievements. This is a gold *corona muralis* (mural crown), decorated with battlements, the reward for the first soldier over the wall in a siege. There was also a civic crown (*corona civica*) of oak leaves for a soldier who saved the life of a fellow citizen. The rarest decoration of all was the glass *corona obsidionalis*, given to a general who relieved a besieged Roman army.

See also
Warfare,
pages 216–19
Religion,
pages 226–7

Religion
In this scene from Trajan's column, Roman soldiers lead a bull, a ram, and a pig around a fort, in a purification ritual known as a *suovetaurilia*. Standing in the center is the emperor, acting as a priest, who will oversee the sacrifice of the animals to Mars, god of war. Religious rituals accompanied every aspect of warfare.

Triumphant Titus
The victorious Titus rode in a golden chariot pulled by four horses, while a slave held a gold *corona triumphalis* (triumphal crown) over his head, repeating the words, "Remember, you are just a man." This was to avoid angering Jupiter, who punished the proud. In this scene from Titus' arch, his chariot is led by Roma herself, while the winged goddess of victory stands behind him.

Booty of Jerusalem
In AD 70 Titus (AD 39–81), son of Vespasian (AD 69–79), crushed a Jewish uprising, sacking the Jerusalem temple. He was awarded a triumphal procession in which his soldiers, wearing laurel wreaths, carried the captured treasures of the temple through Rome to the Temple of Jupiter. This scene comes from the triumphal arch built to commemorate the victory.

Captive princes
In AD 198 Emperor Septimus Severus (AD 193–211) won a great victory over the Parthians, taking 100,000 prisoners and capturing the royal treasury. Here Parthian captive princes are led in the triumphal procession with a white bull, which would be sacrificed to Jupiter. At the end of a triumph, the prisoners were often strangled.

RELIGION

The Roman Gods

The Romans worshipped numerous gods, ranging from the mighty Jupiter Optimus Maximus (Best and Greatest) down to minor household gods, who protected doorways and pantries. The leading gods, including Jupiter, were identified with Greek deities. There were also purely Italian gods, such as Janus, the god of beginnings, and the goddess Roma, the personification of Rome. As the Empire expanded, the Romans came into contact with many foreign gods, such as Isis, from Egypt. These were welcomed into the Roman pantheon. The Romans believed that the more gods their Empire had to protect it, the stronger it would be.

Mars the Advancing

Mars was a god of farming and of war, in which role he was identified with the Greek Ares. As the father of Romulus, legendary founder of Rome, he was one of the chief patron gods of the city. The Roman campaigning season began in March, the month named after him, and from early times Roman armies trained in the Campus Martius, the field of Mars.

Jupiter

Equivalent to the Greek Zeus, Jupiter was the sky god and also the chief god of the Roman state. He is shown here with his sacred eagle, holding the thunderbolts he sent crashing to the earth. His sacred tree was the oak, the tallest tree in the forest, and the one most likely to be struck by lightning.

Vertumnus

A god of seasons and change, Vertumnus watched over the growth of fruit trees. This engraving shows a statue of the god holding a sickle and wearing an apron filled with fruit. Each August, during his festival, the Vertumnalia, Romans brought the first fruit to offer to his statue.

Venus

The goddess of love, Venus, was identified with the Greek Aphrodite. She was the mother of Aeneas, the legendary Trojan hero and ancestor of Romulus. As a result, Venus was another patron of Rome. She was also a goddess of good fortune, called Venus Felix (Venus the Fortunate). As Venus Victrix (Venus the Victorious), she was worshipped by Roman soldiers.

Vesta

The goddess of the hearth, Vesta was identified with the Greek Hestia. Vesta watched over all hearth and altar fires, and a sacred fire was kept constantly burning in her temple. On March 1, the first day of the Roman year, it was ceremonially extinguished and rekindled by rubbing two sticks together—the ancient way of making fire.

Janus

Janus was an ancient Italian god of entrances and beginnings. Just as doors face in two directions, Janus had two faces, looking backward and forward. His temple in Rome was also a passageway, with gates on its east and west sides. These were kept open in wartime and only closed when Rome was at peace—a rare event. January is named after him.

Isis

This copy of a wall painting, from Herculaneum, shows Roman worshippers of Isis, the goddess whose cult was introduced from Egypt. Two rows of worshippers stand either side of an altar singing hymns, while a priest in the center conducts them. The birds by the altar are Egyptian ibises, which were sacred to Isis and kept in her temple.

Household gods

Every Roman family had a shrine, or *lararium*, where statues of the household gods, *lares*, were kept and where food was offered each morning. Shown here are two such, who watched over the family. There were also *penates*, who protected pantries.

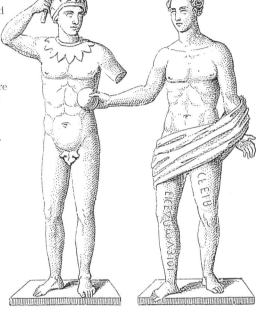

See also
Religion,
pages 224–31

RELIGION

Priests and Priestesses

Roman priests did not form a separate religious community. Priesthood was a part-time activity, usually undertaken by older men of relatively senior status. Roman magistrates and generals acted as priests in the course of their duties, just as the head of a household was a priest in his own home. There were also lifetime priesthoods, organized into four major colleges, and many lesser brotherhoods, called *sodales*. The most important college was that of the *pontifices* (bridge builders), headed by the Pontifex Maximus, the emperor as chief priest. It included fifteen *flamines*, each serving a different state god, and the Vestal Virgins, the only female priesthood. Membership of a priesthood was a great honor. Pliny the Younger (*c.* AD 61–*c.* 113), appointed to the college of augurs (diviners), wrote that he was delighted "because the priesthood is an old-established religious office and has a particular sanctity by being held for life."

Flamen

This is one of the fifteen *flamines*, each assigned to a different state god. The most important were the *flamen Dialis* of Jupiter, the *flamen Martialis* of Mars and the *flamen Quirinalis* of Quirinus. These three *flamines* had to be patricians, while the twelve minor *flamines* could be plebeians. They were selected for office by members of the college of *pontifices*.

See also
Religion,
pages 222–3
Religion,
pages 226–31

Head covered

When officiating as a priest, a Roman man covered his head with his toga. Doing so was a mark of respect for the god. A priest's toga had to be pure—not only clean of dirt, but of contact with anything ritually unclean, such as a corpse. This priest holds a *patera*, a small dish used to scatter incense, wine, or grain on an altar.

Spiked hat

A *flamen* wore a hat with an olivewood spike, tied on with wool, called an *apex*. This was an ancient ritual garment and by the time of the Empire its significance was long forgotten. Yet it was so important that if it fell off during a sacrifice the *flamen* had to resign his office at once.

⬤ Leaping priests

Unlike the *flamines*, priests belonging to the *sodales* were associated with different religious festivals rather than particular gods. The twelve *salii* (leapers or dancers) played a leading role in the Festival of Quinquatrus, on March 15, which opened the army's new campaign season. Dressed as archaic Roman soldiers, they danced through the streets of Rome.

❯ The shields

The *salii* carried twelve ancient shields, called *ancilia*, which were kept in the temple of Mars. One of the shields was believed to have dropped from heaven in the 7th century BC, during the reign of Numa Pompilius. To protect the divine shield, eleven copies were made of it. By the time of the Empire, Romans no longer knew which shield was genuine. This image of one of the shields comes from a Roman gem.

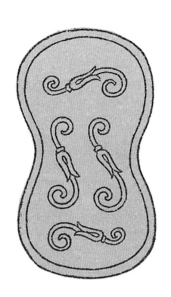

⌄ Vestal Virgins

The only female priesthood in Rome was that of Vesta, goddess of the hearth. She had six priestesses, selected as girls between the ages of six and ten, from leading patrician families. The girls took an oath of chastity and had to serve the goddess for thirty years. The punishment for breaking the oath was to be buried alive. Vestal Virgins had many privileges, including sitting in the front row at the public games.

RELIGION

The Rituals of Sacrifice

For the Romans, as for the Greeks, sacrifice—the offering of a gift, usually an animal, to a god—was the central religious act. Sacrifice followed a strict formula, with a set form of prayers and actions. First the participants and the place of sacrifice were ritually purified with a procession called a lustration (moving around). The officiating priest stood beside the altar, where he offered wine and incense to the god. The animal was then killed with an axe or knife, and cut open. Its entrails were carefully examined for any sign that the sacrifice had been unsuccessful, and the meat was then divided. Part of the offering was burned, for the god, while the rest was cooked and eaten by the celebrants. In this way sacrifice brought humans and gods together in a communal meal.

At the altar
Here the priest stands on the right, with his *patera*, or offering dish, while the victim, a bull, waits patiently on the left. Behind the altar a musician plays a double set of pipes, called *tibiae*. Music was thought to avert evil during the ceremony.

Purification procession
This relief shows a *suovetaurilia*, the sacrifice of a pig (*sus*), a sheep (*ovis*), and a bull (*taurus*). In honour of Mars, the *suovetaurilia* was performed to purify enclosures, including army camps and farmers' fields. If a temple was burned down, a *suovetaurilia* had to be held to reconsecrate the site before rebuilding. The animals were led three times around the place and then sacrificed.

See also
Warfare,
pages 220–1
Religion,
pages 222–5
Religion,
pages 228–31

Killing a bull

The killing of the bull was done quickly and professionally. While two *victimarii* gripped its horns, a third stunned it with a poleax. Once the bull fell to its knees, a *victimarius* cut its throat. The blood was collected in a *patera* to be poured on the altar. The animal was then rolled onto its back and butchered.

Incense

This engraving shows a Roman general preparing to sacrifice a bull on behalf of his assembled army before setting out on campaign. The general stands by the altar, scattering incense in the flames. To his right is a boy attendant, holding the box of incense. Frankincense, imported from southern Arabia, was burned in vast quantities at altars across the Roman Empire.

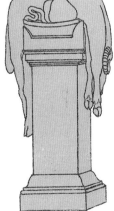

Victimarius

The task of killing the animal belonged to attendants called *victimarii*. They had to be strong to grip a bull by its horns, and they worked stripped to the waist. This *victamarius* wears a garland of leaves and holds the ritual knife used to cut the throat of the victim.

Inspecting the organs

After the animal was cut open, an expert diviner called a *haruspex* inspected its liver, lungs, and heart for any abnormalities. An oddly shaped organ was taken as a sign that the sacrifice had not been accepted by the god. A new animal would have to be offered. Here a dead ram lies on an altar, its lungs beside it.

RELIGION

Augury and Roman Diviners

Like the Greeks, the Romans believed that they could interpret the wishes of the gods through natural signs, including earthquakes, comets, lightning, and the flight and behavior of birds. In Rome there was an official body of expert diviners, called augurs, who were consulted before any important public act was performed, and it was their role to tell whether the gods approved of the act. From the Greeks, the Romans received the idea that gods could also communicate through inspired people in the form of oracles. The word "oracle" referred to both the god's message and the sacred place, such as Delphi in Greece, where it was given. In times of crisis the Senate turned to the *Sibylline Books*, a collection of Greek oracular sayings from southern Italy.

Augur

An augur carried a curved staff, called a *lituus*, which was his badge of office. Facing south, he used the *lituus* to mark out a sacred section of the sky to observe. He then waited for the appearance of birds. The eastern half of the sky was seen as lucky, the west unlucky, so a flight of birds on the augur's left was seen as a good sign. Greek diviners used similar methods, although they faced north rather than south.

Sacred chickens

In Rome there was a flock of sacred chickens, whose feeding behavior provided another method of determining the will of the gods. The chickens accompanied Roman armies on campaign, and before a battle an augur called a *pullarius* (chicken man) offered them grain. If they ate it greedily, it was taken as an excellent sign. Roman soldiers, told the news, could be sure that the gods were with them.

Omens from bees ◀
Like the Greeks, the Romans believed that bee swarms were omens of the future, and often unlucky ones. In his *Natural History*, Pliny the Elder (AD 23–79) wrote, "Bees provide signs of future events both private and public, when a cluster of them hangs down in houses and temples, portents that have often been followed by momentous events." This is a Roman wicker beehive.

The power of the omen
In 249 BC, a Roman consul, Publius Claudius Pulcher, was preparing for a naval battle near Sicily against the Carthaginians. When told that the chickens refused to eat, he was so angry that he had the birds thrown into the sea, exclaiming: "They don't eat, so let them drink!" The Romans suffered a terrible defeat. The consul's treatment of the chickens was blamed and he was sentenced to exile.

See also
Religion,
pages 222–7

Religion,
pages 230–1

Sibylline Books
Here the Pontifex Maximus is accompanied by the keeper of the *Sibylline Books*. This was a collection of ancient Greek verse oracles, from the sibyl, or prophetess, of Cumae. The Romans kept the books in the Temple of Jupiter and consulted them in times of emergency. In the 80s BC both the temple and the books were destroyed in a fire, and the Romans had to build up a new collection of oracles from all over the Empire.

RELIGION

Emperor Worship

Roman emperors were given divine honors with their own temples, priests, and ceremonies. People sacrificed to the *genius*, or life force, of the living emperor, while many emperors and empresses were declared gods after death. The process began when a comet appeared in the sky following the assassination of Julius Caesar. This was assumed to be Caesar's soul joining the gods, and he was deified by the Senate. As a result, Augustus, Caesar's heir, could claim to be the son of a god, and he was deified in turn after death. There was an elaborate funeral ceremony, called a *consecratio* (making sacred), in which the emperor was transformed into a god. Yet most people did not believe that their emperor was divine in the sense that Jupiter or Mars was. Rather, emperor worship was a way of showing loyalty to the Roman state and gratitude to the emperor for his benefactions.

MAVSOLEVM AVGVSTI

Imperial mausoleum
Imperial funerals were held in the Campus Martius, where Augustus built an elaborate tomb for his family in 27 BC. This engraving shows the tomb as it appeared in the 1550s. The original structure was much larger and was planted with cypresses, trees sacred to the dead. It held urns containing the ashes of at least sixteen people, including four emperors: Augustus, Tiberius, Claudius (AD 41–54) and Nerva (AD 96–98).

Hadrian's tomb
Around AD 135 Hadrian built a new imperial mausoleum on the left bank of the Tiber, shown in this reconstruction. It was much bigger than Augustus' mausoleum, which had now been filled. It contained the ashes of most subsequent emperors until Caracalla (AD 188–217). The tomb, later converted into the medieval Castel Sant'Angelo, still dominates the Roman skyline.

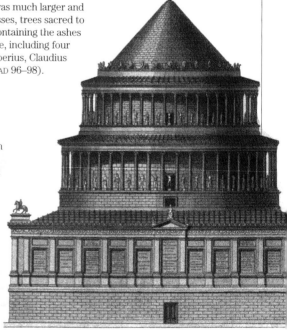

Cult statue
This coin issued by Tiberius shows a cult statue of the divine Augustus, being taken in a procession in a carriage pulled by four elephants. The letters "S.C." stand for *Senatus consulto* (by decree of the Senate). Tiberius issued this coin in AD 36, more than twenty years after Augustus' death. It served as imperial propaganda, designed to enhance Tiberius' own prestige.

Funeral pyre
A coin issued by Emperor Marcus Aurelius celebrates the deification of his predecessor, Antoninus Pius in AD 161. It shows the elaborate funeral pyre of the emperor, which had tiers like a wedding cake. This was made of wooden scaffolding, covered with gold-embroidered hangings and decorated with statues, with a triumphal chariot on top. The emperor's body was placed on the second level, surrounded by spices and incense.

See also
Religion,
pages 222–9

Government,
pages 210–11

Daily life,
pages 270–1

Apotheosis
This carved relief from the base of a column shows the apotheosis (transformation into a god) of Antoninus Pius (AD 138–161) and his wife Faustina (AD 100–141). The pair are carried up to heaven on the back of a winged god, watched by the goddess Roma and a man holding an obelisk, representing the Campus Martius. Two eagles, released to carry their souls, fly alongside them.

Burning the pyre
A 19th-century engraving recreates an imperial funeral, as described by the historian Herodian (*c.* AD 170–240). Following a procession around the pyre by horsemen, the new emperor threw a burning torch into it. As the flames rose, an eagle was released from the topmost level, carrying the soul of the emperor to join his fellow gods. After the fire died down, his ashes were collected in an urn for entombment.

WORK

Bakers and Fullers

Roman bakers and fullers, like other trades, were organized into *collegia*, or guilds. The guilds protected their members' interests and served a religious and political role. Members gathered to celebrate festivals in honor of patron gods, such as Minerva, and to offer their support for particular election candidates. Much evidence about their work comes from Pompeii, where thirty-three bakeries and eleven *fullonicae* (fulleries) have been discovered. The bakeries were identified by mills and ovens, one found still containing the carbonized remains of eighty-eight loaves. The fulleries played the final role in cloth manufacture, cleaning and dyeing newly woven garments. They also acted as laundries, where wealthy Romans sent their clothes to be cleaned or redyed. Paintings on the walls of *fullonicae* depict the different stages of cleaning cloth.

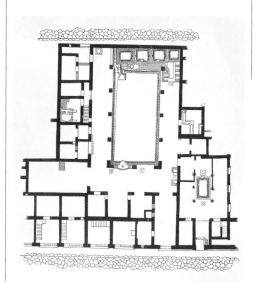

Soaking

The first stage in the fulling process was to soak cloth in stale urine to stiffen it. Fullers collected the urine in earthenware vessels, which they placed on street corners, for passersby to urinate into. The cloth was then washed in a bronze basin in a mixture of water and fullers' earth to remove the grease. This fuller is standing in the basin and treading on the cloth.

Boy fuller

Here a boy is wringing out the cloth or scrubbing it to remove stains. Wall paintings show that children, probably slaves, played an important role in the fulling process.

Sulfur

White cloth was bleached by draping it over a basketlike frame and fumigating it over burning sulfur. This fuller carries the frame and a jar holding the sulfur. The owl on top of the frame was sacred to Minerva in her role as goddess of crafts and commerce.

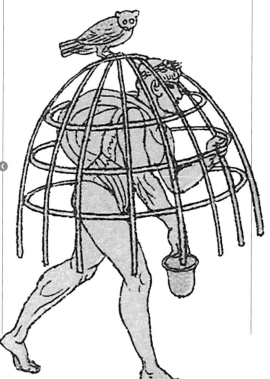

Fullonica

This is the plan of a large *fullonica* in Pompeii. At the top are four large masonry tanks, of descending height, which were used to rinse the cloth. Fresh water flowed from tank to tank. There were also separate rooms for beating, combing, bleaching, dyeing, and pressing the cloth.

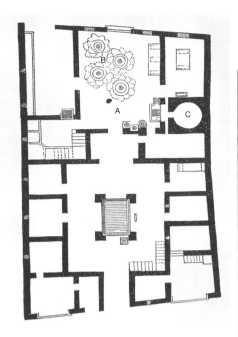

Bakery
This plan shows a small bakery in Pompeii. The area at the top (A) contains four mills of lava (B). To the right is a single large oven (C). The street front, with shops, is at the bottom. This bakery also served as a house for the baker and his family.

Brushing
Garments being finished were brushed to raise the nap evenly over the whole surface. This fuller is brushing a tunic, which hangs from a rope.

Pressing
The final stage was to press the cloth, in a large screw press. The one shown here is from a wall painting, but the remains of a press just like this were found in a *fullonica* in Pompeii. The screw press, also used to crush olives, was a Greek invention.

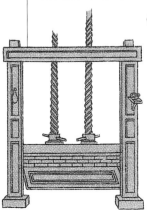

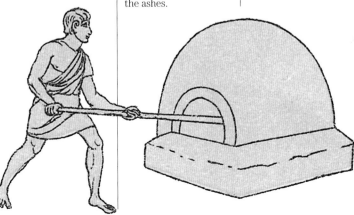

Mill and bakery
Roman bakeries were involved in the whole bread-making process, from grinding the grain in a mill, to kneading dough and baking the bread in an oven. This engraving shows the ruins of a bakery in Pompeii, with the bottom parts of two hopper mills made from lava on the left and a large oven in the background.

Bread oven
Here a baker is using a long wooden paddle to place bread in an oven, which resembles a modern pizza oven. A wood or charcoal fire was burned inside until it reached the right temperature, then the fire was raked out and the loaves placed above the ashes.

See also
Work,
pages 234–5
Costume,
pages 262–5

WORK

Agricultural Work

Most hard physical work was performed by slaves or by oxen and donkeys. Oxen were used to pull carts, plows, and barges along rivers; donkeys were used to turn hopper mills, such as those found in Pompeii. Although the Romans also built watermills, water power was less readily available than donkeys. In *The Golden Ass*, written in the 2nd century AD by Lucius Apuleius (*c.* AD 123–180), the narrator is transformed into a donkey. He describes being put to work in a mill: "I was harnessed to what seemed to me the largest mill of all, my eyes were blindfolded and I was put into a little circular track, along which I was supposed to go round and round without stopping."

Rotary mill

The hopper mill was a Roman invention. It had a lower conical mill stone, the *meta*, with a funnel-shaped upper stone, the *catillus*. A wooden beam, running through the *catillus*, was used to turn it. The miller poured grain in at the top, which fell as flour onto the rim of the *meta*.

Donkey power

Here a donkey turns a hopper mill, driven on by a slave with a whip. Although donkeys worked long hours, they were given a holiday every June 19, during the Festival of Vesta. According to the poet Ovid (43 BC–*c.* AD 18), on this day Roman millers hung garlands of violets around their donkeys and mills.

Horse power

This illustration, from a marble relief in the Vatican Museum, shows a large horse-powered mill. Horses were more expensive to keep than donkeys, so only old and broken-down animals would be used for this purpose. This horse is blindfolded to prevent it being distracted. A miller carries grain to pour in at the top.

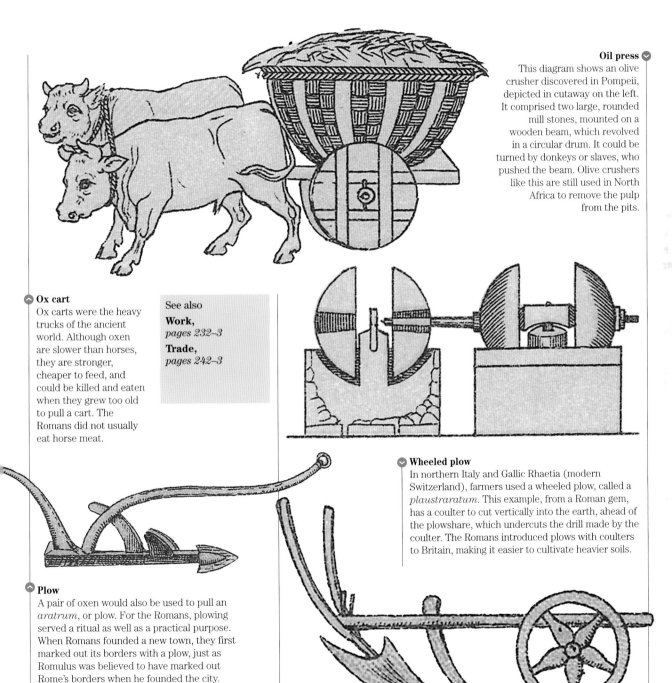

Oil press ⊘
This diagram shows an olive crusher discovered in Pompeii, depicted in cutaway on the left. It comprised two large, rounded mill stones, mounted on a wooden beam, which revolved in a circular drum. It could be turned by donkeys or slaves, who pushed the beam. Olive crushers like this are still used in North Africa to remove the pulp from the pits.

Ox cart
Ox carts were the heavy trucks of the ancient world. Although oxen are slower than horses, they are stronger, cheaper to feed, and could be killed and eaten when they grew too old to pull a cart. The Romans did not usually eat horse meat.

See also
Work,
pages 232–3
Trade,
pages 242–3

Wheeled plow
In northern Italy and Gallic Rhaetia (modern Switzerland), farmers used a wheeled plow, called a *plaustraratum*. This example, from a Roman gem, has a coulter to cut vertically into the earth, ahead of the plowshare, which undercuts the drill made by the coulter. The Romans introduced plows with coulters to Britain, making it easier to cultivate heavier soils.

Plow
A pair of oxen would also be used to pull an *aratrum*, or plow. For the Romans, plowing served a ritual as well as a practical purpose. When Romans founded a new town, they first marked out its borders with a plow, just as Romulus was believed to have marked out Rome's borders when he founded the city. This is a simple early Roman plow with an arrow-shaped iron tip.

TECHNOLOGY

Technological Advances

The Roman Period saw many technological advances, including the invention of concrete, the dome, and underfloor heating systems. The Romans' most lasting achievement was the creation of a network of straight roads with deep foundations. These continued to be used for centuries after the end of the Empire and Europeans still travel along the routes of many of them today. Another skill developed was glassblowing, a technique invented in Syria in the 1st century BC. Roman glassware is exquisite and includes high-status cameo vases as well as everyday vessels. Long before the Industrial Revolution, the Romans also pioneered mass-production, manufacturing vast amounts of molded, decorated red bowls called Samian ware in workshops in Gaul.

L · CAECILI · Q · F
METEL · COS
CXIX
ROMA ¹

Milestone

Roads had milestones, set up every Roman mile, which was approximately 5,000 ft (1,500 m) and represented 1,000 paces. This inscription, from a milestone on the Via Salaria, carries the name of a consul, Lucius Caecelius Metellus, who served in the 2nd century BC, and the distance to Rome: 119 Roman miles 112 miles (180 km).

Roads

Roman roads were built by soldiers, who began by digging a deep, wide trench. After compressing the subsoil, they put down layers of graded materials, whose composition depended on what was available locally. Layers of rubble were interspersed with sand or gravel. The surface metaling might be gravel, cobbles, or slag from ironworking. Roman roads were well drained, with side ditches, and could be used in all weathers.

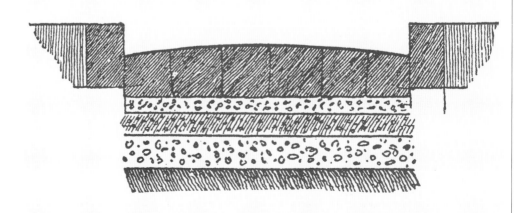

See also
Technology,
pages 238–9
Architecture,
pages 252–3

Glassware
The Romans invented the glass cameo, using different colored layers of glass. A glassblower would make a vase using dark blue glass, wrapped in an outer layer of white glass. Then a sculptor carved reliefs, cutting away the white layer to reveal the blue underneath. This is the Portland Vase, one of just thirteen surviving Roman cameo vases.

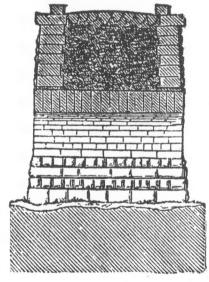

Raised roads
Roman roads were built for military purposes, to enable armies and official messengers to travel quickly in the event of an emergency. As a result, they were always as straight as possible. This road, shown in side view and cross section, has been raised above the surrounding countryside.

Samian ware
From the 1st to the 3rd centuries AD, Samian tableware was produced in workshops in Gaul. The clay was pressed on the interior of a mold, and the vessel was then thrown in the mold, which was turned on a potter's wheel. The shape of a Samian bowl enabled it to be easily stacked, and packed in crates.

TECHNOLOGY

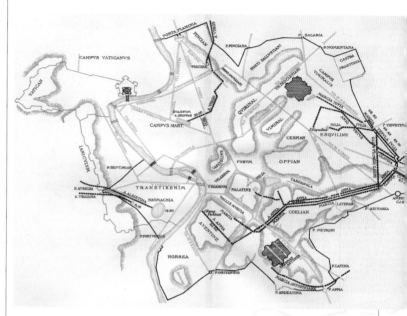

Water Management

The first aqueducts were built by the Greeks in the form of tunnels hewn in rock and ground-level terra-cotta pipes. Hydraulic engineering was taken to a new level by the Romans, who built examples raised on arches to carry water from hillside springs to cities. Rome needed vast quantities of water, for bathhouses, street fountains, toilets, gardens, fire fighting, and mock sea battles. There is a detailed account of the Roman water supply, written by Sextus Julius Frontinus (*c.* AD 40–103), appointed superintendent of Rome's aqueducts in AD 97. Immensely proud of his aqueducts, Frontinus contrasted their utility with the overpraised architectural wonders of Egypt and Greece: "With such an array of indispensable structures carrying so many waters, compare, if you will, the idle Pyramids or the useless, though famous, works of the Greeks!"

See also
Technology,
pages 236–7
Architecture,
pages 252–3

Eleven aqueducts

As the city of Rome grew, more aqueducts were constructed until, by the early 3rd century AD, there were eleven of them, called the Appia, Anio Vetus, Marcia, Tepula, Julia, Virgo, Alsietina, Claudia, Anio Novus, Traiana, and Alexandrina. In total, they supplied some 247,953,736 gallons (1,127,220 m³) of water a day to the city. The geographer Strabo (*c.* 63 BC–AD 24) wrote that "veritable rivers flow through the city and sewers."

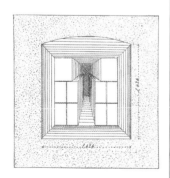

Aqua Appia

This is a cross section of Rome's first aqueduct, the Aqua Appia. It was built in 312 BC by Appius Claudius Caecus (*c.* 340–273 BC), who also commissioned the Appian Way. Because of the low level of the aqueduct's source, almost all of its 10-mile (16.4-km) length was underground. According to Frontinus, it brought 16,219, 872 gallons (73,737 m³) of water to Rome every day.

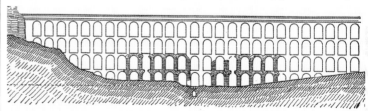

Palace aqueduct

To supply water to the imperial palace, the emperors Domitian and Septimius Severus built this extension to the Aqua Claudia. Spanning the valley between the Coelian and Palatine hills, it had four levels of arches, and stood 138 ft (42 m) high. Aqueducts, carried over high bridges, were partly built for display.

Cloaca Maxima

Rome's first sewer, the Cloaca Maxima, was originally constructed in the 6th century BC, but rebuilt with a stone vault by Marcus Agrippa (*c.* 63–12 BC) in 33 BC. Excess water from Rome's aqueducts flowed through it constantly, diluting the sewage. It was so large that Agrippa was able to travel through it on a boat, making his tour of inspection. This is the sewer's outlet into the Tiber.

Triple aqueduct

Aqueducts were also carried on top of the city's walls. This is a cross section of the Porta Maggiore, the gate where three eastern aqueducts entered Rome together. The drawing shows the Aqua Marcia (bottom), Aqua Tepula (middle), and Aqua Julia (top). The Aqua Marcia water, celebrated for its purity, was the best drinking water in Rome.

Street fountain

Water from the aqueducts flowed into holding and distribution tanks and then through lead pipes to street fountains, the source of drinking water for most Romans. These were provided for the people as *munera* (services) by holders of political office.

Pompeii fountain

The best-preserved public street fountains are in Pompeii, where the whole water system can be traced. Pompeii had a single aqueduct, the water from which flowed into a distribution building, where it was divided into three channels: for private houses, public buildings (such as baths), and street fountains. If water levels dropped, the supply to private houses was automatically cut off before the street fountains.

TRADE

Sea Trade

Although the Roman Empire is celebrated for its well-built road system, trade goods were usually transported by water rather than land—by barges along the rivers of Europe and across the seas in merchant ships. The provision of the Pax Romana (Roman Peace) to the lands around the Mediterranean was a great boost to maritime trade, which Roman rulers promoted by building harbors and lighthouses and clearing the seas of pirates. The Empire was also a market for goods from distant lands, including frankincense from Arabia, amber from the Baltic, silk from China, and spices from India. In his panegyric to Rome, the Greek orator Aelius Aristides (AD 117–81), declared: "So many merchantmen arrive here with cargoes from all over…that the city seems like the common warehouse of the world."

Merchant ship
This relief shows a big-bellied Roman merchant ship, a slow but stable vessel, powered by a single, square sail. Such a ship was only effective with the wind behind it, and sailors had to wait for the correct wind before they could set sail. The sailing season lasted from March to November.

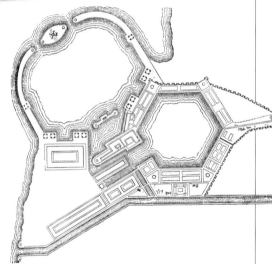

Rome's docks
This plan shows the docks and warehouses of Rome and the different wharves where marble, wine, grain, and olive oil were unloaded. The Horrea Galbana were grain warehouses, named after the Emperor Galba (3 BC–AD 69) who restored them. They were used to store the vast quantities of grain, brought from Egypt and Sicily, which the emperor was expected to distribute to the citizens of Rome.

Ostia
The seaport of Rome was Ostia, on the mouth of the Tiber. Its harbor comprised an outer basin with two walls projecting into the sea, built by Emperor Claudius. Later, Trajan enlarged the harbor with an inner hexagonal basin (shown here bottom right). Goods were unloaded from ships here and then brought by barge up the Tiber to Rome.

North wind

The most unpopular wind with sailors was Boreas, the north wind, shown here as a mature man blowing a conch. Boreas was an angry wind, which blew strongly in winter when ships could no longer take to the sea. The north wind could delay the grain fleet sailing from Egypt to Rome.

South wind

The south wind, called Notos, by the Greeks and Auster by the Romans, is depicted as a young man pouring water from an urn. He was a god who blew in the fall, bringing rain and storms. In the 1st century AD, the poet Statius (AD 45–*c.* 96) wrote: "Auster pours down rain, which keen Boreas with his freezing breath hardens into hail."

Southeast wind

The southeast wind was called Apeliotus. He is shown here as a young man who holds fruit and grain in his cloak. This wind brought refreshing rain in summer. Sailors waiting for the southeast wind would pray to Apeliotus, asking him to blow for them. A Roman book of sailing instructions would not say "sail northwest," but "sail with Apeliotus."

> See also
> **Religion,**
> *pages 228–9*
> **Trade,**
> *pages 242–3*

West wind

Sailors associated the various winds with different gods, each with its own personality. The Tower of the Winds, from Roman era Athens, is carved with eight wind gods. The west wind, Zephyrus, is depicted here carrying flowers in his cloak. A gentle wind, Zephyrus was associated with the coming of spring.

TRADE

The Forum, Markets, and Shops

The main commercial area of every town was the forum. As well as being a center of government and law, it was the location for great markets, held every eight days, when traders set up temporary stalls under colonnades. Such markets were strictly regulated by magistrates, called *aediles*, who made sure that the correct weights and measures were used. In larger cities, there were also huge markets, dealing with particular goods. Rome itself had a Forum Piscarium, or fish market, and a Forum Suarium, where nothing but pork was sold. In every town and city, there were also many small shops with counters opening onto the streets. The shopkeepers were often freedmen who, like the fullers of Pompeii, might be organized in guilds.

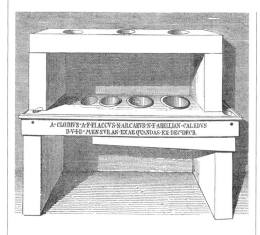

Official measures
This marble measuring device was set up in the forum of Pompeii by Aulus Clodius Flaccus, a magistrate, who had his name inscribed on it. It has five hollows of decreasing size, which represent the official measures to be used by traders in the market.

See also
Work,
pages 234–5
Trade,
pages 240–1

Measuring
The side elevation and view from above indicate how the measuring device was used. Each of the bowls was stopped with a plug, and the goods to be measured poured in until the bowl was filled. The plug could then be removed and the contents poured out. It could be used to check that the traders were giving the correct measures.

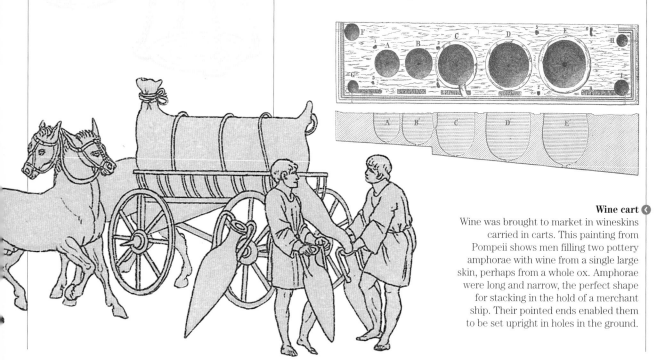

Wine cart
Wine was brought to market in wineskins carried in carts. This painting from Pompeii shows men filling two pottery amphorae with wine from a single large skin, perhaps from a whole ox. Amphorae were long and narrow, the perfect shape for stacking in the hold of a merchant ship. Their pointed ends enabled them to be set upright in holes in the ground.

Scales

These are two types of shopkeepers' scales found in Pompeii. The top one (A), called a *statera*, has a sliding weight, in the form of Minerva, on a crossbar marked with a scale. The lower example (B) is a *libra*, or balance, in which goods were placed on one side and weights on the other.

Knife shop

Tombs of shop owners were often decorated with relief carvings of their workplaces. These were standard carvings rather than individually commissioned works of art. This example shows a cutler's shop, in which the shopkeeper, on the right, is selling a knife to a man in a toga. Behind them are rows of sickles, carving knives, and pruning knives.

Baker's shop

This wall painting, from the large bakery of Sotericus in Pompeii, seems to show the sale of bread. However, the man is wearing a toga and sitting on a raised seat, suggesting a more formal occasion. The toga-clad man, perhaps Sotericus, is probably distributing bread to citizens. Distribution of free bread was an important way of winning political support.

LEISURE

Roman Baths

Roman public baths had their origin in the Greek world, where cities provided simple hip baths from the 4th century BC. Soon after 100 BC, the Romans invented hypocaust (underfloor) and wall-heating systems. This allowed them to build elaborate bathhouses, with different rooms heated to different temperatures, and every Roman town had at least one. More than a place to wash, it was a leisure center, where people relaxed, exercised and met friends. By the 5th century AD, Rome had eleven monumental *thermae*, built by a series of emperors. People could visit them for a nominal charge, which even the poorest could afford, and across the Empire baths played a major role in spreading Roman culture.

Hypocaust

Roman heating technology was unrivaled until modern times, so it is unsurprising that early depictions of baths contain inaccuracies. This 16th-century artist's impression of a hypocaust shows fires directly below the floors of the rooms. In fact, there would be a separate furnace, which heated water and provided hot air that passed through spaces beneath the floors and through box tiles within the walls.

Imperial thermae

This 19th-century map of Rome shows (on the right) three of the imperial *thermae*, built by Diocletian, Titus, and Caracalla, and gives a sense of their monumental scale. The map also shows the public parks of Rome. Like the baths, these were provided by Roman rulers to win popularity. Parks were formally laid out, with colonnades providing shade and neatly trimmed box hedges.

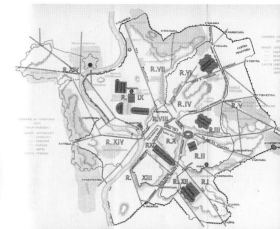

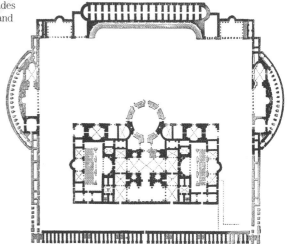

Baths of Caracalla

One of the biggest of Rome's bathhouses was built by Emperor Caracalla. It could hold 1,500 people and required around 4 million gallons (18 million liters) of water a day. The main bath building had a symmetrical plan with large hot, warm, and cold halls laid out on the central axis. On each side were changing rooms and exercise areas.

See also
Leisure,
pages 246–9

Decoration
The interiors of bathhouses were magnificently decorated with mosaic floors, ornamental columns, and walls set with different colored marble tiles. Imperial *thermae* also served as art galleries and were filled with copies of famous Greek statues.

Frigidarium
The sequence of rooms visited depended on the tastes of the bather, and the time of year. In hot summer weather the bather might begin with a visit to the *frigidarium* (cold room), which had a central plunge bath. Many baths also had an outdoor swimming pool, or *natatio*.

Caldarium
This cutaway view shows the *caldarium* (hot room) of the Forum Baths at Pompeii. The floor is raised on stacks of tiles (B), and there is a hot plunge pool on the right (C). On the left is a *labrum*, or basin, for cold water (A). The floor of the *caldarium* was so hot that bathers had to wear wooden-soled shoes.

Oil and strigil
After exercising or bathing, Romans rubbed their bodies in olive oil, often scented, and scraped it off with a curved metal strigil. It was difficult to oil and scrape one's own back, and many bathers had slave attendants to do this for them. Poorer people took turns scraping each other.

Tepidarium
The *tepidarium* (warm room) was heated to a comfortable temperature to prepare the bather moving between hot and cold rooms. This *tepidarium* of the Pompeii baths served as another changing room for men who wanted to go straight to the hot bath. It is richly decorated with stucco and statues of giants between the niches for clothes.

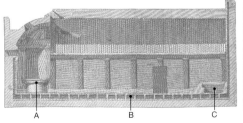

A   B   C

Types of heat
The *caldarium*, shown here, resembled a modern steam bath. It was less decorated than the *tepidarium* because of the damage to stucco caused by the heat and steam. Many baths also had a *laconicum*, a small room providing intense, dry heat. Bathers only spent a minute or two here to break out in a sweat.

LEISURE

Gladiators and Games

Most large Roman towns had an amphitheater where free shows were provided by the ruling classes for the public. Although entertainments included public executions and wild-beast hunts, the most popular were the fights between gladiators. Gladiatorial combat originated with the Etruscans, who staged fights between prisoners of war at funeral games. For Rome's ruling classes, the games, which were mounted at vast expense, came to be seen as a way of winning popularity. There were several types of gladiator, armed in various ways. Much of the excitement came from seeing combat between a lightly armed but fast fighter, such as a Thracian or a *retiarius*, and a slower, better protected gladiator, such as a *murmillo*. Although many fights ended in death, the defeated were often spared and lived to fight again.

The retiarius
On the left here is a *retiarius*, or net man, who was armed as a fisherman with a trident and a net. He tried to ensnare his opponent by throwing a weighted circular net at him. Once he had caught him, he would stab him with the trident. The *retiarius* had to be fast on his feet, so wore no armour except for a shoulder guard called a *galerus*.

The pursuer
The *retiarius* often fought with a *secutor*, or pursuer. He wore an oval helmet, the smooth surface of which was designed to slip through the *retiarius'* net. The helmet's circular eye holes were spaced closely together in order to prevent the trident prongs from entering them.

The Colosseum
The largest amphitheater in the Empire was the 170-ft (52-m) high Colosseum in Rome, built by Emperor Vespasian and his son Titus between AD 72 and 80. It held an audience of 55,000, who sat in rows according to class. For the people of Rome, the Colosseum shows were a strong unifying force. They gave people a chance to see their emperor, who sat in the front row, and to share an exciting experience with him.

To live or die

Here, a wounded Thracian, unable to continue fighting, has dropped his shield and is appealing to the crowd for mercy. If he had fought bravely, the people would shout "*Mitte!*" ("Let him go!"). If they felt he deserved to die, they made a stabbing gesture with their thumbs, crying "*Iugula!*" ("Kill him!"), and the victorious gladiator would finish him off. In the Colosseum this final life-or-death decision lay with the emperor.

Murmillo

The *murmillo* (fish man) was named after the high crest on his helmet, which resembled the dorsal fin of a fish. A heavily armed gladiator, he had the short, stabbing sword, or *gladius*—which gave gladiators their name—a long, curved shield, like a Roman legionary, and a bronze greave on his left leg. Gladiators' chests were often unprotected, increasing the danger and excitement of combat.

Thracian helmet

The arms and armor of some types of gladiator were exaggerated versions of those used by Rome's ancient enemies. Thracian gladiators had griffins on their helmets, like the Thracian warriors who lived north of the Black Sea. The griffin was sacred in Thrace, where it was said to guard the region's celebrated gold mines. With its great size and elaborate decoration, a gladiator's helmet was unlike any armor worn in war.

> See also
> **Society,**
> *pages 214–15*
> **Leisure,**
> *pages 244–5*
> **Leisure,**
> *pages 248–9*

The sica

The Thracian carried a sword, called a *sica*, whose curved shape allowed him to thrust around his opponent's shield and strike his unprotected back. Thracians were lightly armored and fast and very popular with Roman audiences. Graffiti from Pompeii celebrates "Celadus the Thracian, the glory of the girls, who makes all the girls sigh."

Becoming a gladiator

Gladiators were often slaves, criminals, or prisoners of war. There were also free men who became gladiators. Some were driven to it by desperate poverty, while others were attracted by the excitement of the life and the chance to make prize money. On becoming a gladiator, like this *retiarius*, a free man had to swear an oath that he was willing to be "branded, chained, whipped, and killed by the sword."

LEISURE

Chariot Racing

Chariot racing was invented by the Greeks when chariots were still used in warfare. The sport was enthusiastically adopted by the Romans, who built large circus racetracks across their Empire. Roman rulers financed the games, which were provided free to the public. The charioteers belonged to four teams named after the red, white, blue, and green colors they wore. Each had fanatical fans, who gambled on their team winning. Much of the thrill came from the danger of the sport, because chariots often overturned or crashed, and many charioteers died young. The leading charioteer of the 1st century AD was Scorpus, who won 2,048 races before being killed in his chariot at the age of just twenty-six. The poet Martial (*c.* AD 40–*c.* 103) wrote his epitaph: "I am Scorpus, the glory of the noisy circus, the much-applauded and short-lived darling of Rome."

See also
Leisure,
pages 244–7

Circus of Maxentius

This plan, of the Circus of Maxentius, shows the layout of racetracks across the Empire. On the left are the twelve starting gates, arranged in a curved line, allowing each chariot an equal chance to find the best position. The chariots made seven laps in an counterclockwise direction, and each charioteer aimed to get as close as possible to the near end of the *spina* at the start.

The dator ludorum

The races were presided over by the *dator ludorum* (giver of the games), who sat in a box above the entrance, between the starting gates. He gave the starting signal, by throwing a white cloth onto the track. Here a victorious charioteer approaches the box to receive his prize.

Circus Maximus

Rome's largest racetrack, the Circus Maximus, was 1,968 ft (600 m) long and could seat 385,000 people, an audience seven times greater than the Colosseum's. Running down the middle was a 1,130-ft (344-m) long barrier called the *spina* (spine) decorated with statues and monuments, including an obelisk brought from Egypt by Emperor Augustus.

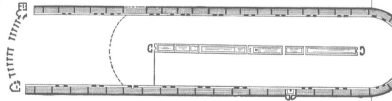

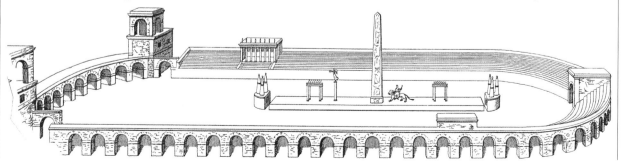

Controlling the horses

The charioteer wrapped his horses' reins tightly around his body and held them in his left hand. He steered by shifting his weight and used a whip to drive the horses on. Here a charioteer reaches the bronze *metae*, or turning posts, where most accidents occurred. If thrown, he might be able to cut himself free with a short, curved knife he carried in his tunic lacing.

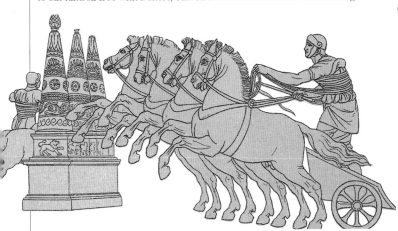

The starting gates

Before the race, each *quadriga* (four-horse chariot) waited in a box called a *carcer* (prison), behind double gates of wood or bronze. At the starting signal an attendant pulled a lever, which jerked out the latches of all the gates at the same instant. The gates, which had springs, flew open and the chariots hurtled out onto the track.

Prizes

While the charioteer's symbolic prize was a palm of victory, he also received silver crowns and gold coins. Charioteers usually began their careers as slaves and, if successful, could quickly earn enough to buy their freedom. Men such as Scorpus were the sporting superstars of the Roman Empire, and their portraits appeared on mosaics and wall paintings, and they were celebrated in poetry.

Seven laps

There were seven laps, counted by removing large wooden eggs and turning carved dolphins around on the *spina*. The dolphins, which were also fountains, were there to honor Neptune, god of horses as well as the sea. The eggs recalled the demi-gods Castor and Pollux, patrons of horsemen, born from a single egg.

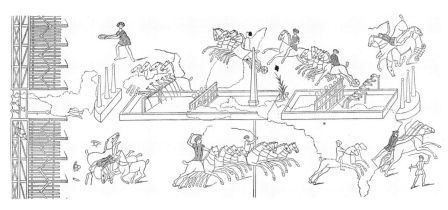

ARCHITECTURE

Roman Interpretation of Greek Forms

The Romans were in awe of Greek architecture and copied its architectural orders. Yet they were selective in what they took from the Greeks, preferring the elaborate Corinthian order over the Doric and Ionic. They also built on a much bigger scale than the Greeks, determined to outdo them. No Roman admired Greek architecture more than Emperor Hadrian, himself a skilled architect. As a young man, Hadrian's admiration for Greece had even earned him the nickname Graeculus, the Greekling. After becoming emperor in AD 117, he embarked on a massive building program. Its centerpiece in Rome was the Temple of Venus and Roma, the two patron goddesses of the city.

Temple of Roma and Venus
Hadrian's temple of Venus and Roma, built between *c.* AD 125 and 135, was the most magnificent temple in Rome. It followed the Corinthian order and was modeled on the Temple of Olympian Zeus in Athens. The Athens temple, begun in the 6th century BC, had only recently been completed by Hadrian. Although it was the biggest temple in Greece, Hadrian's building in Rome was even larger. Its base measured 476 ft (145 m) by 328 ft (100 m).

Inside the Temple of Roma and Venus
Unlike a classical Greek temple, the interior of Hadrian's building had a vaulted ceiling, which allowed a wide space to be enclosed without the need for columns. It was also, unusually, a double temple, in which the statues of Venus and Roma sat back to back. This may have appealed to Hadrian's sense of humor, for Roma, backward, spells *amor* (love).

See also
Architecture,
pages 252–5

Corinthian column

The Corinthian was a Greek development of the Ionic order, sharing the Ionic column's ridges and ornamental base. Unlike the Ionic capital, with its volutes, or scrolls, the Corinthian was decorated with rows of acanthus leaves. Although the Greeks invented this capital, the Romans used it more widely, loving its rich ornamentation. Most Corinthian columns we see in Greece today are from the Roman Period.

Temple of Fortuna Augusta
Across the Empire, Romans built in the Corinthian style. This small temple, from Pompeii, dating from 3 BC, was dedicated to Emperor Augustus. Its eight Corinthian columns support a long portico, or *pronaos*, the ceiling of which is decorated with nine coffers.

The Composite column
The Romans combined Corinthian leaves and Ionic volutes to make the Composite capital, their own invention. At the top of a Composite capital, above the Corinthian acanthus leaves, the corners were decorated with four Ionic volutes.

Tuscan capital
The Romans developed a slender form of the Greek Doric column, sometimes called Tuscan. Unlike Greek Doric, a Tuscan column lacked fluting and had a base and a horizontal ridge below the capital. Although Tuscan capitals were often plain, this example is decorated with an egg-and-dart motif borrowed from the Ionic order.

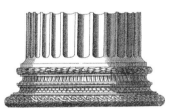

Building Techniques

Unlike the Greeks, who built in stone, Roman builders mostly used concrete and brick, reserving the costlier stone for decorative facades. Roman concrete, invented in the 3rd century BC, combined a mortar made from lime and pozzolana (volcanic sand) with various aggregates. The choice of aggregate depended on the concrete's function. For foundations, builders used heavy limestone rubble, while lighter pumice was used for vaults. The Romans did not invent the arch, which had been used by earlier civilizations, including the Mesopotamians, for drains. Yet they were the first to use arches extensively in above-ground building projects. The use of brick, concrete, vaults, and arches enabled the Romans to build massive structures, including aqueducts, bridges, bathhouses, and amphitheaters.

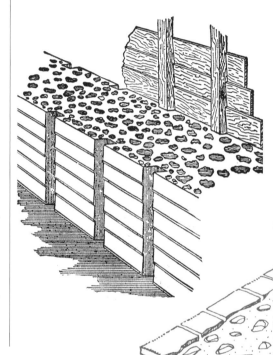

Concrete foundations ◀
For foundations, builders poured concrete between a shuttering of planks nailed to upright lumber. In this illustration, the left side of the shuttering has been removed, revealing the impression left in the concrete by the planks and uprights. Unlike modern concrete, the Roman material was filled with an aggregate of large stones.

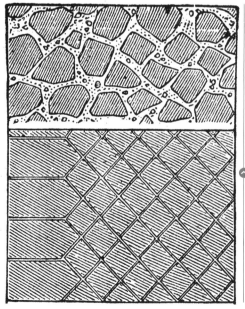

▶ **Stone facings**
For concrete walls, Roman builders used several types of facing, in stone, brick, or a combination of the two. The earliest method, at the top, was *opus incertum*, using irregularly shaped stones. From the 2nd century BC, builders used stones cut into squares, laid at an angle of 45 degrees. This was called *opus reticulatum* (net work).

◉ **Opus testaceum**
From the 1st century AD, *opus testaceum*, using fired bricks, became a common method of facing concrete. Roman bricks, mass-produced in several standard sizes, were longer and flatter than modern ones. However a wall was faced, it was usually covered with white stucco, made from powdered limestone, or marble or limestone panels.

Triumphal arch

A Roman invention, the triumphal arch was originally designed as a victory monument. By the 2nd century AD, arches were also built to celebrate a ruler's civil accomplishments, such as the building of a new road or harbor. This arch, at Beneventum (Benevento) in southern Italy, was erected in honor of Trajan by the Senate in AD 114. It stood over the Via Traiana, a new road, built by the emperor.

See also

Technology,
pages 236–9

Architecture,
pages 250–1

Architecture,
pages 254–5

Interior decoration

From the time of Augustus, the Romans used different colored marbles and granites for columns and inlays. In this artist's impression of a palace interior, the columns with composite capitals are made of porphyry, purple marble from Egypt. The floor is inlaid with panels of colored marble. The barrel-vaulted concrete ceiling is set with square coffers and decorated with flowers.

The Bridge of Aemilius

The Bridge of Aemilius was Rome's first stone bridge, originally built in 179 BC, with stone piers and a wooden superstructure. Thirty-seven years later it was rebuilt with six stone arches. When Augustus restored the bridge in 12 BC, he used a concrete core faced with stone.

The Pantheon

The greatest Roman architectural achievement was the invention of the dome, developed from a number of arches, rotated in a circle. The first domes were built in the 1st century AD, and used for the ceilings of temples, bathhouses, and palaces. The most celebrated dome is that of the Pantheon, a temple built by Hadrian between AD 118 and 125. With a diameter of 142 ft (43.3 m), it was double the size of any known earlier dome and remains the largest unreinforced concrete dome in the world. The Pantheon had a conservative, Corinthian exterior. In Roman times it was hemmed in by other buildings, and a visitor would not even be aware that it had a dome until he went inside. One of the most influential buildings in history, the Pantheon has been imitated by architects from the Renaissance onward.

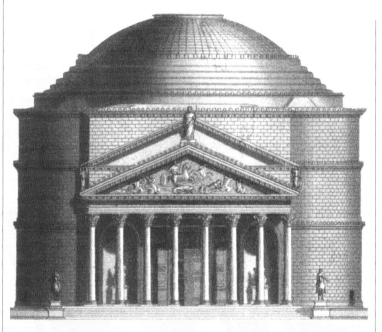

Exterior
The Pantheon's facade has two rows of eight massive Corinthian columns, each 39 ft (11.8 m) tall. These were made of gray-and-red granite brought from quarries in Egypt. Above the columns is an inscription, attributing the Pantheon to Marcus Agrippa, who built the first temple on the site in 27 BC. As a public show of modesty, Hadrian always preserved the names of original builders when he restored temples.

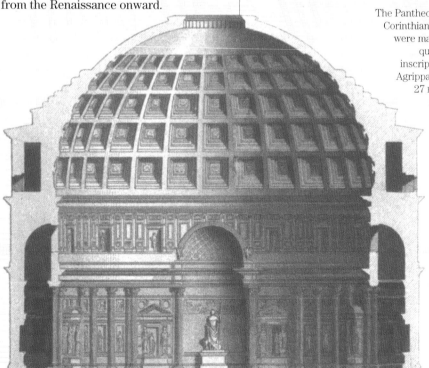

Rotunda
The rotunda's width and height are both exactly 142 ft (43.3 m). It was designed as a sphere, the lower half of which has been stretched out to create a cylinder. The construction of such a large dome, weighing around 4,920 tons (5,000 tonnes), demanded a vast wooden framework, called centering, to support it while the mortar set.

Coffers

The ceiling is set with five rows of ornamental coffers of diminishing size, which reduced the dome's weight. There are twenty-eight in each row, perhaps chosen as the number of days in the lunar calendar. Each coffer has its interior squares aligned to its upper edges, so it can be seen from the ground.

See also
Architecture,
pages 250–3

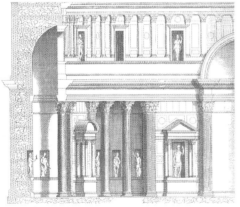

Exedrae

The interior has eight recesses, called *exedrae*, one of them shown in shadow here. These are alternately curved and rectangular. The *exedrae* were for statues of gods, which also stood in niches in the walls. Although it was called the Pantheon (all gods), this may have been a popular nickname rather than the official title. T°he temple's exact function is unclear today.

Oculus

The opening in the ceiling, called an oculus, admits a strong beam of sunlight, which moves around the interior, striking different parts of the rotunda at different times of the day and the year. It may have been used to illuminate specific statues of gods, on their festival days.

ROMAN HOUSES

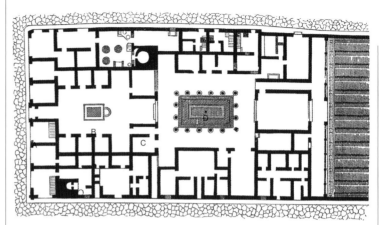

Construction, Arrangement, and Use

Much of what we know of Roman town houses comes from Pompeii, in southern Italy, which was buried in AD 79 by the eruption of Mount Vesuvius. Starting in the 18th century, the city was gradually excavated, revealing many wonderfully preserved buildings. Houses were inward-facing with blank outer walls, and the light was admitted through roof openings and courtyards. The homes of the wealthy were large and divided between public spaces, where visitors were received, and private living quarters. The most richly decorated room, with mosaics, frescoes, and statues, was the atrium, or reception hall. Beyond lay the *tablinum*, the office of the head of the house, and a small garden. There were often two dining rooms, called *triclinia*, one to be used in winter and the other in summer.

House of Pansa

The most magnificent house in Pompeii was the House of Pansa, which occupied almost a whole *insula*, or block. The street entrance (A), left, was flanked by six small shops let out to tenants. The building has a symmetrical plan, with atrium (B), *tablinum* (C), and garden (D) on a central axis. The shaded area on the right, is part of a large vegetable garden, which occupied a third of the *insula*.

See also

Architecture,
pages 252–3

Roman houses,
pages 258–9

Insulae

Pompeii was divided into blocks called *insulae* (islands), which were then subdivided into houses. This plan shows part of an *insula* occupied by two houses, the House of the Centaur on the left and the House of Castor and Pollux on the right. These names were given by the excavators, based on distinctive wall paintings and mosaics. Each house was formed by joining together three smaller ones.

Window

For security, there were few windows on an *insula*'s outer walls. A window often took the form of a narrow slit, designed for ventilation rather than lighting. With their blank outer walls, Pompeiian *insulae* resembled small fortresses.

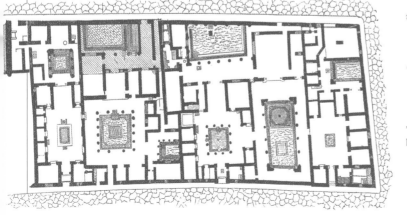

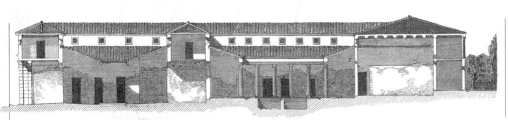

Two floors

The House of Pansa, here in cross section, had two floors, like most Pompeiian houses. On the upper floor are the windows, facing inward, over the atrium and colonnaded garden. The atrium, with an inward-sloping roof unsupported by columns, is Tuscan, as described by Vitruvius (active 46–30 BC) in his book on architecture.

Household shrine

Every family had a household shrine, where statuettes of the gods who protected the home were kept and worshipped. Sometimes this took the form of a simple niche, painted to resemble a temple. This elaborate shrine, in the form of a miniature temple on a podium, is called an *aedicula*.

Tetra-style atrium

This is an artist's reconstruction of a tetra-style atrium, in which the roof opening was supported by four columns. The opening, called a *compluvium*, let in light and channeled rainwater into the *impluvium*, or ornamental pool, below. The walls are lined with busts of the family's illustrious ancestors.

Peristyle garden

Beyond the *tablinum* most of the houses in Pompeii had a small courtyard garden, neatly laid out with hedges, paths, and statues. Its walls were often painted with frescoes of plants, making the garden appear larger. The most common type was the peristyle, with colonnades, providing shade on hot days.

Beware of the dog

On entering a house visitors walked through an entrance corridor (*fauces*), the floor of which was sometimes decorated with a mosaic of a snarling guard dog. This was a deterrent to burglars. This mosaic, from the House of the Tragic Poet, has the words *cave canem* (Beware of the dog) written beneath it.

Atrium and tablinum

This is the atrium of the House of the Tragic Poet, which was Tuscan in style. Beyond the atrium lies the *tablinum*, looking out onto a small colonnaded garden. The *tablinum* was the office of the head of the household where, each morning, he received the visitors who waited in the atrium. Important family documents were kept in a chest in the *tablinum*.

ROMAN HOUSES

Furniture

Roman houses were more sparsely furnished than modern homes, and small items, such as chairs and tables, were moved from room to room as they were needed. Furniture was made of wood, bronze, and marble. In Pompeii wooden items were destroyed by the ash and pumice that buried the city. It was different up the coast at Herculaneum, which was covered in boiling mud. The mud carbonized and preserved organic materials and left complete cupboards, beds, tables, couches, and chairs. The furniture was beautifully made, with decorative ornamentation. Luxury furniture, Hellenistic in style, was introduced to Rome by Gnaeus Manlius Vulso, who paraded bronze couches and pedestal tables captured from the east in his triumph in 187 BC.

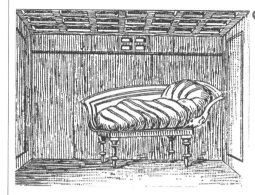

Lectus
There were several types of *lectus*, or couch. This example, with two arms and a solid back, resembles a modern sofa. The cushion is at the right end of the couch, because Romans usually reclined on their left side, leaving their right hand free to hold a scroll or a drink.

Bedroom
Roman houses had many small *cubicula*, or bedrooms, which could have held little furniture other than the bed itself. There were different *cubicula* for sleeping at night and resting in daytime. Mattresses and pillows were stuffed with wool or goose feathers.

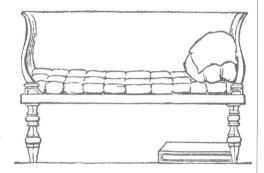

Lighting
Like the Greeks, the Romans lit their homes using small pottery or bronze oil lamps, filled with olive oil and with a short wick. A single lamp does not give much light, so multiple lamps were hung from bronze stands; some stands found at Pompeii had as many as fourteen. This bronze tree stand is 20 in (50 cm) high.

Bed
This is a reconstruction of a Roman bed, based on its metal parts found in the House of Menander in Pompeii. It is made of wood with bronze legs and fittings. The reconstructors assumed that it had leather webbing to support the mattress. However, surviving beds from Herculaneum have a wooden grid across the center.

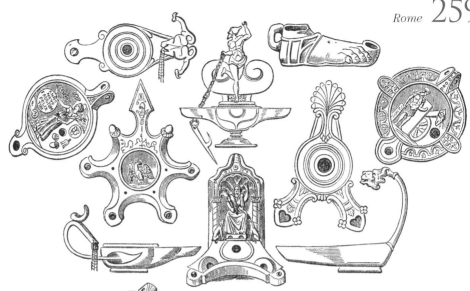

Decorated lamps

This is a small selection of the thousands of lamps found in Pompeii and Herculaneum. They came in many forms and could have single or multiple wicks. Pottery lamps, mass-produced in molds, were decorated with reliefs showing gladiators, chariot races, and mythological and erotic scenes.

Cupboard

Roman cupboards resembled modern ones, with rows of shelves and full-length panel doors. Cupboards were used to store clothing, which was folded rather than hung up in a wardrobe.

See also
Technology,
pages 236–7
Roman houses,
pages 256–7

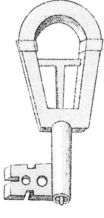

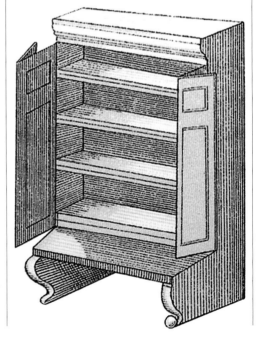

Heating

Rooms were heated using charcoal fires in small, portable, ornamental braziers. This bronze brazier, supported by three fauns with outstretched right arms, is a superb example of Hellenistic art.

Key

Roman families kept their valuables, including money and important documents, in a bronze-and-iron strongbox, usually in the *tablinum*. This Roman key is of the type used for tumbler locks.

FOOD

Food and Entertaining

Superficially, a Roman dinner party resembled a Greek symposium. In both, men and women reclined on couches to eat and drink wine. However, at a symposium only male citizens were present, accompanied by lower status, noncitizen, women. In contrast, both male and female Roman citizens dined together. Unlike a symposium, where guests had equal positions, the Romans had a hierarchy of honor based on the diner's position on the couches. In Greece the dishes were simple, using locally produced ingredients, and the focus was on the second part of the event, the drinking session. The Romans were more interested in the food and would eat up to seven courses of lavishly presented, exotic dishes. A Roman banquet might last eight hours, and the guests were often entertained between courses by musicians and dancers.

Bronze table

Dishes were served on small, round tables, often made of bronze. This example from Pompeii is decorated at the top with skulls and garlands. The legs, ornamented with three sphinxes, terminate in animal paws.

Fast food

During the daytime, Romans ate informally, often at street bars called *thermopolia*. A *thermopolium* had a masonry counter with large earthenware jars set into it, holding hot food and mulled wine. It offered the Roman equivalent of today's fast food.

Triclinium

A *triclinium* held three couches, for nine diners. The couch arrangement created an open space, where the food was served and entertainment provided. The left couch, where the family reclined, with the host at the top, was lowest in rank. The central couch was more honorable, with the very best positions on the right. The arrows show the positions of the diners' bodies.

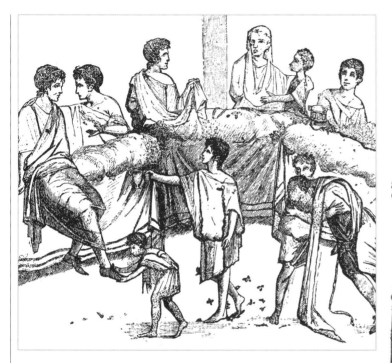

Serving the guests ◄

Serving the guests
Household slaves washed the guests' feet when they arrived, served the dishes, and brought ewers of perfumed water and towels for the diners to wash their hands between courses. This wall painting from Pompeii shows the end of a banquet as the guests prepare to depart. One is helped on with his sandals, while a drunk guest, supported by a slave, bends over to vomit.

Dishes ◄
The Roman love of food is reflected in these wall paintings from Pompeii, showing a fowl, a hare, fish, and some figs. Literary sources describe exotic dishes combining unusual ingredients. Suetonius (*c.* AD 69–*c.* 130), biographer of Vitellius (AD 69), described one dish served to the gluttonous emperor, called the Shield of Minerva. Its recipe called for "pike livers, pheasant brains, peacock brains, flamingo tongues and lamprey milt."

Mulled wine ◄
Wine, always mixed with water, was served in various ways, and might be spiced, sweetened with honey, or heated. This bronze apparatus, used to mull wine, was found in a villa near Stabiae. Wine, poured into the tall churn-shaped container, passed through the hollow walls of the low box, which held hot charcoal. It was poured through a lion's-head tap.

Silver bowl
Roman tableware was ornately decorated and designed to impress the guests. This bowl, ornamented with olive sprigs, is one of seventy beautiful silver vessels found at Hildesheim in Germany, outside the Empire. It is thought to be booty, perhaps seized from a defeated Roman commander by victorious Germanic warriors. If so, it suggests that, even on campaign, Romans dined lavishly.

See also
Work,
pages 234–5
Trade,
pages 242–3

COSTUME

Men's Clothes

In the *Aeneid* the poet Virgil describes the Roman people as "masters of the earth, the race that wears the toga." The woollen toga, Etruscan in origin, was a privilege reserved for male Roman citizens, and it was a central expression of their identity. Like most high-status clothing, it was impractical and uncomfortable to wear, showing that the wearer did not need to perform manual work. A man needed a slave to help him put one on, and he had to move slowly and gracefully with his left arm crooked while wearing it. Yet the toga was required dress for all public occasions, worn in the forum and at public shows. It was worn over a woollen tunic, which was also the basic item of clothing for men of all classes.

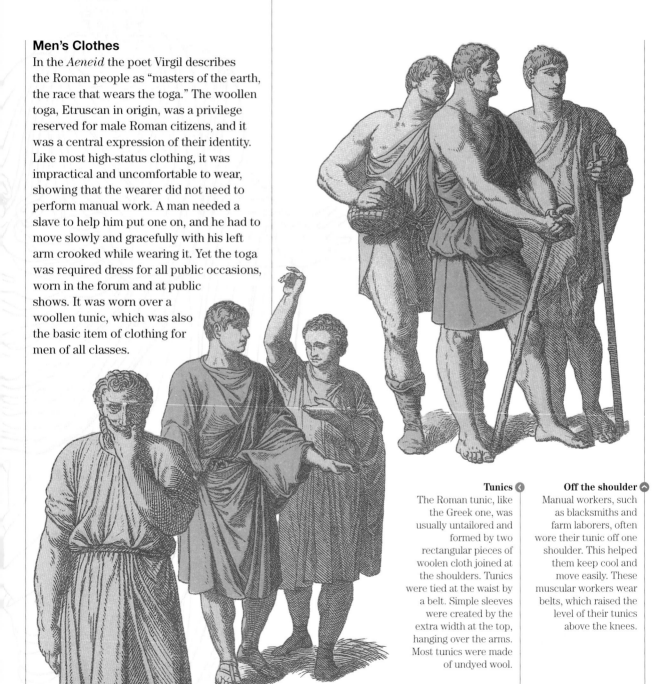

Tunics ◄
The Roman tunic, like the Greek one, was usually untailored and formed by two rectangular pieces of woolen cloth joined at the shoulders. Tunics were tied at the waist by a belt. Simple sleeves were created by the extra width at the top, hanging over the arms. Most tunics were made of undyed wool.

Off the shoulder ◢
Manual workers, such as blacksmiths and farm laborers, often wore their tunic off one shoulder. This helped them keep cool and move easily. These muscular workers wear belts, which raised the level of their tunics above the knees.

Types of toga
Ordinary citizens wore a plain *toga virilis*, made of white wool. Magistrates and boys of high birth wore a *toga praetexta*, which had a purple edge. Men in mourning dressed in a dark *toga pulla*, while those standing for elections wore a *toga candida*, whitened with chalk (the origin of the word 'candidate'). When acting as a priest, a man covered his head with the toga.

See also
Society,
pages 212–13
Work,
pages 232–3
Costume,
pages 264–5

The sinus
The Roman passed the toga around his back, under his right arm, and over his left shoulder again, so that its rear pointed end hung slightly higher than the front one. This wearer is pulling the front edge over, creating a large fold called a *sinus* (lap). The *sinus* was sometimes used as a pocket to carry documents or other small items.

Wearing a toga
The toga was a semicircular piece of woolen cloth, 18 ft (5.5 m) long and 9 ft (2.7 m) wide in the middle. A Roman began by draping it over his left shoulder, with its straight edge against his neck and the pointed end in front touching the ground. This man is shown without his tunic to make the process clearer.

The umbo
The final stage was to create a smaller fold, called an *umbo* (navel), by pulling part of the underlayer in front up over the top of the *sinus*. The *umbo* was decorative, but also helped to hold the toga in place. In this statue of Emperor Septimius Severus, you can see the large *sinus* fold on the left and the smaller *umbo* resting on top of it.

COSTUME

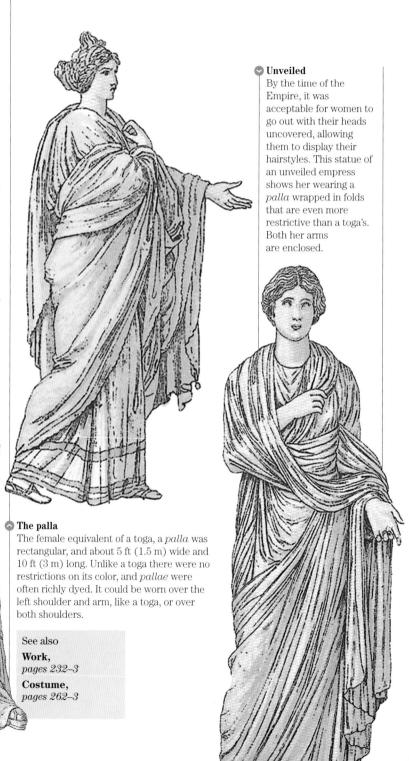

Women's Clothes and Jewelry

Roman women wore a linen tunic that reached the knees, beneath a foot-length *stola*, or dress, made of wool, linen, or silk. Outdoors, they wrapped themselves in a shawl-like mantle called a *palla*. For a wealthy woman, getting dressed in the morning was an elaborate process, requiring the help of two or three household slave girls. The slaves applied her makeup, including white foundation made from chalk or lead, and eyeliner of soot mixed with animal fat. They helped her choose her jewelry for the day. The most elaborate task was dressing the lady's hair, which was often arranged in complex curls or braids. The satirist Juvenal (active late 1st and early 2nd centuries AD) described a rich lady's fury at her hairdresser: "The slave girl arranging her coiffure will have her own hair torn out, poor creature...'Why isn't this curl in place?' the lady screams."

◢ Veil

The *palla*, like a toga, could be drawn up over the head like a veil. Portrait statues of ladies of the imperial family often show them veiled with their *pallas*. This was a traditional gesture, for veiling had been the custom during the Republican Period. In the 2nd century BC, the consul Sulpicius Galba even divorced his wife for going out unveiled.

◣ The palla

The female equivalent of a toga, a *palla* was rectangular, and about 5 ft (1.5 m) wide and 10 ft (3 m) long. Unlike a toga there were no restrictions on its color, and *pallae* were often richly dyed. It could be worn over the left shoulder and arm, like a toga, or over both shoulders.

◢ Unveiled

By the time of the Empire, it was acceptable for women to go out with their heads uncovered, allowing them to display their hairstyles. This statue of an unveiled empress shows her wearing a *palla* wrapped in folds that are even more restrictive than a toga's. Both her arms are enclosed.

See also
Work,
pages 232–3
Costume,
pages 262–3

Wigs

Fashions in women's hairstyles changed constantly, and were often led by the empress, whose portrait could be seen on coins and statues. Many wealthy women wore wigs, and there was a fashion for blonde hair, from German slave girls. This woman wears a wig of braided blonde hair, piled into a tube.

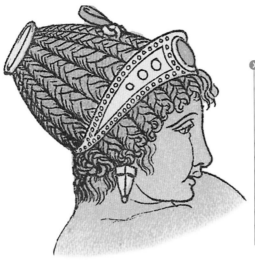

Hairpins

Women held their hair and wigs in place with hairpins, made from gold, silver, ivory, and bone. The tops were often delicately carved with images. A popular subject, as here, was the head of a woman with an elaborate hairstyle. This was sometimes a portrait of the empress whose style was being imitated.

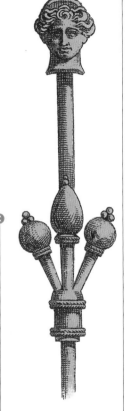

Flavian hairstyle

Hairstyles were at their most elaborate under the Flavian Dynasty (AD 69–96). Flavian empresses wore their hair in a mass of ringlets, piled high at the front. This was often a hairpiece, held in place with a row of bone pins. This hairstyle was satirized by Juvenal, who wrote: "See the tall edifice rise up on her head in serried tiers and storeys!"

Severan hairstyle

This is the Severan hairstyle, which came into fashion in the early 3rd century AD. It was introduced by Julia Domna (AD 170–217), the Syrian wife of Septimius Severus. Her hair resembled a tight helmet with two waved wings on either side of her face. This was probably a wig. In some coin portraits her own hair can be seen protruding from underneath.

Snake bracelets

Rich women wore a large amount of jewelry made from gold and precious stones, including Indian emeralds and pearls and Baltic amber. Bracelets and armbands often took the form of snakes, which were regarded as protective talismans. Because a snake sheds its skin, it was an emblem of renewal.

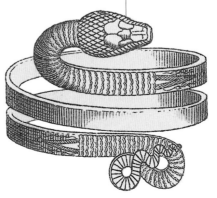

DAILY LIFE

Roman Family

Although our word "family" comes from the Latin *familia*, the Roman notion of the word was very different from a modern "nuclear family." A traditional Roman family was headed by the oldest male, the *paterfamilias* (father of the family). He had authority over all family members, including his children, grandchildren, and slaves. He selected husbands and wives for his children, arranging their marriages with another *paterfamilias*. His adult sons might have wives and children, but they would not be heads of their own families until he died. Daughters often remained under their father's authority even after they married. The family also included the dead ancestors, whose tombs were regularly visited and whose portraits stood in the house.

Bridal ring
Weddings took place in June, sacred to Juno, goddess of wives and mothers. Before the wedding there was a betrothal ceremony. The groom gave his bride a ring, worn on the finger used for wedding rings today. The writer Aulus Gellius (*c.* AD 125–*c.* 180), attempting to explain the custom, wrote: "When the human body is cut open, a very delicate nerve is found which starts from this finger and travels to the heart."

See also
Costume,
pages 262–5
Daily life,
pages 268–71

Dressing the bride
A wall painting from Pompeii shows a mother helping her teenage daughter dress for her wedding. The bride's hair was traditionally arranged in six locks. She wore a white tunic, held at the waist with a woolen "knot of Hercules," which only her husband was permitted to untie.

Husbands and wives

Tomb carvings show husband and wife standing beside each other, emphasizing their close partnership. Epitaphs often praise ideal wives with the words: "She stayed at home, she worked at her wool." Yet, over time, women became increasingly independent. By the early Empire, a wife had the right to divorce her husband. She could maintain control of her dowry, which would be returned to her in the event of divorce.

The wedding

This bride wears a traditional flame-colored veil, called a *flammeum*. The ceremony took place in the bride's house, where the families gathered, and the couple's right hands were linked by a maid of honor. After sacrificing a pig, a wedding feast was held. The groom then led his bride to her new home, where he carried her over the threshold. This was to avoid her tripping, which would be an unlucky omen.

Children

The purpose of marriage was to produce children. Boys were more highly valued than girls, because they would keep the family name going and win honor. Girls had to be provided with dowries, although they were useful in making alliances with other families. A terra-cotta relief, on the right, shows two slaves carrying a *lectica* (litter), the Roman equivalent of a baby carriage.

Empress Livia

Livia (58 BC–AD 29) was the wife of Emperor Augustus, who promoted her public image as the devoted wife and mother. Livia dressed modestly, and even spun and wove wool for her husband's tunics. Behind the scenes, she was very influential; it was rumored that she plotted against Augustus' chosen heirs in favor of Tiberius, her son from a previous marriage. Caligula, referring to her scheming, called her *Ulixes Stolatus* 'Odysseus in a *stola*').

DAILY LIFE

Children

More is known about the lives of children in Roman times than for almost any other period before the 19th century. Evidence includes toys from graves, portraits of boys and girls, mosaics and reliefs of children playing and going to school, and even a book, *Onomasticon* by Julius Pollux (active 2nd century AD), describing children's games. In their letters Romans often talk affectionately of their children. Marcus Cornelius Fronto (*c.* AD 100–70) wrote to his son-in-law about his infant grandson: "The one word your little Fronto continually says is 'Give!' (*da*). I hand over whatever I can... He shows signs of his grandfather's character too: he is particularly greedy for grapes... He is also very keen on little birds: he loves young chicks, pigeons, and sparrows... From my earliest childhood, I too was enthralled by these birds."

Ball games

Children played with balls of wood or leather stuffed with feathers or horsehair. Most games were based on throwing and catching. In his book *Onomasticon*, Julius Pollux, the Greek tutor to Emperor Commodus (AD 161–92), describes several ball games.

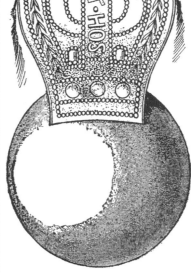

Bulla ◀
Babies of citizen status were given a bag-shaped gold or silver amulet, called a *bulla*, to wear around their necks. Like the *crepundia*, the *bulla* was apotropaic, warding off the evil eye, but was also a mark of status. When a boy assumed the *toga virilis*, between the ages of fourteen and seventeen, he set aside his *bulla*, dedicating it to the *lares* at the household shrine. Girls did this on the eve of their wedding day.

See also
Daily life,
pages 266–7
Daily life,
pages 270–1

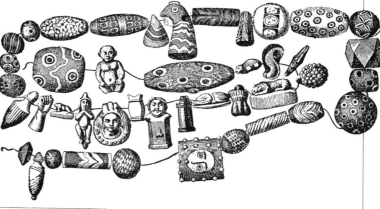

Crepundia
Newborn babies were not named until the eighth day after birth, in the case of girls, and the ninth day for boys. A purification ceremony was held in the home, where a sacrifice was offered to the gods. The parents gave the baby a set of toys, called *crepundia*, which were also believed to protect it from the evil eye (*fascinatio*). Belief in the evil eye, common in ancient Greece and Italy, survives in these countries today.

Dolls

Girls played with dolls made from pottery, bone, or wood, often with jointed limbs. Many dolls have been found in children's tombs. For boys there were gladiator dolls, the Roman equivalent of Action Man.

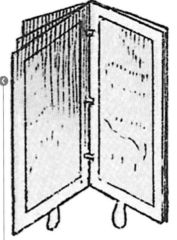

Discipline

Teachers frequently beat their pupils, as this wall painting of a school from Pompeii demonstrates. In one of his epigrams, the poet Martial complained of the noise from a neighboring school: "What's your quarrel with me, horrible schoolteacher, hateful to boys? The cocks have not yet broken the silence, and already your threatening grumbles and beatings thunder."

Education

Boys and girls learned to read and write, using a wax tablet and a stylus. They were usually taught at home by their parents or by a slave tutor. For many boys, there were also three levels of formal education: elementary school, grammar school, and rhetoric school. These schools were small and privately run, often by Greek freedmen, who charged a small fee for their lessons.

Literature

The *grammaticus*, or grammar teacher, taught Greek and Latin language and literature, in particular the poetry of Homer and Virgil. Educated Romans were expected to be bilingual, and the ability to quote the great poets was the mark of a cultivated man. Books were written on papyrus scrolls, read from left to right. After reading a column, the reader rolled it up with his left hand, unrolling a new column on the right.

Death and Funerals

The Romans believed that the dead belonged to a collective body of gods or spirits, called *manes* (spirits of the dead). It was essential to be given a proper funeral and a tomb, which would serve as a home for the spirit of the departed. The unburied dead were thought to become restless spirits, called *lemures*, who would haunt the living. During a funeral, the body was washed and laid out and a coin placed in the mouth. It was then placed on a couch or bier and carried in a procession to the tomb. In the late republic and early Empire, cremation was the usual way of disposing of the dead. From the 1st century AD, the practice of inhumation slowly spread across the Empire until, by the 3rd century AD, it was almost universal.

Pyramid tomb
Prominent Romans were buried in magnificent tombs, which took many architectural forms. This marble-faced pyramid tomb was built around 18 BC outside Rome for Caius Cestius, a minor senator. The Romans of the time were obsessed with Egyptian-style monuments and art.

Street of tombs
The dead were buried outside town in tombs on either side of the road. This kept the spirits at a safe distance from the living. It was the ideal location for a lasting memorial, which could be seen by travelers and was easily visited by relatives. Romans who could not afford their own tomb might join a burial society and reserve a place in a communal one. Shown here is the street of tombs outside Pompeii.

See also
Religion,
pages 230–1
Daily life,
pages 266–9

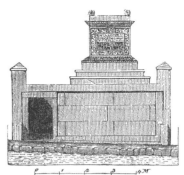

Tomb of Naevoleia Tyche

In the 1st century AD a rich Pompeiian businesswoman, Naevoleia Tyche, set up a grand tomb for herself, her husband, Caius Munatius Faustus, and their freedmen. Above the inscription, which describes Naevoleia herself as a freedwoman, there is a relief portrait of her. Beneath the inscription is a relief of funeral ceremonies.

Paying the ferryman

When Naevoleia's tomb was opened, it was found to contain several glass urns in lead cases. Each held ashes, bones, and a coin. Although Roman belief was that spirits remained in or around their tombs, they took the Greek idea that the dead were rowed across a river to the underworld. The coin was the fee for Charon, boatman of the dead.

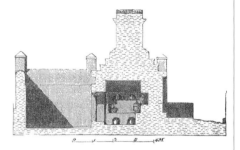

Tomb chamber

This cross section of Naevoleia Tyche's tomb shows the chamber where the urns holding the ashes of the dead were placed. The chamber was seen as a collective home for the dead. Members of burial societies held regular feasts, so that they could become acquainted with their companions in the next life.

Funeral triclinium

This funeral *triclinium*, used for banquets, stands among the tombs of Pompeii. Romans remembered their dead loved ones during festivals and on the birthday of the deceased. They would visit the tomb and share a meal with the dead. The most important festival was the Parentalia, in honor of dead parents, between February 13 and 21.

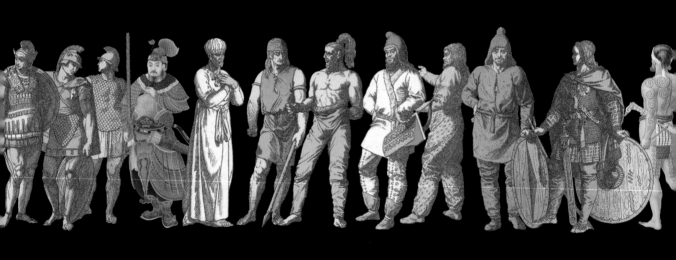

OTHER CIVILIZATIONS

INTRODUCTION

From a traditional Western perspective, the preeminent ancient civilizations were those of Mesopotamia, Egypt, Greece, and Rome. However, many other cultures existed on every continent in ancient times, not least those that vied with the Mediterranean cultures and Mesopotamia in the Middle East and Western Asia, notably the Persian Achaemenids, Parthians, and Sasanids. In Europe, while classical Greece and Rome loom large, cultures including the Minoans, the Etruscans, the Celts, and the Germanic peoples also flourished.

Some of the earliest civilizations were in southern and eastern Asia. Beginning some seven thousand years ago, Chinese civilization developed in the valley of the Huang River; and in 221 BC the country was unified under a single emperor. In India, as in Mesopotamia and Egypt, civilizations developed around the fertile floodplain of a major river, here the Indus. Over nearly four thousand years many sophisticated cultures emerged, including the Indus Valley and Aryan civilizations and the Mauryan, Kushan, and Gupta Empires.

Besides Egypt, the kingdoms of Kerma, Kush, and Meroë developed along the banks of the Nile, while Aksum in Ethiopia became a major power in East Africa. Farming and ironworking were developed in West Africa and spread to most of sub-Saharan Africa from the 6th century BC.

In the Americas civilizations developed disconnected from events elsewhere. Complex societies emerged in Mesoamerica and along the western coast and highlands of South America, producing the fine art and architecture of the Olmecs, Maya, Chavín, Moche, and many others.

THE WORLD
500 BC

In 500 BC the world stood poised on the
brink of major changes. The demands of
expanding populations, together with
advances in technology, led to increased
trade and cultural interchange.
As democracy and science developed
in Greece, remarkable new religions
and philosophies were flowering in
the east, including Buddhism,
Jainism, Confucianism, and Taoism.

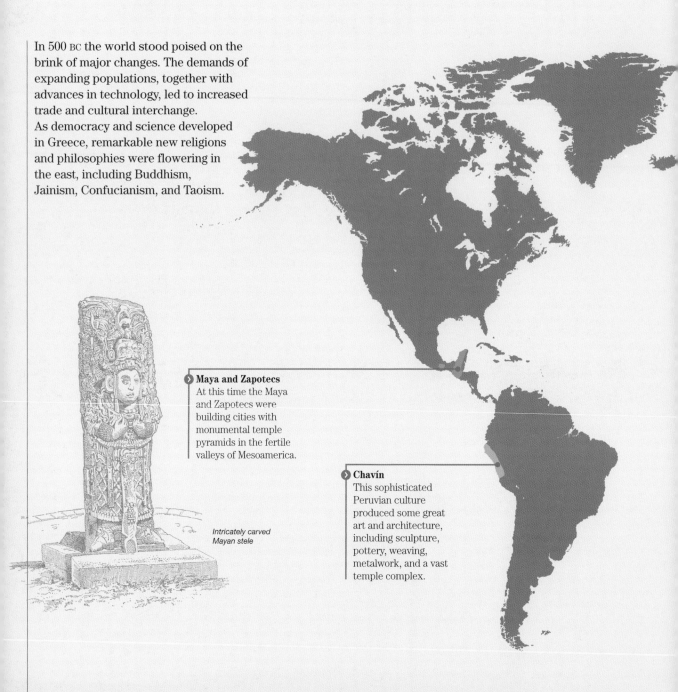

*Intricately carved
Mayan stele*

Maya and Zapotecs
At this time the Maya
and Zapotecs were
building cities with
monumental temple
pyramids in the fertile
valleys of Mesoamerica.

Chavín
This sophisticated
Peruvian culture
produced some great
art and architecture,
including sculpture,
pottery, weaving,
metalwork, and a vast
temple complex.

Shield, showing typically complex Celtic knotwork

Etruscans

The city states of Etruria in central Italy grew wealthy from mining and trading in metals and were an important influence on the Romans.

Nineteenth-century reimagining of Etruscan warriors

Scythians

These fearsome mounted warriors from western Central Asia were the major power of the steppelands during the middle of the 1st millennium BC.

China

The Zhou Dynasty was in terminal decline, and China was about to be engulfed by a long power struggle known as the Warring States Period.

Celts

The Celts were talented artists and fierce warriors from the northern Alps. By 500 BC, they were spreading their culture through western Europe.

The Achaemenid Empire

The largest Empire the world had yet seen, this spanned three continents from Libya in the west to the Indus in the east.

India

Northern India was split into sixteen kingdoms, dominated by Magadha (modern Bengal and Bihar), while southern India was populated by isolated tribal peoples.

Meroë

The kingdom of Meroë flourished in Nubia. Meroë was heavily influenced by Egyptian culture.

Phoenicians

The Phoenicians were a major seafaring power in the Mediterranean during the 1st millennium BC. They founded Carthage, an early rival of Rome.

Carthaginian coin, depicting an elephant on one side

The Egyptian-inspired pyramids of Meroë

SOUTH ASIA
3500 BC–AD 550

c. 3500 BC

Farming begins in the Indus Valley. The first farmers live in mud-brick houses and grow legumes, fruit, cotton, wheat, and barley, and raise cattle, sheep, and goats.

c. 3100 BC

The first towns appear in the Indus Valley. The towns trade grain and other foods with highland peoples, who offer them timber, metal, and semiprecious stones.

Early tablet with Sanskrit text

c. 1500 BC

The Aryans, a central Asian people related to the Persians, migrate to India. They gradually dominate the indigenous population, extending their control over the whole of northern India.

1500–900 BC

The Aryans develop a language, Sanskrit, and compose a set of sacred poems called the Vedas. These are the earliest scriptures of Hinduism.

c. 563

Siddhartha Gautama, the spiritual teacher who founded Buddhism, is born. The Buddha taught that a person can achieve enlightenment by suppressing worldly desires.

c. 540 BC

Vardhamana Mahavira, the founder of Jainism, is born in Bharat, India. Over the next 1,000 years, Jainism spreads to central and western India.

c. 500 BC

The dominant *mahajanapada* is Magadha, under its powerful *raja* Bimbisara. Aryan towns, including Ujjain and Kausambi, grow into cities.

340 BC

The Nanda Dynasty controls much of central and northeastern India.

326 BC

Alexander the Great, the Macedonian king, conquers northwestern India. However, before he can invade Magadha, his army mutinies and he is forced to retreat.

Buddha with his disciples

305 BC

Chandragupta fights a great battle with Seleucus. The two kings make a treaty and a marriage alliance. Seleucus offers Chandragupta control of the whole Indus Valley.

293 BC

Chandragupta abdicates in favor of his son Bindusara, who extends the Mauryan Empire deep into southern India.

268 BC

Bindusara dies and is succeeded by his son Ashoka, who continues the expansionist policies of his father and grandfather.

Bust of Alexander the Great

240 BC

The Third Buddhist Council helps to establish Buddhist doctrine and lays the groundwork for the expansion of the religion.

232–185 BC

The Mauryan Empire is ruled by a succession of weaker kings and gradually loses territory.

230 BC–AD 220

The Satavahana Empire dominates southern and central India. The Satavahanas establish peace and order in their Empire and manage to resist numerous foreign invaders following the fall of the Mauryan Empire.

135 BC

Nomadic descendants of the Yueh-Chi from the central Asian steppes migrate southwest to conquer the Greek kingdom of Bactria. They form themselves into five chiefdoms, the most powerful of which is Kushan or Kuei-shuang.

73 BC

The last Shunga king, Devabhuti (reigned 83–73 BC), is overthrown by his minister Vasudeva Kanva, who establishes his own Dynasty.

Carved seals from
Mohenjo Daro

c. 2600 BC

The first cities are built. The largest, at Harappa and Mohenjo Daro, have populations of up to 50,000. There are also smaller cities at Ganweriwala, Rakhigari, and Dholavira.

2000–1700

Indus Valley civilization comes to an end. No one can be sure why. Theories include climate change, plague, foreign invasion, and overpopulation.

1000–800 BC

The Aryans settle on the plain of the Ganges river. They live there as semi-nomadic *janas* or clans. Each *jana* is ruled by a *raja*.

Early bronze of the god Shiva

c. 900 BC

The *janas* form into settled tribal kingdoms called *janapadas* (meaning "foothold of a tribe"). They build settlements of wood and sun-dried mud.

c. 700 BC

The *janapadas* merge to form sixteen *mahajanapadas*, or great realms, that stretch across the whole of northern India. They include Kasi, Kosala, Anga, Magadha, Vajji, and Malla.

500s BC

A written form of Sanskrit is developed. The Vedas are written down. The four main texts are the Rigveda, the Yajurveda, the Samaveda and the Artharvaveda.

c. 500 BC

From this time the Vedic deities are superseded by three powerful gods, Vishnu, Shiva, and Shakti, and the religion of Hinduism emerges in its current form.

364 BC

Mahapadma Nanda, founder of the Nanda Dynasty, takes control of the Magadha kingdom. The Nandas build a vast army and set about creating an Empire.

Lion capital, Ashoka's column

321 BC

A young soldier from Magadha, Chandragupta Maurya, inspired by Alexander, raises an army and seizes the throne from Dhana, the unpopular Nanda king.

311 BC

By this date, Chandragupta Maurya has conquered the whole of northern India as far as the Indus. This brings him into conflict with the Macedonian general and ruler Seleucus.

c. 261 BC

After witnessing the terrible death and suffering caused by his conquest of Kalinga, Ashoka converts to Buddhism. He rejects warfare and tries to live according to Buddhist principles.

c. 250 BC

Ashoka's Buddhist missionaries arrive in Sri Lanka and establish Buddhism as the state religion.

190 BC

Demetrius, a Bactrian Greek king (reigned 190–167 BC), establishes a Dynasty that rules northwestern India until around 94 BC.

185 BC

The Mauryan Dynasty, now in control of only Magadha in eastern and northcentral India, ends when the last Mauryan king, Brihadrata, is overthrown by Pushyamitra Shunga, one of his generals. Shunga establishes his own Dynasty.

26 BC

The Kanva Dynasty is brought to an end by the Satavahanas of southern India.

AD 50

The Kushans, under Kujala Kadphises, defeat the northern Sakas and extend their territory into northwest India.

c. AD 75–100

Kujala Kadphises' successor, Vima Kadphises, conquers the Indus Valley and much of the Ganges plain. The Kushan Empire now stretches from the Aral Sea in the north to the Ganges in the south.

AD 100–130

The Kushan Empire reaches its height under Kanishka (reigned *c.* 100–130). Kanishka is a great sponsor of the arts. His Empire grows wealthy through control of trade routes between China and the West.

Camels, essential on early trade routes

C. AD 225

Following the death of the eighth Kushan ruler, Vasudeva I (191–225), the Kushan Empire splits into western and eastern halves.

AD 225–240

The Persian Sasanid Empire conquers the western Kushan Empire. The Kushan Dynasty is replaced by Persian vassals known as Kushanshas.

AD 320

The Gupta Dynasty is founded by Chandra Gupta I (reigned AD 320–335). Through a marriage alliance, Chandra Gupta wins control of Magadha.

Hanuman and his army, in a story from the Ramayana

AD 335

Chandra Gupta I dies and is succeeded by his son Samudra Gupta (reigned 335–380). Samudra Gupta extends the Empire right across northern and eastern India.

Sasanid sculpture of a mounted nobleman

AD 380–415

The Gupta Empire reaches its zenith under Chandra Gupta II, often referred to as the Golden Age of India, a time of enormous creativity in the arts and sciences.

5th century AD

Hinduism recovers in India under the devout Guptas. The great Hindu epics the *Ramayana* and *Mahabharata* reach their final form. *Puja*, or image worship, inspires temple building and beautiful sculptures of Hindu gods.

C. AD 400

India's most famous poet Kalidasa writes his plays and poetry.

AD 415–455

Kamaragupta is an effective ruler, whose peaceful reign is marred near the end by attacks from a rival Dynasty, the Pushyamitras.

AD 450s

The Gupta Empire is attacked by the Ephthalites, or White Huns, a nomadic people from Central Asia.

C. AD 455–467

Skanda Gupta, the last great Gupta emperor, defeats the Pushyamitras and drives out the White Huns.

AD 480s

The White Huns manage to break through Gupta defences in the northwest.

AD 499

The scholar Aryabhata, who is believed to be the first to come up with the concept of zero, puts forward his theories of astronomy, including his idea that the earth moves around the sun.

C. AD 500

The White Hun king Toramana and his successor Mihirakula conquer several provinces of the Gupta Empire.

AD 505–511

The White Huns overrun northern India and sack the Gupta capital, Pataliputra.

AD 511

The Gupta Empire collapses. Gupta territory is reduced to little more than its heartland, Magadha. India is once again divided into small kingdoms.

AD 540–550

The reign of Vishnu Gupta, the last recognized king of the Gupta Dynasty.

c. 40,000 BC

Australoid people from China and Southeast Asia use boats or rafts to reach New Guinea and Australia (then part of one giant landmass) in a series of island-hopping voyages.

c. 4500 BC

Peoples from the Philippines, Indonesia, and Melanesia begin to settle many of the islands of Micronesia. They live by growing yams, breadfruit, and taro in the fertile volcanic soil.

c. 4th millennium BC

The Austronesian-speaking peoples originally from Taiwan successfully cultivate rice. This causes their population to swell, prompting their expansion into the Philippines, Malaysia, and Indonesia.

c. 2000 BC

By this time, the Austronesians have become the dominant people in the Philippines, Malaysia, and Indonesia.

c. 2000 BC

Austronesians begin colonizing the coastal areas and islands of New Guinea, mingling with the original Australoid settlers who had been there since *c.* 40,000 BC.

c. 1600 BC

The interaction between the Austronesians and Australoid people in New Guinea produces Lapita culture, characterized by its reddish brown clay pottery decorated with elaborate repeated patterns.

c. 1600–1000 BC

The Lapita use sail- or paddle-powered canoes to begin to settle Melanesia.

c. 13th century BC

The Lapita invent the outrigger canoe. A wooden float is attached to the canoe, making it more stable and enabling more cargo to be carried. This allowed them to make much longer voyages.

c. 13th century BC

The Austronesians settle the coast of modern-day Vietnam.

Moai sculptures, Easter Island

c. 1000 BC

Lapita culture spreads eastward through Melanesia, reaching the Bismarck Islands, New Caledonia, Fiji, Samoa, and Tonga.

c. 500 BC

Lapita culture has disappeared by this time. In the west it has merged into traditional Australoid culture; in the east (Fiji, Samoa, and Tonga) it develops into Polynesian culture.

c. 200 BC

The brilliant navigational skills of the Polynesians enable them to make long-distance voyages across the Pacific. By 200 BC, they have spread eastward to Tahiti, the Tuamotu archipelago, and the Marquesas Islands.

Polynesian outrigger canoe

c. AD 200

Austronesians from Indonesia sail west across the Indian Ocean in outrigger canoes and become the first people to settle Madagascar off the coast of Africa.

Tattooed Oceanic warrior

c. AD 300

The Polynesians reach Easter Island. Here they later carve the famous giant Moai sculptures from compressed volcanic ash.

c. AD 400

The Polynesians settle the Hawaiian islands. They bring with them pigs, dogs, chickens, and crops, such as taro, sweet potatoes, coconut, banana, and sugarcane.

c. AD 400

The Funan Empire, which emerges in the 1st century AD, dominates mainland Southeast Asia. Based in the Lower Mekong, it extends as far as Malaysia and Burma.

AD 800–1000

Polynesians reach Aotearoa (New Zealand), the Solomon Islands, and, possibly, the west coast of the Americas.

CHINA AND EAST ASIA
75,000 BC–AD 589

c. 75,000 BC

Modern humans arrive in China.

c. 30,000 BC

People from Siberia and Korea first settle in Japan.

c. 14,000–400 BC

Jomon culture develops on Japan's largest island, Honshu. They use stone tools and make clay vessels and figures with distinctive cord-patterned markings.

c. 5000–3000 BC

Yangshao culture emerges in northwestern China. The Yangshao live in villages, farm millet, and raise pigs, sheep, and goats.

c. 3000 BC

The Jomon people of Japan begin to supplement their hunting-and-gathering lifestyle with farming. They settle in semipermanent villages.

2698 BC

According to legend, Emperor Huangdi, the Yellow Emperor, establishes Chinese civilization.

2205 BC

China's first Dynasty—again, according to legend—is the Xia, founded by Yu the Great. However, the legend of the Xia has been supported by archaeological finds in Henan Province, suggesting the existence of an early Bronze Age civilization in this region.

1122 BC

The Shang ruler Di-xin is overthrown by Wu of Zhou in western China, who establishes his own Dynasty. The Zhou rule western China directly, leaving the eastern states under the control of trusted noblemen, a period known as the Western Zhou.

771 BC

The ruler of Shen, one of the eastern states, kills the Zhou king and sacks his capital, Fenghao.

770 BC

The Zhou move their capital east to a new capital at Luoyang. Control over their lands is reduced and, with their royal line broken, their legitimacy is weakened. This marks the start of the Eastern Zhou Period.

300 BC

Settlers begin to arrive in Japan from Korea and China. They bring with them new skills, such as rice paddy farming, mining, and metalworking.

Fantastical engraving of a Zhou chariot

Shi Huangdi, first emperor of China

221 BC

Zheng becomes the first emperor of a unified China. He adopts the title of Shi Huangdi.

Rice paddy farming

206 BC

Zhao Gao is overthrown by Ziying, grandson of Shi Huangdi. He, in turn, is defeated by rebel leader Liu Bang, who founds the Han Dynasty under the name Han Gaozu.

206–195 BC

Han Gaozu is a skillful ruler who repeals many of Shi Huangdi's authoritarian laws while maintaining a strong, centralized state.

206 BC–AD 9

During the Former Han Period, the capital is at Chang'an in western China. China expands into modern-day Tibet, Vietnam, and North Korea, but suffers frequent raids to its northern border by Xiongnu nomads from Mongolia.

124 BC

The Han establish the Imperial University to educate future government officials in Confucian ideals.

108 BC

The Han conquer northern Korea. Subsequent Chinese settlement brings elements of Han culture to the peninsula.

Horseman, late Han Dynasty

Goats were domesticated from the 5th millennium BC

c. 3000 BC

Yangshao culture, known for its red, black and white pottery painted with geometric designs, reaches the peak of its development.

c. 3200–1900 BC

Longshan culture flourishes in the Huang (Yellow) River Valley in eastern China. They farm rice and raise cattle and sheep. The Longshan are highly skilled potters, make copper implements and build China's first cities.

c. 2000 BC

The Jomon people of Japan learn how to build boats for fishing.

1766 BC

The Shang Dynasty is founded. They build cities, including Eritou, Luoyang, and Zhenzhou, develop a pictographic form of writing, and go to war in horse-drawn chariots.

c. 1500 BC

Seminomadic farmers occupy most of Korea.

Confucius and followers

770–480 BC

During the first part of the Eastern Zhou, known as the Spring and Autumn Period, the Empire fragments. The Zhou kings control a small royal domain with nominal authority over their other territories. The nobles become de facto rulers of independent states.

c. 551–479 BC

The great Chinese philosopher Confucius lives through the turmoil of the later Zhou Period. This inspires his ethical system in which individuals develop a sense of moral responsibility.

480–221 BC

The second period of the Eastern Zhou is the Warring States Period. The emperor's authority is no longer recognized, and the separate states engage in open warfare.

300 BC–AD 300

During the Yayoi Period in Japan, the first villages and towns are built of wood and stone. The Yayoi weave cloth textiles and use iron tools and weapons. Japan's first cities emerge.

246–221 BC

During the Warring States Period, the stronger states gradually absorb the weaker ones. From 246 BC, Ying Zheng, king of the western state of Qin, wages a series of battles until, by 221 BC, Qin reigns supreme.

221–210 BC

Shi Huangdi replaces the nobles of the conquered states with loyal government officials and runs China as a strongly centralized state.

210–207 BC

Er Shi, the second emperor of the Qin Dynasty, is a weak ruler and unable to deal with nationwide rebellions. In 207 BC Er Shi is overthrown by his adviser Zhao Gao.

Yayoi pottery shard

Early Indian Buddhist stupa

140–87 BC

Under Emperor Wudi, Confucianism becomes the official Chinese state philosophy, and Confucian scholars are elevated to senior government positions.

133–53 BC

Over a long series of military campaigns the Han gradually pacify the Xiongnu, reducing them to tributary status by 53 BC.

57 BC–AD 668

Three kingdoms, Goguryeo, Baekje, and Silla, the first settled states of Korea, dominate the Korean Peninsula and parts of Manchuria.

1st century AD

Buddhism reaches China, probably spread by merchants traveling along the Silk Road from India and Central Asia.

AD 9

The military campaigns of the Han weaken the Chinese economy, causing great hardship. A reformist official called Wang Mang seizes the throne and declares a new Dynasty, the Xin.

AD 9–23

Wang Mang rules China. His arrogance antagonizes allies and tributary states and his disastrous land reforms weaken the economy and cause uprisings.

Early plan of an idealized Chinese city

AD 23

Peasant bands ransack the capital Chang'an and kill Wang Mang.

AD 88–188

The rulers that follow Zhang are weak. Power passes to rival court factions—eunuchs, the families of empresses, and Confucian scholar officials as well as to provincial warlords.

AD 189

The warlord Yuan Shao attacks Luoyang; this causes the break up of the Empire and open warfare between regional warlords.

AD 220

Xian, final Han emperor, is forced to abdicate. No warlord is able to unify China; it splits into three kingdoms.

AD 263

The Wei general Sima Yen launches a three-pronged attack on Shu and captures its capital Chengdu. The emperor Liu Shan surrenders, and the kingdom of Shu comes to an end.

AD 264–279

Sun Hao, emperor of Wu, grows increasingly tyrannical, killing or exiling all who oppose him.

AD 265

General Sima Yen usurps the Wei throne and declares himself Emperor Wudi, the first of the Jin Dynasty.

AD 306–310

A Xiongnu chieftain, Liu Yuan, begins his conquest of northern China. He founds the state of Han Zhao.

AD 306

Sima Yue, cousin of Emperor Wudi and one of the Eight Princes, defeats his rivals and wins the power struggle, but only by recruiting from the nomad peoples of Central Asia, encouraging them to invade. Northern China is weakened and depopulated by the civil war, leaving the Jin vulnerable.

AD 311–316

Liu Yuan conquers the two Jin capitals, Luoyang and Chang'an, but is unable to impose his rule across all northern China.

AD 397–534

Conscious of the fact they are not Chinese, the Toba deliberately adopt Chinese culture and rule like a traditional Chinese Dynasty.

AD 420–479

In southern China, the Eastern Jin Dynasty is overthrown by one of their generals, Liu Yu, who founds the Southern Song Dynasty.

AD 479–502

The Southern Song Dynasty comes to an end when Xiao Daocheng usurps the throne from Emperor Shun and founds his own Dynasty, the Southern Qi, as the Emperor Gao.

AD 538–710

During the Asuka Period of Japanese history, the Yamato political system emerges. The patchwork of clan kingdoms transforms into a united Japan under a single emperor, who bestows land and titles on clan chieftains in return for their loyalty.

AD 556

In southern China the Liang emperor Jing is forced to yield the throne to Chen Baxian, who founds a new Dynasty, the Nan Chen, as the Emperor Wu.

AD 557

A powerful landowning family based in the northwest of China, known as the Northern Zhou, takes control of Western Wei and then expands into western China, the former Shu kingdom.

AD 577

The Northern Zhou conquers Eastern Wei, reunifying northern China.

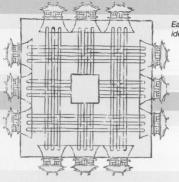

Painting of a prince, Asuka Period, Japan

Warrior from the later Han Period

AD 25

The Han Dynasty is reestablished under Liu Xiu (reigned AD 24–57), who establishes his capital at Luoyang, east of Chang'an. This marks the start of the Later Han Period, which lasts until AD 220.

AD 57–88

Liu Xiu is succeeded by his son Ming (reigned AD 57–75) and grandson Zhang (reigned AD 75–88), both competent rulers who oversee a modest recovery in the Empire's wealth and power.

AD 220–280

The Three Kingdoms Period: Wei in the north is the most powerful; Wu to the south is larger but weaker; weakest is the western kingdom of Shu. Wars between the kingdoms are frequent and bloody.

c. AD 250–538

During the Kofun Period, Japan is increasingly influenced by Chinese technology, religion, and culture. Honshu and Kyushu develop into a patchwork of small kingdoms.

AD 258–263

Shu politics becomes increasingly corrupt and dominated by eunuch factions.

AD 279–280

Wudi of Jin launches a five-pronged attack on Wu. The Wu forces collapse and the Wu capital Jianye falls. China is reunified under the Jin.

AD 291–306

After Wudi's death in AD 291, a violent power struggle erupts in northern China, known as the Rebellion of the Eight Princes, devastating the land.

4th century AD

By the 4th century, there are 24,000 Buddhist monks and almost 2,000 Buddhist monasteries in China.

AD 316–386

Northern China becomes a patchwork of short-lived, part-Chinese, part-nomad states known as the Sixteen Kingdoms. Widespread famine and lawlessness force large numbers to flee to southern China.

AD 317–420

Meanwhile in southern China, the Jin Dynasty, known as the Eastern Jin, continues for another 104 years under eleven successive emperors.

AD 386–397

During an eleven-year military campaign Toba, one of the nomad-Chinese states, manages to unify northern China under its rule, reestablishing the Wei state.

Standing Buddha, Wei Period

6th century AD

Mahayana Buddhism becomes one of China's main religions. From China, Buddhism spreads to Korea and from there to Japan.

AD 557

The Southern Qi falls following a rebellion by General Xiao Yan, who founds his own Liang Dynasty.

AD 534

Pro-Toba and pro-Chinese factions in the Toba court split apart, sparking civil war. Wei splits into eastern and western halves.

Sixth-century brick pagoda, China

Yang Jian, pictured in his garden with his wives

AD 581

Yang Jian, known posthumously as Wendi, a nomad Chinese general, usurps the Wei throne and founds the Sui Dynasty.

AD 589

Wendi crosses the Yangtse River and overthrows the Nan Chen Dynasty in the south. After almost 400 years of division, China is once again united under one ruler.

THE MIDDLE EAST AND WESTERN ASIA 3000 BC–AD 637

c. 3000 BC

Civilization emerges in Phoenicia (present-day Lebanon). The Phoenicians speak a semitic language similar to Hebrew, developing a twenty-two-letter alphabet, the basis of all modern alphabets.

3rd millennium BC

The Phoenicians, a great seafaring people, develop ports at Byblos, Berot, Sidon, and Tyre and trade cedarwood, grain, fruit, cattle, and, most famously, purple dye with Egypt.

Egyptian trading vessel

c. 1500–1200 BC

The port cities of Phoenicia emerge as independent city-states, but militarily weak. They spend most of this period dominated by either Egypt or the Hittites.

13th century BC

The Phoenician city states win their independence and begin establishing colonies in the western Mediterranean, especially in Tunisia, Sicily, and Sardinia.

c. 13th century BC

Some of the Hebrew tribes settle in Egypt, where they are forced into slavery by the pharaoh. According to tradition, they are freed by Moses, who leads them back to Canaan.

928 BC

Solomon's successor Rehoboam's tax demands provoke a rebellion, and the Hebrew kingdom splits in two, with Israel in the north and Judah in the south.

c. 800–600 BC

The Phoenician city-states are dominated by Assyria.

Figure from an Assyrian bas-relief

8th century BC

By the 8th century, two groups of Aryans have settled in Iran—the Medes in the northwest and the Persians in the south.

7th century BC

Persia is ruled by Hakhamanish, whose name is Hellenized as Achaemenes. His successors are known as the Achaemenids. For most of the 7th and early 6th centuries, Persia is dominated by the Medes.

609 BC

The Egyptians win the Battle of Megiddo and occupy Judah.

Fanciful 19th-century rendering of a Persian war chariot

550 BC

Cyrus the Great (reigned 550–529 BC) defeats the Median king Astyages at the Battle of Pasargadae, then captures the Median capital at Hamadan. Cyrus unites the Persians and Medes under his rule.

550–539 BC

Cyrus the Great builds a vast Empire, capturing Lydia in western Anatolia, the Greek cities of Ionia, and large areas of Central Asia.

521–513 BC

Darius I (reigned 521–486 BC) campaigns against the Scythians of Central Asia. By 518 BC, he has extended the Empire east as far as the Indus. In 513 BC he conquers Thrace in southeastern Europe.

Carthaginian terra-cotta urn

500 BC

The most powerful Phoenician colony, Carthage, forms a new maritime Empire, consisting of former Phoenician colonies in the western Mediterranean.

410–147 BC

Carthage wages a series of wars with the Greeks and then Rome for control of Sicily. The Romans finally conquer Carthage's colonies and destroy the city.

4th century BC

The Parni, a nomadic people from Central Asia, move into Parthia in northeastern Iran.

The ruins of Ur

16th century BC

Aryans, a people from Central Asia, begin migrating to modern-day Iran—a name that means land of the Aryans.

c. 1500 BC

The Hebrews migrate from Ur in Mesopotamia to Canaan. According to tradition they are led by Abraham, whose grandson Jacob takes the name Israel. Each of Israel's sons founds a tribe.

Engraving of a Biblical Hebrew priest

c. 1020 BC

The Hebrew tribes unite under a single monarch, Saul (reigned c. 1020–c. 1006).

c. 1005–965 BC

Saul's anointed successor David conquers neighboring tribes, establishing Hebrew control over Canaan. David captures Jerusalem from the Jebusites and makes it his capital.

c. 965–928 BC

David's son Solomon builds a temple in Jerusalem.

724 BC

The Assyrian ruler Sargon II destroys Israel by transporting the entire population to Assyria. The remaining Israelites of Judah come to be known as Jews.

Assyrian battle chariots

722 BC

The Assyrians destroy the northern kingdom of Israel.

605 BC

At the Battle of Carchemish, the Babylonians defeat Egypt and oust them from the Levant. Judah becomes a vassal state of Babylonia.

6th century BC

Phoenicia is conquered by the Babylonians, and its colonies are forced into independence.

587 BC

Following a rebellion by the Jews, the Babylonians destroy Jerusalem and deport many thousands of Jews to Babylon.

Cross section of terraced gardens, Babylon

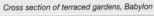

539 BC

Cyrus the Great captures Babylon. Some 50,000 Jews return to their homeland. They rebuild Jerusalem, including Solomon's Temple.

529–522 BC

Achaemenid emperor Cambyses II, son of Cyrus the Great, adds Egypt and Libya to the Empire's dominions.

500–480 BC

Carthage grows rich through its trade in gold, silver, tin, and iron. It allies itself with the Etruscans and fights Syracuse for control of Sicily.

494–480 BC

The Ionian Greeks, supported by Greece, rebel against Achaemenid rule. Darius and his successor Xerxes attempt to conquer Greece, but are decisively defeated at Marathon (490 BC) and Salamis and Plataea (480 BC). Achaemenid expansion comes to an end.

480 BC

The Greeks of Syracuse defeat a Carthaginian invasion at Himera in Sicily.

336–323 BC

Alexander the Great of Macedon conquers a 3,000-mile (5,000-km) Empire stretching from Greece to India. He dies in 323 BC.

323–321 BC

Perdiccas, as regent to Alexander's infant successor Alexander IV, takes control of the Empire, but is killed in 321 BC. Antipater becomes regent and appoints satraps to govern each part of the Empire.

321–301 BC

Wars of the Diadochi: Alexander's rival successors,, the Diadochi, fight to obtain larger shares of Alexander's Empire. Out of this struggle emerge, by 301 BC, three Hellenistic states.

323–301 BC

On Alexander the Great's death, his general Antigonus "the One-Eyed" gains control of the eastern Mediterranean and most of the Middle East.

312 BC

Seleucus, a former general of Alexander, establishes the Seleucid Dynasty controlling the eastern part of the Empire.

305 BC

Ptolemy, another general, consolidates his hold over Egypt and Palestine. He founds a Dynasty that will rule Egypt for the next 275 years.

223–198 BC

A Seleucid revival begins under Antiochus III (reigned 223–187 BC). He reconquers Bactria and Parthia (209 BC). Then, in 198 BC, he wins Phoenicia and Palestine from Egypt. The Seleucid Empire reaches its greatest zenith.

Portrait of Seleucus, from a coin

197 BC

Antiochus' attempt to take over territories in Europe and Asia Minor is repelled by the Romans.

170–124 BC

Parthian expansion continues under Mithradates I (reigned 170–138 BC) and his successors. By 124 BC, the Parthian Empire stretches from the Euphrates in the west to Herat, Afghanistan, in the east.

163–63 BC

Judah is an independent Jewish state under Judah Macabee's family, the Hasmoneans.

160s BC

The Seleucid Empire is wracked by civil war as rival claimants fight for the throne.

Parthian bas-relief

60 BC

The Seleucid Dynasty ends as the Empire's last dominions, including Judaea, are absorbed by the Romans.

30 BC

Egypt becomes part of the Roman Empire when the final Ptolemaic ruler, Cleopatra VII, kills herself.

53 BC–AD 115

The Parthians wipe out a Roman army at Carrhae (53 BC). The Roman heavy infantry is no match for the highly mobile Parthian horse archers. To avenge the defeat, the Romans launch a series of attacks on Parthia.

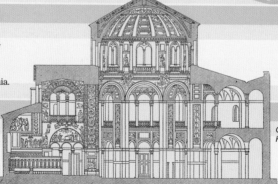

AD 66–135

The Jews rebel against Roman rule in AD 66–70 and again in AD 132–135. In AD 135, the Romans reconquer Jerusalem and turn it into a Roman city.

AD 241–272

Under Shapur I the Sasanids defeat the Kushans to take Sogdiana, Bactria, and northwest India. By the 270s, their Empire stretches from the Euphrates to the Indus.

Cross section of Hagia Sophia, Byzantium

AD 531–579

The Sasanid Empire revives under Khosru I, who destroys the Ephthalite Empire and reconquers the eastern provinces.

AD 602–610

The Byzantine Empire is brought to its knees as Avars, Slavs, and Sasanids overrun its territories.

AD 607–618

The Sasanid emperor Khosru II (reigned 591–628) launches an all-out invasion of the Byzantine Empire, overrunning Syria and Palestine in 608 and Egypt in 618.

280–261 BC

Antiochus I, successor to Seleucus, wins victories over the Galatians in Asia Minor, but loses territory to Ptolemy II of Egypt.

196–171 BC

As Seleucid power crumbles, Parthia retakes its former territories and goes on the offensive. The Seleucids gradually lose territory to both the Romans and Parthians.

110–87 BC

Under Mithradates II the Parthians fight off a Scythian invasion to the east while expanding at Seleucid expense into Armenia and northern Syria to the west.

Romanticized 19th-century depiction of a Parthian warrior

261–246 BC

Antiochus II, successor to Antiochus I, wins back many of the territories his father had lost, but loses Bactria to his own satrap, Diodotus I.

175–163 BC

The Seleucid king Antiochus IV tries to ban Judaism. The Jews, led by Judah Macabee, rebel.

80–30 BC

Egypt under the later Ptolemies suffers from civil wars and native revolts.

238 BC

Arsaces I, king of the Parni, topples the Seleucid satrap Andragoras and declares Parthia an independent kingdom.

Throne-chair from the Ptolemaic Period

Byzantine mosaic frieze

c. 4 BC–AD 29

The life of Jesus of Nazareth. According to tradition, Jesus performs miracles and preaches about the coming of the Kingdom of God.

AD 115–198

The Romans retake Armenia and Mesopotamia from the Parthians in 115–117. Emperor Hadrian later abandons them, but under Septimius Severus the Romans reconquer Mesopotamia in AD 198.

c. AD 30–130

Jesus' disciples spread his message among the Mediterranean Jewish communities. Paul encourages non-Jews to become Christians. Alexandria, Antioch, Jerusalem, and Rome become important centers of Christianity.

AD 224

Ardashir I (reigned c. 220–240), vassal King of Persia, defeats the Parthians at Hormizdagan and kills the emperor. Soon afterward, Ardashir founds the Sasanid Dynasty.

AD 395

After the death of Emperor Theodosius, the Roman Empire is formally split between east and west, marking the beginning of the Byzantine Empire.

AD 610–620

The reforms of Heraclius (reigned 610–641) transform the Byzantine army and administration. Greek replaces Latin as the Empire's official language, marking a decisive break with the old Roman Empire.

AD 490s

White Huns (Ephthalites) take Sogdiana and Bactria from the Sasanids and kill the Sasanid emperor, bringing instability to the Empire.

AD 622–627

The Byzantines under Heraclius turn the tide against the Sasanids and destroy the Sasanid army at Nineveh in 627. Khosru II flees and the Empire sinks into anarchy.

AD 502–532

Byzantine–Sasanid wars: A series of conflicts break out between the two Empires, ending with a peace treaty negotiated in 532.

AD 637

The Sasanid Empire is destroyed by Muslim Arab armies, which take control of Persia.

290 THE WORLD
AD 1

By AD 1 the Romans had established themselves as the dominant force in Europe, North Africa, and the Middle East. Meanwhile, India remained divided into small kingdoms and China was enduring the death throes of the first Han Dynasty. While Buddhism was spreading into East Asia, in the West, a new religion, Christianity, was soon to emerge, inspired by the teachings of Jesus of Nazareth.

Early stele from Teotihuacán

Teotihuacán
During the 1st century AD, the city of Teotihuacán (in modern Mexico) underwent rapid growth. It would soon be the largest cultural, religious, and commercial centre in Mesoamerica.

Maya
Maya civilization was in its Late Preclassic Period, a time in which powerful city-states emerged and conflict was probably frequent. The preeminent city was El Mirador in modern Guatemala.

Moche
Moche, in northern Peru, was the first state to emerge in South America. Ruled by priest-kings, Moche produced fine pottery, murals, textiles, and jewelry.

Deep bas-relief carvings on a Mayan platform

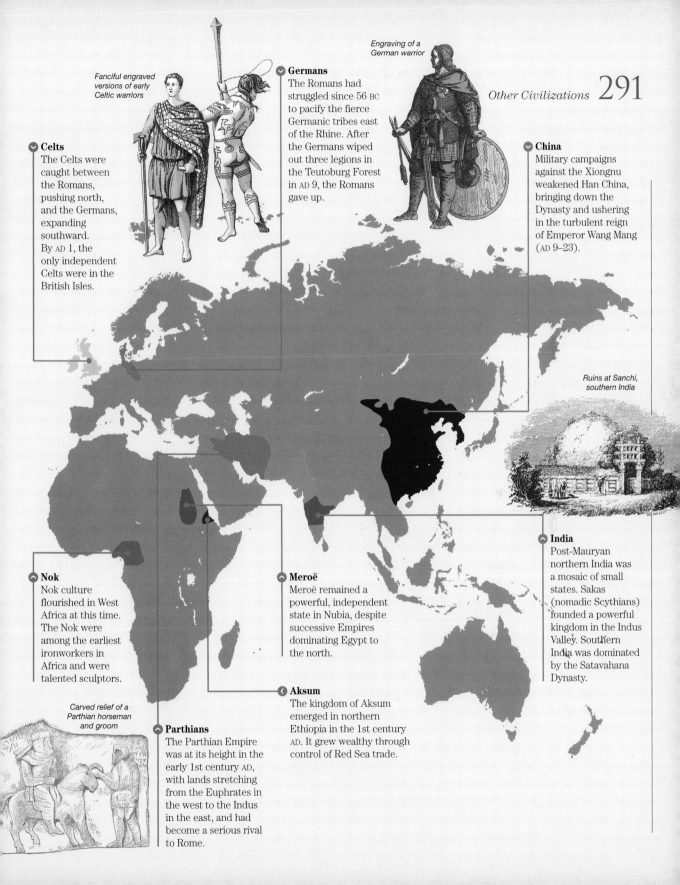

Celts
The Celts were caught between the Romans, pushing north, and the Germans, expanding southward. By AD 1, the only independent Celts were in the British Isles.

Fanciful engraved versions of early Celtic warriors

Germans
The Romans had struggled since 56 BC to pacify the fierce Germanic tribes east of the Rhine. After the Germans wiped out three legions in the Teutoburg Forest in AD 9, the Romans gave up.

Engraving of a German warrior

China
Military campaigns against the Xiongnu weakened Han China, bringing down the Dynasty and ushering in the turbulent reign of Emperor Wang Mang (AD 9–23).

Ruins at Sanchi, southern India

India
Post-Mauryan northern India was a mosaic of small states. Sakas (nomadic Scythians) founded a powerful kingdom in the Indus Valley. Southern India was dominated by the Satavahana Dynasty.

Nok
Nok culture flourished in West Africa at this time. The Nok were among the earliest ironworkers in Africa and were talented sculptors.

Meroë
Meroë remained a powerful, independent state in Nubia, despite successive Empires dominating Egypt to the north.

Aksum
The kingdom of Aksum emerged in northern Ethiopia in the 1st century AD. It grew wealthy through control of Red Sea trade.

Carved relief of a Parthian horseman and groom

Parthians
The Parthian Empire was at its height in the early 1st century AD, with lands stretching from the Euphrates in the west to the Indus in the east, and had become a serious rival to Rome.

EUROPE
6500 BC–AD 481

c. 6500 BC

European farming begins in Greece and the Balkans, possibly brought there by migrants from the Fertile Crescent. It spreads around the Mediterranean, reaching Spain by *c.* 5000 BC.

Sheep farming began in Europe in the 5th millennium

c. 4500–3900 BC

Farming arises in western and northern Europe with the beginning of dairy production, sheep shearing, and the use of oxen as traction.

3rd millennium BC

Henges are constructed in northwestern Europe—most famously Stonehenge in Wiltshire, England (from *c.* 2200 BC). Their function may be religious, astronomical or both.

Stonehenge, from a 19th-century engraving

c. 2100 BC

By the late 3rd millennium, there is a growing uniformity of culture across Europe. Societies are hierarchical. Rich elites are buried in large earth mounds called barrows.

c. 2000–1700 BC

The Minoans develop a hieroglyphic script, superseded by a syllabic script. Neither has been deciphered.

c. 1200 BC

Iron is first used in Europe. Iron is starting to replace bronze in Greece by 1000 BC, and in the rest of Europe by 750 BC.

c. 1000–600 BC

Groups of Celts begin to migrate, spreading Urnfield culture across western Europe as far as northern Spain.

c. 1000–500 BC

Germanic peoples from Scandinavia and northern Germany migrate to the south and west, dominating Celtic settlers in southern Germany.

616–509 BC

An Etruscan noble family, the Tarquins, rule Rome.

6th century BC

The Etruscans expand into northern Italy and the Adriatic coastline. Powerful city-states emerge in Italy.

509 BC

The Romans establish a republic.

Early Germanic tribesmen

Bronze Etruscan wheeled brazier

c. 450–400 BC

La Tène culture spreads through trade and migration across central and western Europe, reaching Britain and Ireland by around 400 BC.

Romanticized 19th-century version of early Celtic warriors

c. 400 BC

Celtic tribes invade northern Italy. They settle in the fertile Po Valley, a region that the Romans call Cisalpine Gaul.

301 BC

At the Battle of Ipsus (301 BC) Antigonus faces the combined armies of Ptolemy, Seleucus, and Lysimachus. He loses his life and most of his territories.

294 BC

Antigonus' son Demetrius (reigned 294–283 BC) manages to regain control of Macedonia.

c. 3100–2500 BC

During this period, plowing begins, wool becomes the main raw material for textiles, wheeled vehicles come into use in northern Europe, and irrigation systems are developed in the arid south, allowing intensive agriculture.

c. 2600 BC

Cycladic sculptors start producing beautiful marble figurines, many depicting female shapes possibly representing a mother goddess.

c. 1700 BC

The Minoan palaces and towns fall into ruins, possibly because of an earthquake. They are rebuilt soon after, and this "Second Palace Period" is the time of greatest Minoan influence and prosperity.

c. 750 BC

Hallstatt culture, the second great Celtic culture emerges in central Europe. Hallstatt is one of Europe's first iron-using cultures and is known for its hill forts and elaborate burial sites.

474 BC

An Etruscan fleet is destroyed off Cumae by the ships of Hieron I of Syracuse.

c. 400 BC

Celtic tribes invade the Lower Danube region.

350–250 BC

The Etruscan city-states fall under Roman control.

281–279 BC

In the early 3rd century, the Celts of the Lower Danube move further south into the Balkans and Greece, attacking Delphi and conquering Thrace.

c. 3000 BC

Cycladic culture develops on a number of islands in the southern Aegean. It is known for its pottery and fine metalwork.

c. 2500 BC

The Unetice culture of central Europe is the first to use bronze. Its use spreads to southeastern Europe by 2300 BC, to western Europe by 1800 BC and to Scandinavia by 1500 BC.

c. 1450 BC

The Minoan palaces and towns are destroyed for a second time, this time by invading Mycenaeans, who also colonize the Cyclades. Minoan and Cycladic cultures come to an end.

c. 750–500 BC

Hallstatt culture spreads across France, Spain, Portugal, Germany, the Low Countries, and southern Britain.

c. 450 BC

La Tène, the third and final flowering of Celtic culture, develops from Hallstatt culture in France, Switzerland, and Germany. It is known for its swirly, curvilinear art style, used to decorate weapons, jewelry, and other artifacts.

c. 3000 BC

Minoan culture develops on Crete. The Minoans grow wealthy through trade. They build fine palaces, the biggest of which is at Knossos. These may be centers of government for individual city-states.

c. 2300 BC

Chiefdoms are established across most of Europe by this time. Fortifications and weapons found at sites in southern and central Europe suggest warfare is common.

c. 1350 BC

Urnfield culture, the earliest Celtic culture, appears in central Europe. Urnfield people cremate their dead and bury the ashes in urns in enormous cemeteries.

7th century BC

Etruscan civilization emerges in the northwest central area of the Italian peninsula. It develops writing and the pottery wheel.

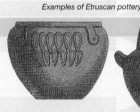

Examples of Etruscan pottery

c. 350 BC

The first contact between the Mediterranean and German civilizations occurs when the Greek explorer Pytheas of Massilia explores the coasts of Germany and Scandinavia.

276–215 BC

Antigonus II Gonatas (reigned 283–239 BC), son of Demetrius, consolidates the Antagonid hold over Macedonia and most of Greece.

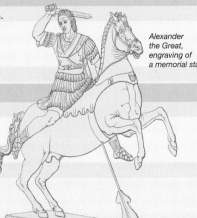

Alexander the Great, engraving of a memorial statue

278–277 BC

Three Celtic tribes migrate east to Asia Minor (modern Turkey), where they create the Kingdom of Galatia.

270–230 BC

This is the high point of Celtic culture, with their communities flourishing throughout Europe and as far east as Asia Minor.

215–168 BC

The Antigonid Dynasty suffers a series of defeats by the Romans. The Dynasty ends in 168 BC, and Greece is absorbed into the Roman Empire.

206–133 BC

The Romans wage a long campaign against the Celtiberians in Spain until their stronghold is taken at Numantia in 133 BC. A small Celtiberian pocket continues in northwestern Spain until 19 BC.

Celtic metal torque, elaborately worked metalwork

56 BC

Caesar conquers the Germanic tribes to the west of the Rhine, the only Germans to be brought under permanent Roman rule.

56 BC–AD 9

The Romans attempt to pacify the Germanic tribes to east of the Rhine.

9 BC

The Romans defeat the Celts of Pannonia (modern Hungary), almost the last independent Celts in continental Europe. From this time the Celts become increasingly Romanized and their culture survives only in Britain and Ireland.

Bust of Caesar, dressed as a Roman general

C. AD 200

Germanic tribes begin to reorganize themselves. Tribes merge to form larger, more effective fighting forces. Rhineland tribes, for example, become the Franks.

AD 235–284

With the Roman Empire in upheaval and its borders often left undefended, Germanic tribes, such as the Goths, Vandals, and Alemanni, make frequent raids on the Empire.

Attila the Hun, from a western engraving

AD 372

The Huns, a nomadic people from Central Asia, invade the kingdom of the Ostrogoths (a branch of the Goths) in Dacia, southeastern Europe. The Ostrogoths seek refuge within the Eastern Roman Empire in Thrace.

AD 378

The Ostrogoths in Thrace are mistreated, so they rise up, killing the Eastern Roman emperor Valens at the Battle of Adrianople.

AD 401

The Visigoths reach northern Italy, but are checked at Pollentia by a Roman force.

AD 406

A coalition of German tribes, including Goths, Vandals, Suevi, Burgundians, and Alans, invade Italy under their chieftain Radagaisus, attacking Florence before the Romans are able to drive them away.

AD 406–409

The advance of the Huns prompts a number of Germanic tribes—Vandals, Suevi, Alans, Franks, Burgundians, and Alemanni—to cross the Rhine and sweep into Gaul.

AD 441

The Huns, under Attila, seize the Balkans and all Roman lands east of the Rhine.

C. AD 450

Angles, Saxons, and Jutes begin to settle southern Britain, creating new kingdoms and a new Anglo-Saxon culture.

AD 451

The Huns invade Gaul, but are defeated by an alliance of Romans and Germanic tribes under the command of the Roman general Aetius.

230–220 BC

The Greeks expel the Celts from Galatia and Thrace.

230–206 BC

The Carthaginians start to eject the Celtiberians, a Hallstatt Celtic culture of Spain.

220–192 BC

The Romans attack the Celts of Cisalpine Gaul. The Celts resist until 192 BC, when their final base at Bononia (modern Bologna) is taken.

113 BC

Two Germanic tribes from Jutland, the Cimbri, and the Teutones destroy a Roman army at Noreia in the eastern Alps.

109–101 BC

The Cimbri and Teutones move west and defeat the Romans in southern Gaul (modern France). The tribes then split—the Cimbri move to Spain and the Teutones to northern Gaul. Thus divided, the Romans defeat them by 101 BC.

58–51 BC

Roman general Julius Caesar conquers the Celts of Gaul.

AD 9

An alliance of Germanic tribes, led by Arminius, wipe out three Roman legions in the Teutoburg Forest. After this the Romans cease trying to conquer the Germans. Instead, they forge military and commercial alliances with friendly border tribes.

AD 43–410

Celtic culture in Britain comes under attack following the Roman invasion in AD 43. However, the Romans cannot subdue Britain's northern and western extremities and Celtic culture survives in Cornwall, Wales, and Scotland throughout the occupation.

Coins showing Caesar in a victor's wreath

AD 367–370

The Roman province of Britain comes under simultaneous attack from Picts from Scotland, Scotii from Ireland, and Saxons from Germany.

AD 370

Theodosius restores order to Britain, building coastal defenses and forts and repairing Hadrian's Wall.

AD 370s

The Western Roman Empire suffers a decline in manpower and is forced to contract out the defense of its borders to loyal Germanic border tribes.

AD 382

The Ostrogoths overrun Thrace and Pannonia and Emperor Theodosius is forced to make peace, ceding them territory.

AD 395

The Visigoths (the other branch of the Goths) invade Greece and Dalmatia under their chieftain Alaric.

Ostrogoth warrior

AD 409–415

Many of the Germanic tribes cross the Pyrenees to settle in Spain.

AD 410

Alaric's Visigoths sack Rome. Emperor Honorius is forced to make a humiliating peace. He offers them Aquitaine and southern Gaul, forming the basis of a Visigothic kingdom. In return he asks them to attack the Germanic tribes that have settled there.

Visigoth warrior

AD 470s

With the Western Roman Empire shrunk to little more than the Italian peninsula, the final emperors are puppets of Germanic generals.

AD 476

The last Roman emperor, Romulus Augustulus, is deposed by Odoacer, who proclaims himself King of Italy.

AD 481

A Frankish kingdom, under the Merovingian Dynasty, is established in eastern France, western Germany, and the Low Countries.

CENTRAL ASIA
6000 BC–AD 511

c. 4000 BC

Horses, initially reared for their meat, begin to be used for transportation.

4th millennium BC

The first wheeled vehicles are developed in southern Russia. Horses are bred for strength in order to pull ever larger vehicles.

3rd millennium BC

Horses are strong enough to pull war chariots. Spoked wheels are developed by the Andronovo culture of western Siberia. These replace solid wheels, making chariots more maneuverable and enabling them to dominate battlefields.

c. 2100–1750 BC

The Oxus civilization develops in southwestern Central Asia. It develops irrigation systems to make the arid soil more productive. This enables some towns to develop into cities engaged in craft production, elaborate burials, and monumental platforms similar to the ziggurats of Sumer.

c. 1750 BC

The precarious irrigation systems of the Oxus civilization collapse and many towns are abandoned.

c. 1500–1000 BC

The Srubnaya people north of the Caspian Sea develop bits and bridles, enabling them to start riding horses. This allows steppe peoples to manage herds over vast distances.

c. 1000 BC

Horse-riding spreads through Central Asia, leading to the rise of nomadic pastoralism—nomadic groups move their herds of sheep, goats, horses, and camels between summer and winter pastures, greatly increasing the grazing land available to them.

Elevation of a Sumerian ziggurat

c. 950–700 BC

The Cimmerians, from the Russian steppe north of the Black Sea, are the first nomad power of Central Asia.

c. 730–700 BC

The Scythians, Iranian speakers from western Central Asia, migrate to Cimmerian territory. They fight the Cimmerians for some thirty years, eventually driving them south into Anatolia.

Scythian warriors, from a 19th-century engraving

Mounted Sarmatian archer

c. 700–350 BC

The Scythians establish a powerful Empire from southern Russia to the Persian borders. They excel at horse riding. They make fine jewelry, and elaborate burial chambers for their elite.

c. 350 BC

Scythian power wanes, and their people are gradually absorbed by another people of Iranian descent, the Sarmatians.

c. 350–50 BC

The Sarmatians gradually migrate west where they threaten the Roman Empire. In the course of this migration they absorb other ethnic groups and lose their distinctive identity.

3rd century BC

The Xiongu, a coalition of Turkic tribes, rise to dominance on the eastern steppes. Formidable horse riders, they use a short, composite bow, ideal for mounted warriors.

c. 150–100 BC

The Xiongu carry out frequent raids against Han China, extracting large amounts of tribute. The Han retaliate, reducing them to tributary status by 53 BC.

c. AD 370–395

The Huns, a warlike Turkic people from the western steppes, create an enormous Empire. From their homeland they move west, destroying a tribe of Alans, devastating the Ostrogothic kingdom, and ravaging Armenia.

c. AD 420–453

The Huns unite under a single king—first Oktar, then Rugila, then joint kings Bleda and Attila. Bleda dies in 445, leaving Attila in sole charge. Thus united, the Huns mount a fearsome assault on Europe, very nearly destroying the Roman Empire.

c. AD 450–511

The White Huns, or Ephthalites, from Central Asia conquer Sogdiana and Bactria from the Sasanids (490s) and attack and destroy the Gupta Empire in northern India (505–511).

AFRICA
7000 BC–AD 400

7th millennium BC

Farming in Africa first develops in the eastern Sahara. To survive the long periods of drought, people begin planting the seeds of their favorite plants, including wheat and barley.

c. 5000 BC

Cattle, sheep, and goats are domesticated in the central Sahara, allowing a form of nomadic pastoralism as herders drive their animals between pastures.

c. 3500 BC

Complex society emerges among farming communities on the banks of the Nile in Nubia. The Nubians are heavily influenced and often conquered by the Egyptians to the north.

c. 3000 BC

The Saharan climate grows drier, and desertification spreads, forcing herders southward into the semiarid Sahel. From here, cattle herding spreads east to the Ethiopian highlands and from there to southern Africa.

Barley, an early cultivated crop

Ruins of the Meroë civilization

c. 1700–1500 BC

The kingdom of Kerma flourishes in Upper Nubia. Its capital, Kerma, is the first Nubian city. It is surrounded by defensive walls and moats and contains a palace, a religious sanctuary and about two hundred houses.

c. 1500–900 BC

Kerma is conquered by Pharaoh Thutmose I, and Nubia falls under Egyptian control.

c. 900–590 BC

The Kingdom of Kush emerges in Nubia in about 900 BC, with its capital at Napata.

728–664 BC

The Kushite king Piankhy conquers Egypt. He and his successors become the 25th Dynasty of Egyptian pharaohs. After sixty-four years in control the Kushites retreat from Egypt in the face of Assyrian invaders.

664 BC–AD 350

Kush, which becomes known as Meroë after 590 BC, continues to flourish as a powerful independent state. Its people build pyramids, develop an alphabet based on Egyptian hieroglyphics, and trade in iron, copper, and gold.

590 BC

The capital of Kush is moved from Napata to Meroë farther to the south. This may be in response to an Egyptian invasion of Lower (northern) Nubia.

c. 100 BC

The introduction of camels to the Sahara transforms North African culture. Camels enable long-distance trade, and their suitability for warfare allow nomadic tribes to mount devastating raids on sedentary communities.

1st century AD

The kingdom of Aksum emerges in northern Ethiopia. Its power and wealth stem from control of the Red Sea port of Adulis, an important center of trade. The Aksumites build impressive fortresses and stone monuments.

c. AD 1–500

Bantu-speaking peoples spread their culture through much of central and southern Africa. They bring knowledge of farming and ironworking, as well as their languages, to many parts of the continent.

Table Mountain, a characteristic South African landscape

AD 300–350

Meroë declines in power following attacks by desert nomads. In 350 Meroë is conquered by Aksum.

c. AD 330–356

Aksum reaches the height of its power under King Ezana, who conquers Meroë. Ezana is the first African king to convert to Christianity.

500 BC–AD 400

Nok culture flourishes in West Africa. The Nok people are among the earliest ironworkers in Africa. They are best known for their terra-cotta figurines of humans and animals.

MESOAMERICA
12,000 BC–AD 1000

c. 12,000 BC

The earliest settlers in Mesoamerica arrive during the Pleistocene epoch. Much of the land is covered in glaciers. They live by hunting big game and gathering wild plant foods.

c. 9000 BC

The glaciers melt, sea levels rise, many large mammals become extinct. Mesoamerican people begin hunting and trapping small game and trying to cultivate certain plants.

c. 1500 BC

Olmec people establish simple farming communities along the Gulf Coast of Mexico.

c. 1250 BC

Olmec chiefdoms emerge. These are communities of a few thousand, ruled by a hereditary elite. They engage in craftwork and trade, build ceremonial pyramids, and create huge stone heads.

c. 1200–1000 BC

Mayan civilization emerges in the highlands of Guatemala and begins spreading to the lowlands of Yucatán by 1000 BC.

c. 1000–600 BC

The Maya drain the swamps and channel water in canals, creating sufficiently fertile farmland to support a complex society.

c. 900–700 BC

San Lorenzo goes into decline. Some of the huge stone heads are defaced, possibly by the Olmecs themselves.

c. 800–400 BC

La Venta is the most influential Olmec site during this period. It is dominated by a 100-ft (30-m) high cone-shaped clay mound, which may represent a volcano.

c. 350–300 BC

The Olmec site of La Venta goes into rapid decline. Some monuments are destroyed. By 300 BC, the Olmecs have disappeared as a distinct culture.

c. 300 BC

Teotihuacán is founded as a small farming village, one of many in the fertile central valley of Mexico.

AD 36

An engraved monument is erected at El Baúl in the southern highlands of Guatemala. This is the first of many built in this area, an important center of Mayan writing.

c. AD 150

Tikal, a small Mayan city, expands rapidly. Large ceremonial buildings are constructed.

Terra-cotta heads found at Teotihuacán

3rd century AD

The Mayan writing culture of southern Guatemala declines, possibly following a volcanic eruption, and no new engraved monuments are built.

AD 378

A long war between Tikal and the nearby city-state of Uaxactun culminates in a big battle. Tikal wins and Uaxactun is captured by a general called Smoking Frog.

AD 411–457

Tikal, the most powerful Mayan city-state of the Classic Period, reaches its apogee under King Stormy Sky. It dominates the region economically and politically and has trade links throughout Mesoamerica.

c. AD 500

Teotihuacán reaches the height of its power. With a population of around 150,000, it is the largest and most influential cultural, religious and commercial centre in Mesoamerica.

AD 600–650

Teotihuacán begins to decline in the early 7th century, perhaps because of overcultivation of the surrounding land.

AD 682–723

Tikal revives under King Ah Cacau, but never manages to regain its former status.

c. AD 750

Teotihuacán is sacked and burned, possibly during an invasion or rebellion by the nearby city of Cholula. The population falls sharply from this time.

Ruined pyramids of the Sun and Moon, Teotihuacán

c. 5000–2700 BC

Mesoamericans learn to cultivate a number of crops, including corn, beans, squash, bottle gourd, chile peppers, tomatoes, avocado, and cotton.

c. 2700–2300 BC

Maize is domesticated, leading to the first sedentary farming communities. The fertile soil can produce four crops a year, enabling the development of the first complex societies.

c. 2000 BC

The earliest Mesoamerican ceramics appear around this time in the Tehuacán Valley, the Valley of Oaxaca, and the Pacific coastal region of Soconusco.

Maize, a staple crop in Mesoamerican cultures

Maya ruins at Uxmal

c. 1150–700 BC

The Olmec site at San Lorenzo flourishes as a major trading center. The Olmecs build ceremonial structures on raised platforms, courtyards, and a ball court.

600–400 BC

The Maya build cities with monumental temple pyramids. Influenced by the Olmecs, they become experts at craftwork, astronomy, and mathematics and develop hieroglyphic writing.

c. 500 BC

Zapotec states emerge in the Oaxaca Valley of southern Mexico. The most developed is Monte Albán. The Zapotecs build stone pyramids, develop hieroglyphic writing, and a calendar.

300 BC–AD 250

During this Late Preclassic Period, Mayan city-states emerge. Many have fortifications, indicating frequent warfare. El Mirador, the most powerful city, has a population of around 80,000.

c. 200 BC–AD 200

Monte Albán flourishes as the center of Zapotec rule in the Oaxaca Valley.

1st century BC

Teotihuacán undergoes rapid growth when refugees arrive there following a volcanic eruption in Cuicuilco. Teotihuacán is transformed into a grand city built on a grid, containing a ceremonial center that includes two enormous temple pyramids.

c. AD 200–250

Tikal, whose wealth is based on trade in obsidian, is rebuilt and further expanded by its ambitious rulers.

AD 300–900

The Classic Period of Mayan history. Mayan kings rule from palaces in city centers. The city-states grow wealthy from trade. They worship some 150 gods, practice animal and human sacrifice, and are skilled astronomers and mathematicians.

Toltec pottery

AD 562

Tikal declines after its defeat by the city-state of Caracol.

Bas-relief from the Classic Mayan Period

c. AD 800

Monte Albán declines and Zapotec influence wanes.

9th century AD

The Classic Period of Mayan history comes to an end when the city-states in the central lowlands begin to fail. Populations decline, building work ceases, and the cities are abandoned.

AD 950

By this time all the major Mayan cities of the central lowlands are in ruins. The cause of this sudden end to Mayan civilization remains a mystery.

AD 1000

Northern Mayan cities, such as Chichén Itzá, Uxmal, and Mayapan continue to flourish until AD 1000, when the area is invaded by Toltecs from central Mexico.

c. 12,000 BC

The earliest human settlements in South America date to this time. The Paleo-Indians of the central and southern Andes live by hunting mastodon and prehistoric llama and gathering plants, such as maize, beans, and squash.

c. 11,000 BC

Human occupation of Gran Cacho in south central South America (including parts of Argentina, Paraguay, and Bolivia) begins at this time.

Llamas were domesticated by 500 BC

c. 9200–7800 BC

Humans settle in the Amazon Basin around this time. They are hunter-gatherers who eat fruit, brazil nuts, fish, tortoises, snakes, birds, and larger land mammals.

6th millennium BC

The islands of the Caribbean are inhabited by this time.

c. 3750–1800 BC

The earliest complex societies in South America emerge on the coast of Peru, supported by the unusually rich marine resources. They build temples and ceremonial centers.

Chavin gold: a pectoral ornament

1st millennium BC

Rivers are diverted from the Andes to the arid coastal lowlands, expanding the available farmland. Trade networks develop between farming and highland communities. Monumental ceremonial centers, such as Garagay, are built.

c. 500–400 BC

During the second stage of Chavín culture, the ceremonial center at Chavín de Huantár grows in importance. The Chavín domesticate the llama and increase their links with other civilizations.

c. 800 BC

Chavín culture emerges in Peru. The Chavín carve stone, weave, paint cloth, and produce elaborately decorated pottery and jewelry. They create an enormous ceremonial center at Chavín de Huantár.

c. 400–250 BC

Chavín culture reaches its height during the third stage, known as Jarabarriu. The population grows, and roads and trading routes are developed.

c. 200 BC

Moche culture arises in the coastal desert of northern Peru. The Moche people are talented craftspeople, producing pottery, murals, textiles, and jewelry.

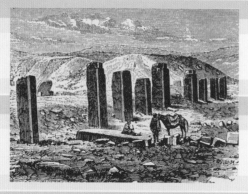

Tiahuanoco, "The American Stonehenge"

c. 100 BC

The city of Moche is founded. It contains a large ceremonial center with two enormous mud-brick pyramids and a cemetery containing royal tombs.

c. AD 400

The city of Huari emerges in the Peruvian Andes near modern Ayacucho. Its people build a major road network and South America's first terraced fields.

c. AD 536–594

A period of drought followed by intense rain and flooding may have disrupted the Moche way of life and weakened their civilization. The city of Moche is abandoned and the capital is moved to Pampa Grande.

c. AD 600

The Nazca people create enormous etchings—the Nazca Lines—on the desert surface, depicting animals and geometric shapes that can be appreciated only from the air.

A stylized monkey, a part of the Nazca lines

c. 10,600 BC

The earliest inhabitants of southern South America settle the northern pampas. They use stone tools and hunt animals, such as the giant ground sloth and prehistoric horse.

c. 10,400 BC

The earliest human settlements in the Brazilian Highlands date to this time. They live by eating manioc, sweet potatoes, palm fruits, pine nuts, and maize, and hunting birds, rabbits, armadillos, deer, and tapirs.

c. 10,000 BC

By this time, humans are dispersed through-out mainland South America apart from the Amazon Basin.

c. 2300 BC

Farming begins in the northern Andes. Maize is cultivated on the southwest coast of Ecuador.

c. 2000–1 BC

People living in the Amazon Basin begin supplementing fishing and hunting with the cultivation of root crops.

c. 1900 BC

Farming begins in Peru. Cotton, squash, gourds, and some root crops are cultivated. Mountain dwellers begin to herd alpacas and llamas.

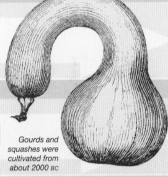

Gourds and squashes were cultivated from about 2000 BC

c. 800–500 BC

During the first stage of Chavín culture, known as Urabarriu, Chavín de Huantár has a population of a few hundred and the ceramics show the influence of other cultures.

Ruins at Tiahuanaco

c. 300 BC

The first human settlements arise at Tiahuanaco in southern Peru, near Lake Titicaca.

c. 250–200 BC

Chavín culture suffers a rapid decline. New building work ceases. Chavín styles of pottery and metalwork disappear. By 200 BC, the culture has vanished.

Huari figure, 8th century

c. AD 200

The Moche expand, spreading their culture by conquest along the coast and establishing fortified settlements at sites such as Loma Negra and Huaca del Brujo.

c. AD 200

The Lord of Sipán rules the Moche at around this time.

AD 200–800

The Nazca people flourish on the desert coast of modern Peru to the south of Moche. They make decorated pottery bowls and musical instruments and weave textiles.

c. AD 400

The city of Tiahuanaco is built. It contains a ceremonial and administrative center with temples, tombs, and palaces as well as housing for 40,000 people.

AD 450

The Moche state reaches its height with a population as high as 650,000.

AD 400–700

Tiahuanaco builds an Empire that dominates the southern Andes and southern coastal desert.

AD 600–800

The warlike Huari conquer Moche in the 7th century and the Nazca in the early 9th. They create an Empire covering a large area of northern Peru.

c. AD 800–900

The Huari culture begins to decline. The city of Huari is abandoned by AD 900.

c. AD 1000

The city of Tiahuanaco is abandoned, possibly following prolonged drought.

c. AD 1000

The Caribbean and northern Andean peoples have, by this time, developed a life centered on towns and cities, ruled by local elites.

By AD 500, the Western Roman Empire
had collapsed and Europe had fragmented
into Germanic tribal kingdoms, while the
eastern Byzantine Empire remained intact.
Meanwhile, White Huns from Central
Asia were destroying the Gupta
Empire of northern India and
severely destabilizing the Sasanids
of Persia. China, divided between
north and south, was shortly to be
unified under the Sui.

Teotihuacán
The city of Teotihuacán
in central Mexico was at
the height of its power,
and covered 7¾ sq miles
(20 sq km).

Ruins at Teotihuacán

Maya
Tikal was the most
powerful Mayan city with
a population of around
100,000. Other major
regional powers
included Palenque,
Yaxchilán, Copán,
and Calakmul.

*Carved Mayan
ceremonial stone*

South America
By AD 500, several powerful kingdoms
coexisted on the coast and highlands
of Peru, including Moche, Nazca,
Huari, and Tiahuanaco.

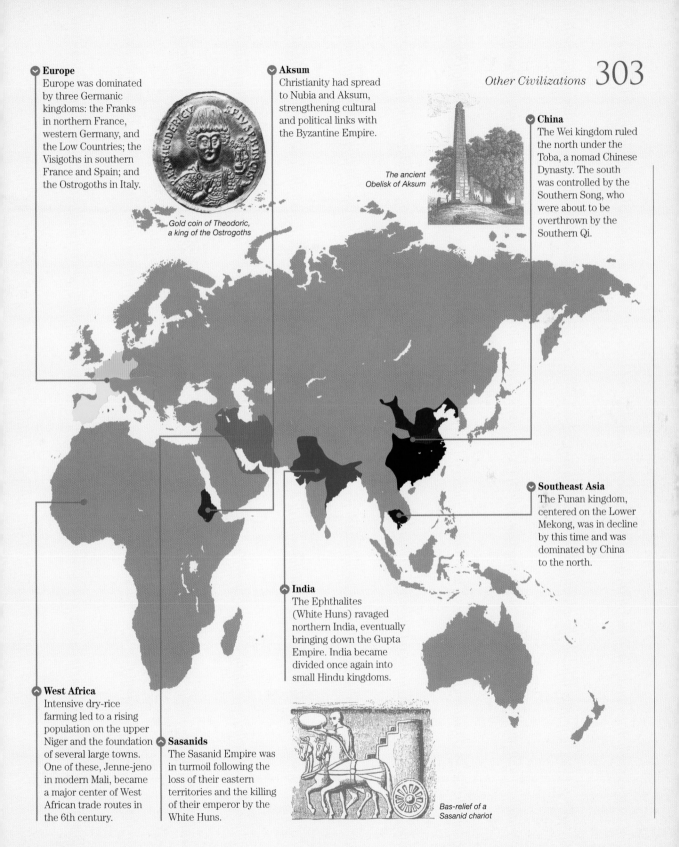

Europe

Europe was dominated by three Germanic kingdoms: the Franks in northern France, western Germany, and the Low Countries; the Visigoths in southern France and Spain; and the Ostrogoths in Italy.

Gold coin of Theodoric, a king of the Ostrogoths

Aksum

Christianity had spread to Nubia and Aksum, strengthening cultural and political links with the Byzantine Empire.

The ancient Obelisk of Aksum

China

The Wei kingdom ruled the north under the Toba, a nomad Chinese Dynasty. The south was controlled by the Southern Song, who were about to be overthrown by the Southern Qi.

Southeast Asia

The Funan kingdom, centered on the Lower Mekong, was in decline by this time and was dominated by China to the north.

India

The Ephthalites (White Huns) ravaged northern India, eventually bringing down the Gupta Empire. India became divided once again into small Hindu kingdoms.

West Africa

Intensive dry-rice farming led to a rising population on the upper Niger and the foundation of several large towns. One of these, Jenne-jeno in modern Mali, became a major center of West African trade routes in the 6th century.

Sasanids

The Sasanid Empire was in turmoil following the loss of their eastern territories and the killing of their emperor by the White Huns.

Bas-relief of a Sasanid chariot

ACHAEMENID DYNASTY Dynasty of Persian rulers (7th century–480 BC), the greatest of whom was Cyrus II.

ACHILLES Youthful "hero" of Homer's *Iliad*, destined to die shortly before the moment the Greeks defeated the Trojans.

AEDILE In ancient Rome, one of the lesser magistrates responsible for public order and cleanliness, markets, the safety of public buildings and thoroughfares, and the staging of festivals.

AKHENATEN Ancient Egyptian pharaoh of the 18th Dynasty (*reigned c*. 1353–*c*. 1334 BC), founder of a new artistic and religious movement that was obliterated by his successors.

AKHETATEN City founded out in the desert by Pharaoh Akhenaten, 365 miles (585 km) south of modern Cairo. Its remains are now the archaeological site of Tell el-Amarna.

AKKAD Central region of ancient Mesopotamia, basis of the first great Mesopotamian empire.

AKSUM Kingdom that emerged in what is now northern Ethiopia during the 1st century AD. It controlled traffic and trade in the Red Sea.

ALEXANDER THE GREAT Son of Philip II of Macedon (*reigned* 359–336 BC), Alexander III's primary purpose was to defeat the Persians once and for all. Which he did, at the battles of Granikus, Issus, and finally Gaugamela. He went on to carve out a vast empire, but died, aged thirty-three, in Babylon in 323 BC.

AMPHORA Large vase or ceramic jar for containing wine, olive oil, honey, or other fluids.

AMUN Ancient Egyptian creator god revered in Thebes, who became chief national deity and patron of the pharaohs of the 18th Dynasty.

APOLLO In the ancient Greek pantheon, Apollo was god of enlightenment and human achievements—including medicine, law, music, prophecy, art, and righteous retribution.

ARYANS Central Asian people speaking an Indo-Iranian language. From *c*. 1500 BC they slowly migrated en masse southward, eventually spreading over much of India.

ASSUR *see* **ASSYRIA**

ASSURBANIPAL Last great king of Assyria (*reigned* 668–627 BC), grandson of Sennacherib.

ASSYRIA Northern region and kingdom of ancient Mesopotamia, named after the national god Assur.

ATHENE or **ATHENA** Patron deity of Athens from very early times (before the arrival of Zeus and the Olympians), her divine attributes changed over the centuries as Greek culture changed—so she could be goddess of war (especially as Pallas Athene) and victory, but also goddess of household crafts and skills, and wisdom.

ATTICA Large peninsula in southeast Greece, originally the combined territories of twelve small communities, but by the 6th century BC the unified territory that was the Athenian state, with Athens as its capital and center of government.

AUGUSTUS Title ("revered one," "destined one") taken as a name by Julius Caesar's heir and successor, previously known as Octavian, first Roman emperor.

AUXILIARY A soldier in the Roman army who was not a citizen of Rome; a mercenary soldier.

BABYLON Town, then city, then city-state and at times empire capital in ancient Mesopotamia, regarded as "the holy city of Babylonia" by 2300 BC.

BABYLONIA Southern region of ancient Mesopotamia, centered on the city of Babylon.

BASILICA In ancient Rome, a public building used initially for judicial and later for religious purposes.

BIREME Type of wooden ship that had two banks of oars on each side, pioneered by the Phoenicians, but adapted and enlarged by first the Greeks (to triremes) and then the Romans (to quadriremes and quinquiremes).

CAESAR Clan "surname" of Julius Caesar, after his death taken as a title by successive Roman emperors.

CANOPIC JARS Urns in which organs of human corpses undergoing mummification were stored by ancient Egyptians.

CASSIUS DIO Roman author (*c*. AD 153 or *c*. 163/4–after 229) whose eighty-volume history of Rome largely survives intact and remains uniquely valuable.

CASTOR AND POLLUX Roman names of the ancient Greek zodiacal "heavenly twins," Gemini.

CELTS Originally central European people speaking any of several Celtic languages. Their earliest culture, from *c*. 1350 BC, was the Urnfield; their second great culture was the Hallstatt, from *c*. 750 BC; and the third was La Tène, from *c*. 450 BC; but by late Roman times they were almost entirely confined to areas just outside the northwestern borders of the empire.

CENTAUR Mythical figure with the body of a man to the waist joined to the body of a horse at the neck.

CHALDEA Area around the Sumerian city of Ur in southern Mesopotamia.

CHAVÍN Culture that emerged in what is now Peru *c*. 800 BC; it lasted for 600 years.

CIRCUS In ancient Rome, a circuit or race course, especially a chariot racetrack.

COELIAN (CAELIAN) HILL The southeasternmost of the seven hills of Rome.

COHORT Major division of a Roman army legion comprising legionaries or auxiliaries.

CONSUL Holder of the highest elected political office in the Roman Republic and the Empire.

CORINTH In ancient Greece, a city sited on the spit of land that connected the Peloponnese with the mainland.

CROOK AND FLAIL In ancient Egypt, the two symbols of the pharaoh's authority.

CROWNS OF EGYPT A pharaoh might wear the white crown (*hedjet*) of Upper Egypt, the red crown (*deshret*) of Lower Egypt, the double crown (*pschent*) of the combined kingdom, or the blue crown (*khepresh*) that signaled he was the leader of a nation at war.

CUNEIFORM Ancient script of characters formed by wedge-shaped reed ends impressed in clay.

CYCLOPS In Greek mythology, a giant with a single eye in the middle of the forehead.

CYRUS II Persian emperor (*reigned* 560–*c.* 530 BC), greatest ruler of the Achaemenid Dynasty.

DACIA An area that in ancient Roman times covered what is now Romania and Moldova and parts of Ukraine, Hungary, and Bulgaria.

DELIAN LEAGUE Association of around 150 ancient Greek city-states under the leadership of Athens, founded in 478 BC to continue war against the Persians and avoid strife between them.

DELPHIC ORACLE *see* **ORACLE AT DELPHI**

DELTA Huge triangular part of ancient and modern Egypt surrounding the Nile River from Cairo to the Mediterranean Sea. It is effectively the same as Lower Egypt.

DENARIUS Coin in ancient Rome.

DI MANES In ancient Rome, spirits of departed family members honored as minor gods.

DISH-COVER TOMB Mesopotamian sarcophagus with a brick floor and earthenware cover.

DOMITIAN Highly unpopular but ruthlessly efficient Roman emperor (*reigned* AD 81–96).

DORIANS A widespread Hellenic people.

ELAM Ancient civilization of linked kingdoms just to the east of Mesopotamia.

ELEUSINIAN MYSTERIES Torchlit night rituals carried out on the Eleusis coast in honor of the Greek goddess Demeter, patroness of agricultural fertility.

ERECHTHEUS Legendary Athenian king.

ERIDU Earliest and southernmost city-state/kingdom of ancient Mesopotamia.

ETRUSCANS The Etruscan civilization emerged in what is now central north-western Italy in the 7th century BC.

FORUM Civic center used for judicial, governmental, and commercial operations.

GAUL Area of western Europe covering what is now France, Belgium, and parts of Switzerland, Germany, and Holland.

GERMANIC TRIBES Germanic-speaking peoples. Tribes included the Cimbri, Teutones, Franks, Goths, and Vandals.

GILGAMESH Hero of the ancient Akkadian *Epic of Gilgamesh.*

GREAVES Metal shin guards used by warriors of ancient Greece and Rome.

GUPTA EMPIRE Empire that at its height controlled much of India, founded by Chandra Gupta I (*reigned* AD 320–35).

GUTI or **GUTIANS** Invaders of ancient Mesopotamia from the east between 2193 and 2112 BC.

GYNAIKONITIS In ancient Greece, the household area devoted to womenfolk— used when the menfolk were entertaining courtesans in their quarters (the *andron*).

HADRIAN Emperor of Rome AD 117–38. He was an excellent military strategist who concentrated on expanding the Empire only as far as possible to protect it.

HAMMURABI King of ancient Babylon 1792–1750 BC.

HAN DYNASTY Ruling dynasty in China founded by Han Gaozu in 206 BC.

HAPY Ancient Egyptian god of the annual flooding of the Nile.

HATHOR Egyptian goddess of love, beauty, fertility, mystery, and darkness.

HATSHEPSUT Female Egyptian pharaoh (*reigned* 1479–1458 BC).

HEPHAESTUS Greek god of the forge.

HERACLES or **HERCULES** Semidivine ancient Greek and later Roman hero.

HERMES Greek god whose major divine attribute was the ability to cross boundaries. He was himself a messenger of Zeus between the gods, the earth, and the underworld. He was also god of thieves, liars, and tricksters.

HIEROGLYPHICS Pictogram script.

HITTITES Anatolian people who established a kingdom *c.* 18th century BC in what is now central Turkey.

HORUS Ancient Egyptian falcon-headed god of the sky and daylight.

HUANGDI The legendary "Yellow Emperor" said to have established Chinese civilization in 2698 BC. *See* **SHI HUANGDI**.

HUNS Warlike Turkic people from the steppes of western Asia who from AD *c.* 370 migrated westward sweeping other kingdoms before them. Their most famous leader was Attila (*reigned* AD 434–53).

HYKSOS Western Asiatic rulers of Egypt for around a century from 1650 BC.

INTERMEDIATE PERIODS In Egypt, periods of political disunity and decline.

ISHTAR Babylonian love and fertility goddess, but also goddess of war.

ISIS Ancient Egyptian goddess, ideal wife (of Osiris), and mother (of Horus).

ISRAELITES Semitic tribe, originally descendants of Mesopotamian migrants to Palestine and Egypt *c.* 1500 BC.

KARNAK Area of Thebes near Luxor that was the site of a vast temple complex.

KHUFU, GREAT PYRAMID OF At Giza, erected *c.* 2560 BC, and the only one of the Seven Wonders of the (Ancient) World still standing.

KRATER Ancient Greek bowl for mixing (*krater*, "mixer") wine with water.

KUSHAN EMPIRE Empire founded by central Asian nomad descendants.

LAMASSU The Assyrian winged bull with a heavily bearded man's head, statues of which were generally sited in pairs as palace or temple guardians.

LEGIONARY In the Roman army, a Roman citizen professional soldier.

LICTOR A lictor enforced measures of respect paid to the magistrate and punished sentenced offenders.

LUXOR Area of Thebes that was the site of huge temple complexes.

MAAT In ancient Egypt, the concept (and goddess) of order, truth, and decency.

MAGHADA Area of India now occupied by much of Bengal, Bihar, and eastern Uttar Pradesh.

MARDUK Patron deity of ancient Babylon.

MARK ANTONY Friend, lieutenant, and eventual co-avenger of Julius Caesar.

MAURYAN EMPIRE Empire that controlled much of India 321–230 BC, founded by Chandragupta Maurya.

MAYA Complex civilization of Central America. Its Classic Period was AD 300–900.

MEDES Ancient Iranian people who defeated the Assyrians in 606 BC.

MEGIDDO Royal Canaanite city dominating the Plain of Jezreel.

MEMPHIS Ancient Egyptian city of Ineb-Hedj, renamed later by the Greeks.

MEROVINGIAN DYNASTY Rulers of the Frankish kingdom between the 5th and 8th centuries AD.

MIDDLE KINGDOM In ancient Egypt, the period from the 11th Dynasty to the 14th, inclusive (2040–1650 BC).

MINOANS Early Cretan culture from *c.* 3000 BC.

MINOTAUR Legendary creature, half man, half bull, housed in a labyrinth beneath the Minoan Palace of Knossos in Crete.

MOCHE Powerful culture that arose *c.* 200 BC in what is now northern Peru.

MYCENEANS Proto-Greek Aegean trading culture 1450–*c.* 1200 BC.

NABU Babylonian god of wisdom.

NEBUCHADNEZZAR II Ruler of Babylon *c.* 605–562 BC.

NEFERTARI Chief wife of ancient Egyptian pharaoh Ramesses II.

NEFERTITI Wife (and sister) of ancient Egyptian pharaoh Akhenaten.

NEPTUNE Originally a Roman god only of water, but later a god of the sea.

NEW KINGDOM In ancient Egypt, the prosperous period from the 18th Dynasty to the 20th, inclusive (1570–1070 BC).

NINEVEH Ancient city in Assyria.

NOK CULTURE Civilization in what is now central Nigeria *c.* 500 BC– *c.* AD 200.

NUBIA Land that comprised the Nile Valley south of Aswan and the First Cataract down to the Sixth Cataract, not far from modern Khartoum in Sudan.

OLD KINGDOM In Egypt, the period from the 3rd Dynasty to the 6th, inclusive (2686–2134 BC) (the "pyramid period").

OLMECS Early farming culture, later important trading nation, along the Gulf Coast of Mexico *c.* 1500–*c.* 300 BC.

ORACLE AT DELPHI High priestess or Pythia, who announced the words of the oracle within a fume-filled mountain cave.

OSCILLA Decorative Roman disks carved with the faces of deities for luck.

OSIRIS In ancient Egypt, the divine lord of the dead and granter of life after death.

PAPYRUS Paperlike material.

PARTHENON Temple of the goddess Athene the Virgin (Greek: *parthenos*) at Athens, built in 480 BC. For a time it served as treasury of the Delian League.

PARTHIA An area corresponding roughly to modern Iran, Iraq, and the Gulf states.

PELOPONNESIAN WARS Two wars between Athens and Sparta in 460–446 BC and 431–404 BC.

PERICLES Statesman, orator, and military leader of Athens *c.*461–429 BC.

PHOENICIANS Trading people on what is now the coast of Lebanon *c.*1550–300 BC.

POMPEY Gnaeus Pompeius (106–48 BC), awarded the title Magnus, leader of the later Roman Republic.

POSEIDON Greek god of streams, coastal waters, seismic disturbances, and horses.

PRAETOR Senior Roman civic official.

PTOLEMID DYNASTY Dynasty founded by Ptolemy, general to Alexander the Great. It lasted 305–30 BC.

PUNIC WARS Series of three wars between Rome and the Phoenicians of Carthage between 264 and 146 BC.

QADESH (BATTLE OF) Either of two battles. The first (*c.* 1301 BC) was between Pharaoh Seti I and the Hittites under Mutawallis, and divided Syria-Palestine between the two powers. The second (1274 BC) was a bloody stalemate between the Egyptian forces of Ramesses II and the Hittites.

QUAESTOR Roman official who oversaw state monies, including taxes and fines.

RA Ancient Egyptian sun deity.

RAMESSES II Egyptian pharaoh (*reigned* 1279–1214 BC).

ROTUNDA Ancient Roman form of dome.

SAMNITES Tribes that ruled the south central Apennines, 600–290 BC.

SANSKRIT Early form of Indo-Iranian language developed from the 2nd millennium BC.

SARGON I King of ancient Akkad 2334–2279 BC, founder of the Akkadian Empire.

SARGON II King of Assyria 722–705 BC.

SASANIDS Ruling Iranian dynasty founded by Ardashir I (*reigned c.* AD 220–40).

SELEUCID DYNASTY Dynasty founded by Seleucus, Alexander the Great's general.

SENNACHERIB Son of Sargon II, king of Assyria 704–681 BC.

SESTERCE Ancient Roman coin of a value of one-quarter of a denarius.

SHAMASH Solar deity of Babylon.

SHANG DYNASTY Ruling dynasty in China 1766–1122 BC.

SHI HUANGDI Title of Zheng, first emperor of a unified China (*reigned* 221–210 BC).

THEBES Ancient Egyptian capital for a time in the Middle and the New Kingdoms.

THOTH Ibis-headed ancient Egyptian god of wisdom, learning, and magic.

THRACE Large area covering what is now northeastern Greece, southern Bulgaria, and European Turkey.

THUTMOSE III Greatest military pharaoh of ancient Egypt (*c.* 1479–1425 BC).

TIAMAT Babylonian goddess of the saltwater depths and primordial chaos.

TIBERIUS Stepson of Augustus, and Roman emperor for twenty-three years (AD 14–37).

TOLTECS Ruled central Mexican Empire between the 10th and 12th centuries AD.

TRAJAN Roman emperor AD 98–117.

TRIBUNE Roman official who represented the common people against corruption or coercion in high places.

TROJAN WAR War fought on a 100-days-per-year basis over ten years between mainland Greeks and Trojan Greeks at the city of Troy in *c.* 1194–1184 BC.

TROY Ancient city in what is now coastal Anatolia in northwest Turkey.

UR Ancient city in Chaldea.

URAEUS Cobra figurine on the front of the headdress of an Egyptian pharaoh.

URUK Very early city in ancient southern Mesopotamia – its modern name is Warka.

VALLEY OF THE KINGS Valley across the Nile from Thebes in which tombs of pharaohs and nobles were constructed during the New Kingdom (16th–11th century BC).

VALLEY OF THE QUEENS Valley not far from the Valley of the Kings, in which wives and children of the pharaohs of the 18th, 19th, and 20th Dynasties were entombed.

VESPASIAN Roman emperor AD 69–79, having been a successful military commander in Britain and Judaea. His imperial successors Titus (*reigned* 79–81) and Domitian (81–96) were both his sons.

VISIGOTHS The Germanic tribe of the Western Goths who disrupted the Roman Empire in the late 4th century AD and, under Alaric, sacked Rome in 410.

VITELLIUS For eleven and a half months emperor of Rome in AD 69. A notorious glutton, Vitellius was eventually deposed (and killed) by followers of Vespasian.

ZAPOTECS Culture that emerged in southern Mexico *c.* 500 BC.

ZEUS Chief of the Olympian gods, introduced as effectively the third set of ancient Greek deities in the overall Greek pantheon, much later than basic nature gods, such as Ouranos, and later even than, for instance, Demeter and Poseidon. He represented the light of day, under which everything was seen and known, implying ultimate power.

ZIGGURAT A stepped pyramid made of baked bricks and usually topped with a shrine to a tutelary deity, often all within a large temple precinct or complex in ancient Mesopotamia. Possibly the inspiration both for the Tower of Babel and for Jacob's Ladder in the Judeo-Christian Bible.

This book approaches the past through illustrations, dating from the late 18th to the early 19th centuries. These illustrations are beautiful in themselves, yet they also tell a fascinating story about the rediscovery of the material culture of the ancient world.

In one sense, ancient history was never forgotten, shaping the development of the West through the Bible and classical writers, such as Plutarch and Cicero. Yet until the 17th century, ancient history was usually seen as a play in modern dress. Shakespeare in Julius Caesar, for example, presents a Rome where clocks strike and men wear doublets and "sweaty night caps." In the same period historians concentrated on the written records of the past rather than ancient art or material remains. They were concerned not with evoking life in the past, but with drawing moral lessons from history.

Even so, from the late 16th century a new attitude to the past began to emerge, as antiquarians such as William Camden (1551–1623) in Britain, and Roger de Gaignières (1642–1715) in France, documented ancient remains. From the 1740s, wealthy travelers from northern Europe visited Italy on the "Grand Tour," and many brought back classical sculptures to decorate their homes and gardens. The high points of the tour were Rome, Pompeii, and Herculaneum, then being excavated, and Hadrian's palace at Tivoli. The collections of men, such as Charles Townley (1737–1805), including sculpture from Tivoli, would form the basis of national museums.

In 1762 Nicholas Revett (1720–1804) and James "Athenian" Stuart (1713–88) published The Antiquities of Athens, *whose beautiful illustrations inspired a neoclassical revival in architecture. Two years later, the German scholar Johann Joachim Winkelmann (1717–68) brought out the* History of Ancient Art, *a hugely influential work, which first distinguished between the styles of Greek and Roman sculpture.*

In 1798 Napoleon Bonaparte invaded Egypt, accompanied by a team of 160 scholars, who documented wall paintings, temples, and tombs. Their work was published as the magnificent Description de l'Égypte, *which came out in twenty-three, leather-bound volumes between 1809 and 1818. Many of the Egyptian illustrations in the present volume ultimately derive from this work.*

The 19th century saw wholesale plundering of ancient sites. In 1801–5, Thomas Bruce, the seventh Earl of Elgin (1766–1841), stripped the Parthenon of much of its sculptural decoration, which was shipped to London. Later, in 1815–20, Giovanni Belzoni (1778–1823), the flamboyant ex-circus strongman, smashed his way into Egyptian tombs, removing sculptures and sarcophagi to be exhibited in London. The British were rivaled by the French and the Germans, who were building up their own museum collections in Paris and Berlin.

The period saw the beginnings of the new science of archaeology. One of the pioneering figures was Austen Henry Layard (1817–94) who, in the 1840s, discovered the ancient Assyrian capitals Nimrud and Nineveh. Previously, the Assyrians had been known only as names in the Bible. Layard's excavation of four palaces, and removal of dozens of sculptures and reliefs, caused immense excitement in 19th-century Britain. The grisly Assyrian reliefs, showing the flaying of captives, seemed to provide proof of the truth of the Bible accounts.

In the 1870s, the German archaeologist Heinrich Schliemann (1822–90), determined to prove that Homer's Iliad *was real history, drove a trench through a great mound at Hissarlik in Turkey, revealing the ancient city of Troy, which had been rebuilt several times. In the process Schliemann destroyed the 13th-century-BC level for which he was searching. He was more successful in Mycenae, where he discovered fabulous treasures, including the so-called Mask of Agamemnon, dating from the Greek Bronze Age.*

Fueled by exciting archaeological discoveries, the 19th century saw a huge public appetite for the ancient world. In an age before modern mass communication, people drew most of their knowledge from illustrated volumes. Works such as Auguste Racinet's Le Costume historique *(1888) and Friedrich Hottenroth's* Trachten Haus- Feld- und Kriegsgeräthschaften der Völker alter und neuer Zeit *(1891) focused on clothing, but also depicted jewelry, interior design, and everyday artifacts. This page (right) from Hottenroth's work, for example, includes tools, plows, mills, carts, and merchant's scales, as well as wall paintings showing the work of a laundry in Pompeii.*

It is not surprising that 19th-century illustrators made mistakes sometimes. Indeed, part of the charm of the illustrations lies in these mistakes. For example, on page 173, we have a Greek trireme rigged like a 19th-century sailing ship, and on page 225, we see Roman priests wearing strange dunces' caps. Despite these occasional errors, the 19th-century images show a new awareness that the material culture of the past was very different from that of the present. As L. P. Hartley put it in his famous opening line to The Go-Between *(1953), "The past is a foreign country: they do things differently there."*

ANDREWS, C., *Ancient Egyptian Jewellery*, British Museum Press, 1996

ARNOLD, D., *The Encyclopedia of Ancient Egyptian Architecture*, I. B. Tauris, 2003

ASCALONE, ENRICO, *Mesopotamia*, University of California Press, 2007

AUBOYER, JEANNINE, *Daily Life in Ancient India: From Approximately 200 BC to 700 AD*, Weidenfeld & Nicolson, 1965

BAINES, J. and MALEK, J., *Atlas of Ancient Egypt*, Andromeda, 1980 (Or revised as *Cultural Atlas of Ancient Egypt*, Facts on File Inc., 2000)

BIRLEY, ANTONY R., *Marcus Aurelius: A Biography*, Routledge, 1993

BOARDMAN, J. *The Greeks Overseas: Their early Colonies and Trade*, Thames & Hudson, 1999

BOARDMAN, JOHN (ed.), *The Oxford History of the Roman World*, Oxford University Press, 2001

BREWER, D. J. and TEETER, E., *Egypt and the Egyptians*, Cambridge University Press, 1999

BRIANT, PIERRE, *From Cyrus to Alexander: A History of the Persian Empire*, Eisenbrauns, 2006

BRUHNS, KAREN OLSEN, *Ancient South America*, Cambridge University Press, 1994

BUXTON, R., *The Complete World of Greek Mythology*, Thames & Hudson, 2004

CAMP, J. M., *The Archaeology of Athens*, Yale University Press, 2001

CONNOLLY, PETER, *Greece and Rome at War*, Greenhill Books, 1998

CONNOLLY, PETER and DODGE, HAZEL, *The Ancient City: Life in Classical Athens and Rome*, Oxford University Press, 1998

DALLEY, STEPHANIE (ed.), *The Legacy of Mesopotamia*, Oxford University Press, 1998

DAVIDSON, JAMES, *Courtesans and Fishcakes: The Consuming Passions of Classical Athens*, HarperCollins, 1997

DAVIS HANSON, V., *A War Like No Other: How the Athenians and Spartans fought the Peloponnesian War*, Methuen, 2007

DE SELINCOURT, AUBREY (trans.), MARINCOLA, JOHN (ed.), *Herodotus: The Histories*, Penguin Classics, 1996

DODSON, A. and IKRAM, S., *The Tomb in Ancient Egypt*, Thames & Hudson, 2008

ELLIS, PETER BERRESFORD, *The Celts: A History*, Carroll & Graf, rev. ed. 2004

FITTON, J. L., *The Minoans*, British Museum Press, 2002

GAHLIN, LUCIA, *Egypt: Gods, Myth and Religion*, Lorenz Books, 2001

GRANT, MICHAEL (trans.), *Tacitus: The Annals of Imperial Rome*, Penguin Classics, 1971

GRAVES, ROBERT (trans.), *Suetonius: The Twelve Caesars*, Penguin Classics, 2007

GREEN, PETER, *Alexander of Macedon, 356–323 BC. A Historical Biography*, University of California Press, 1991

GREEN, PETER (trans.), *Juvenal: The Sixteen Satires*, Penguin Classics, 1967

GROUSSET, RENÉ, *The Empire of the Steppes: A History of Central Asia*, Rutgers University Press, 1970

HENNIG, MARTIN, *A Handbook of Roman Art*, Phaidon Press, 1983

HINTZE, FRITZ and URSULA, *Civilizations of the Old Sudan: Kerma, Kush, Christian Nubia*, B. R. Grüner, 1968

HOPKINS, KEITH, *A World Full of Gods: Pagans, Jews and Christians in the Roman Empire*, Phoenix, 2000

IKRAM, S. and DODSON, A., *The Mummy in Ancient Egypt*, Thames & Hudson, 1998

JONES, PETER, *The World of Rome: An Introduction to Roman Culture*, Cambridge University Press, 1997

KEMP, B. J., *Ancient Egypt: Anatomy of a Civilization*, Routledge, 1989, rev. ed. 2005

LEHNER, M., *The Complete Pyramids*, Thames & Hudson, 1997

LLOYD, SETON, *Foundations in the Dust: The Story of Mesopotamian Exploration*, Thames & Hudson, rev. ed. 1980

LOEWE, MICHAEL and EDWARD L. SHAUGHNESSY, *The Cambridge History of Ancient China: From the Origins of Civilization to 221 BC*, Cambridge University Press, 1999

MANLEY, B., *The Penguin Historical Atlas of Ancient Egypt*, Penguin, 1996

MCINTOSH, JANE R., *Ancient Mesopotamia: New Perspectives*, ABC Clio, 2005

MORKOT, R., *Egypt: Land of the Pharaohs*, Odyssey Books, 2005

NEILS, J., *The British Museum Concise Introduction: Ancient Greece*, British Museum Press, 2008

OATES, JOAN, *Babylon*, Thames & Hudson, rev. ed. 1986

OPPENHEIM, A. L., *Ancient Mesopotamia: Portrait of a Dead Civilization*, University of Chicago Press, 1964

OPPER, THORSTEN, *Hadrian: Empire and Conflict*, British Museum Press, 2008

OSBORNE, R., *Archaic and Classical Greek Art*, Oxford Paperbacks, 1998

PARTRIDGE, R. B., *Fighting Pharaohs: Weapons and Warfare in Ancient Egypt*, Peartree Publishing, 2002

PINCH, G., *Magic In Ancient Egypt*, British Museum Press, 1994

POLLOCK, SUSAN, *Ancient Mesopotamia: The Eden That Never Was*, Cambridge University Press, 1999

RADICE, BETTY (trans.), *The Letters of the Younger Pliny*, Penguin Classics, 1963

REEVES, C. N., *The Complete Tutankhamun*, Thames & Hudson, 1990

REEVES, C. N. and WILKINSON, R. H., *The Complete Valley of the Kings*, Thames & Hudson, 1996

ROBINS, G., *Art of Ancient Egypt*, London: British Museum Press, 1997

ROBINS, G., *Women in Ancient Egypt*, British Museum Press, 1993

SAGGS, H. W. F., *The Greatness That Was Babylon*, Sidgwick & Jackson, 1988

SAGGS, H. W. F., *The Might That Was Assyria*, Sidgwick & Jackson, 1984

SCHOFIELD, L., *The Mycenaeans*, British Museum Press, 2007

SCOTT-KILVERT, IAN (trans.), *Plutarch: The Age of Alexander*, Penguin Classics, 1973

SCOTT-KILVERT, IAN (trans.), *Plutarch: The Rise and Fall of Athens: Nine Greek Lives*, Penguin Books, 1960

SHAPIRO, H. A. (ed.), *Archaic Greece*, Cambridge University Press, 2007

SHARER, ROBERT J. and LOA P. TRAXLER, *The Ancient Maya*, Stanford University Press, 6th ed. 2006

SHAW, I. (ed.), *The Oxford History of Ancient Egypt*, Oxford University Press, 2000

SHAW, I. M. E. and NICHOLSON, P. T., *The British Museum Dictionary of Ancient Egypt*, British Museum Press, 1995

SPAWFORTH, T., *The Complete Greek Temples*, Thames & Hudson, 2006

TALBERT, RICHARD J. A. (trans.), *Plutarch on Sparta*, Penguin Classics, 1988

TAYLOR, J. H., *Death and the Afterlife in Ancient Egypt*, British Museum, 2001

WARNER, REX (trans.), *Thucydides: History of the Peloponnesian War*, Penguin Classics, 1972

WARNER, REX (trans) and GEORGE CAUKWELL (ed.), *Xenophon: The Persian Expedition*, Penguin Books, 1949

WILKINSON, R. H., *The Complete Gods and Goddesses*, Thames & Hudson, 2003

WILKINSON, R. H., *The Complete Temples of Ancient Egypt*, Thames & Hudson, 2000

WOOD, MICHAEL, *In Search of the Trojan War*, BBC Books, 2005

General editor

DOMINIC RATHBONE is Professor of Ancient History in the Department of Classics at King's College London, where he has taught Greek and Roman history since 1985. His main research interests are Roman Egypt, the agrarian history of Roman Italy, and private and public finances in the Roman Empire. He has worked on excavations of Roman villas in Italy and has directed a survey of Greco-Roman village sites in the southwest Fayyum in Egypt. He has published on a variety of related subjects, such as Roman estate management, banking, and economics in Egypt and in Italy.
Contribution: Introduction (*pages 6–11*)

Contributors

PETER CHRISP is a scholar who has written widely on historical subjects, with a particular emphasis on the ancient world. He has a long-standing interest in ancient Rome, and has visited most of the major sites, from Hadrian's Wall to Leptis Magna and Ephesus. He was a senior writer on Culture Online's "Icons of England" website, and also cowrote the text for the 2006 Summer Exhibition, "Edges of Rome," at London's Globe Theatre, looking at Shakespeare's reinterpretation of Roman history.
Contribution: Rome (*pages 200–71*), Illustrating Civilizations of the Ancient World (*pages 308–11*)

LUCIA GAHLIN is a lecturer in Egyptology for the Universities of Bristol and Exeter. She is a Trustee of the Egypt Exploration Society, Chair of the Friends of the Petrie Museum, and Deputy Director of Bloomsbury Summer School, all based in London. She was the Small Finds Registrar at the archaeological site of Amarna in Middle Egypt, and has worked extensively in the Petrie Museum of Egyptian Archaeology.
Contribution: Egypt (*pages 12–83*)

GEORGE HART took degrees in Classics and Egyptian Art and Archaeology at University College London, before joining the staff of the British Museum, where he was for many years Principal Lecturer on the museum's collections from Egypt, Greece, the Levant, and the civilizations of the Mediterranean world.

He was Chairman of the Friends of the Petrie Museum of Egyptian Archaeology between 1988 and 2000, and is a Lecturer for the National Association of Decorative and Fine Arts.
Contribution: Greece (*pages 130–99*)

ANDREW KIRK was educated at Oxford University and is Senior Editor at Liverpool University Press. He has written four books, three on historical subjects, and has a long-standing interest in ancient history, having visited the principal centers of Mesopotamian history in Iran and Iraq as a student.
Contribution: Mesopotamia (*pages 84–129*)

ALEX WOOLF graduated in history from the University of Essex and has since written numerous works of ancient history, including books on the Romans, Anglo-Saxons, and Vikings. In 2004 he edited Marshall Cavendish's highly acclaimed eleven-volume encyclopedia, *Exploring Ancient Civilizations*.
Contribution: Other Civilizations (*pages 272–303*)

All illustrations have been reproduced from the following, except where noted below:

COELL, DR. H., *Illustrierte Mythologie*, Leipzig, 1872

DURUY, VICTOR, *Histoire Des Grecs,* Tomes I, II & III, Librairie Hachette, Paris,1889

ERMAN, ADOLF, *Life in Ancient Egypt*, Macmillan, London, 1894

FIRTH, JOHN BENJAMIN, *Augustus Caesar and the Organisation of the Empire of Rome*, Putnam, New York, 1903

GRAFTON, CAROL BELANGER, *Egyptian Designs*, Dover Publications, New York, 1993

GUHL, E. & KONER, W., *The Life of the Greeks and Romans*, Chatto & Windus, London, 1889

HECK J. G., *Iconographic Encyclopaedia*, Volumes I & II, Rudolph, Garrigue, New York, 1851

HOTTENROTH, FRIEDRICH, *Trachten, Haus-Feld- und Kriegsgeräthschaften der Völker alter und neuer Zeit*, Stuttgart, Verlag von Gustav Weise, 1884

JOHNSTON, HAROLD WHETSONE, *The Private Life of the Romans*, Scott, Foresman and Company, Chicago, 1903

JONES, OWEN, *The Grammar of Ornament*, Bernard Quaritch, London, 1910

LANCIANI, RODOLFO, *The Ruins and Excavations of Ancient Rome*, The Riverside Press, Cambridge, 1897

LAYARD, A. H., *Nineveh and Its Remains*, Volumes 1 & 2, John Murray, London, 1849

OATES, JOAN, *Babylon*, Thames & Hudson, London, 1986

OVERBECK, J., *Geschichte Der Griechischen Plastik*, Volumes 1 & 2, Leipzig, 1894

OVERBECK, JOHANNES, *Pompeji*, Leipzig, 1884

PARIS, PIERRE, *Manual of Ancient Sculpture*, H. Grevel, London, 1890

PERROT, GEORGES & CHIPIEZ, CHARLES, *Histoire De L'Art Dans L'Antiquité*, Tomes IX & X, Librairie Hachette, Paris, 1911

RACINET, ALBERT, *Le Costume Historique*, Librairie de Firmin-Didot, Paris, 1888

RAGOZIH, ZENAIDE A., *The Story of Nations Assyria*, G. P. Putnam's Sons, New York, 1887

RAGOZIH, ZENAIDE A, *The Story of Nations Chaldea*, G P Putnam's Sons, New York, 1886

RAWLINSON, GEORGE M. A., *The Seven Great Monarchies*, Volumes 2 & 3, John B Alden, New York, 1884

REINACH, SALOMON, *Peintures De Vases Antiques*, Librairie de Firmin-Didot, Paris, 1891

ROLLINS, *Ancient History*, Ward, Lock, London, 1892

SAGGS, H. W. F., *The Greatness that was Babylon*, Sidgwick & Jackson, London, 1962

SIETSEMA, ROBERT, *Designs of the Ancient World*, Hart Publishing Company, New York, 1978

SMITH, WILLIAM, *A Smaller Dictionary of Greek and Roman Antiquities*, John Murray, London, 1880

WILKINSON, J. GARDNER, *The Ancient Egyptians*, Volumes 1, 2, & 3, John Murray, London, 1878

The publisher would like to thank the following for their permission to use images. Every effort has been made to acknowledge the pictures. We apologize if there are any unintentional omissions: AKG Images: 294 (bl); British Library: 285 (tc); Erich Lessing: 282 (br). Alamy/Mary Evans Picture Library: 277 (br). Art Archive/Musée du Louvre, Paris/Dagli Orti: 297 (cr); Laurie Platt Winfrey: 284 (b). Bridgeman Art Library/Bibliotheque Nationale, Paris, France/Archives Charmet: 285 (br); Louvre, Paris, France/Giraudon: 87 (tr), 90 (t). Corbis/Charles & Josette Lenars: 282 (cr). Scala Archives/Kimbell Art Museum, Fort Worth, Texas/Art Resource, NY: 301 (bl). TopFoto: 300 (bc); Feltz: 303 (tr); The Granger Collection, NYC: 285 (tr), 288 (tl), 303 (tl); RHR: 300 (cl); Charles Walker 300 (br).